In a world where celebrity seems to have replaced character as the measure of a woman's life, *In Her Steps* comes as a refreshing change. Denise Marie Siino masterfully weaves words and well-chosen details from a diverse group of women across the ages—famous and obscure—to inspire us to become all God intends for us to be. I plan to have my daughters and their friends read this book!

—Patti Pierce, executive director, Women at the Well

The power of women inspiring women! *In Her Steps* introduces us to some true *heroines*—strong women who have stepped out in faith and changed their world. As as we read about their lives, we dare to believe that we, too, can make a significant contribution—that's the power of this motivating book. These women's life stories will ignite your imagination and encourage you to live more courageously and expectantly. This book will remind you that, whether through history-making exploits, self-sacrificing courage, or simply quiet acts of devotion, every one of us has the making of a hero. An inspiring must-read for any woman who yearns to make a difference . . . and isn't that all of us?

—Nancy Stafford, actress ("Matlock"), speaker, and author of
The Wonder of His Love: A Journey into the Heart of God and
Beauty by the Book: Seeing Yourself as God Sees You

Women of Courage and Valor

In Her Steps

Denise Marie Siino

BROADMAN
& HOLMAN
PUBLISHERS

NASHVILLE, TENNESSEE

Ten-digit ISBN: 0-8054-3165-9
Thirteen-digit ISBN: 978-0-8054-3165-0

Published by Broadman & Holman Publishers
Nashville, Tennessee

Dewey Decimal Classification: 248.843
Subject Heading: HEROES AND HEROINES
WOMEN—BIOGRAPHIES
CHURCH HISTORY—BIOGRAPHIES

1 2 3 4 5 6 7 8 9 10   10 09 08 07 06 05

To my husband and hero, Jack,
who encourages me to aim high

Table of Contents

Preface

There's no getting around saying it: the women in this book are my heroes. As I have worked as a journalist and lived as a Christian, their lives have heavily influenced my thinking and my actions. They have changed my life. This compilation is by no means exhaustive. As I plunged into the topic of women's history, I learned about hundreds, probably thousands, of *known* women who have done extraordinary things, let alone the women whose stories remain obscure. To create this book, with few exceptions, I only had to research the ones who have meant the most to me.

The chapters that follow are not simply an inventory of accomplishments or accolades, which, in my opinion, never helped anyone live differently. Rather, each is a story woven out of a woman's life, highlighting events great and small that propelled each individual forward to her God-given destiny. In writing the chapters, I was confronted with the task of choosing which details of a woman's life to include and which to omit. This was an extraordinarily difficult process because they all lived such remarkably full lives that leaving out any information at all seemed disrespectful of the woman and unfair to you, the reader. Faced with a dilemma, I decided to let my overall goal for the book be my guiding light: to enable you to lead a heroic life, if you so choose. To that end I felt I needed to show not only where each woman had come from and where she ended up, but also the mental and physical pathways that she followed to get there—the decisions she made, the failures and hardships she experienced, the triumphs she won.

My hope for each of you is that, in the following pages, you will find inspiration and hope to live your life to the fullest under the banner of Jesus Christ. Not every story in this book is going to light your fire. But when you come across one that does, meditate on it. Contemplate the choices the heroine made and where that choice led her. Pray over her life, asking God to help you make her choices yours as well.

Then go out into the world, and *live*.

—Denise Marie Siino

Acknowledgments

First and foremost, I want to acknowledge the one and only true and living God—Father, Son, and Holy Spirit—for giving me the gift of language and teaching me how to use it. I am also grateful to my husband, Jack, without whose love I could never have written this book. I am indebted to Sheila Ramirez, Marilyn Jensen, Janet MacDonald, and the Orange Writers Circle, who were my second set of eyes. I am deeply thankful for Linda Klassen, whose friendship and wisdom have guided me through many uncertainties. Finally, I am appreciative of Internet technology, which turned this project from a laborious endeavor to something much less time-consuming and very rewarding.

Introduction

As a child, I was not raised on Bible stories. I knew nothing about the heroes and heroines of the Christian faith. But I enjoyed reading and in grade school was introduced to the heroes of Greek mythology. These characters captivated me and formed my understanding of *hero*: the offspring of mortal-divine parentage or a mere human favored by the gods with supernatural powers, who went about saving others from the perils of their day. Men like Perseus, Odysseus, and Heracles stood apart from others by the glory of their heroic acts—acts that fueled my imagination and filled my dreams.

Yet, while believing that heroes did not actually exist, I hungered to live my life in a way that emulated those I read about. In the introduction to *Christian Mythmakers*, Rolland Hein states, "In an inmost region of our beings we sense that our lives are part of a great story forming, with the quality of our actions determining the level upon which the finished story will exist."[1] Robert Coles might call this "sensing" *idealism*. In his book *The Call of Service: A Witness to Idealism*, idealism, the willingness to live in a way that makes us more than the sum of our parts and empowers us to better our world, is described as a "deeply human impulse," something we all need and for which we inwardly yearn.[2]

When I was seven, idealism expressed itself in me in an age-appropriate fashion—playacting. The first time I saw a horse up close was following a Christmas parade in the San Gabriel Valley, California, where a white Lipizzaner stallion nibbled at my hair while its rider, sitting high

1

up above, mingled with the crowd. Shortly after that, my schoolmates and I spent hours during recess pretending to be a band of wild horses, always with me as the courageous stallion, swift and clever as Pegasus, protecting and defending the herd as we crossed the dangerous territory that was our school yard. As a teenager, however, I found myself in predicaments that were over my head. Not only did my image of a hero change to that of a knight whose mission in life was to save young women in distress, but I was the young woman, and I needed saving! How badly I wanted heroes to be real. It was then that I turned to God for help.

Over the ensuing years, reading the stories found in Scripture and working in the field of journalism, I began to realize that heroes do exist. Real people. Real peril. Real courage that surpassed anything I had mustered in those imaginative moments of my childhood. To my surprise many of the stories I heard involved women of faith. Their names can be found in the annals of antiquity as well as yesterday's newspaper, from every location around the globe. The valiant midwives who refused to kill and lied to protect newborn Hebrew boys from a raging Egyptian pharaoh; the female martyrs of the early Christian church; the nineteenth-century British missionary to India who fought against the undertow of culture to save young girls from prostitution and a hopeless future; the little Dutch woman who, during World War II, risked everything under horrific conditions to help her Jewish neighbors; the current-day Indian missionary to the United States who could not ignore the injustice of legalized abortion or the ravaging emotional pain it caused women who were led to believe it was the cure-all for their predicament.

All these women, and many others whom you will read about in this book, have relied on their faith to shape history. There are countless others, too, whose names you may never read. Hidden heroes, as Max Lucado calls them.[3] These people may not be the larger-than-life figures we often associate with heroes, but to the lives they touch, they are heroic in the fullest sense of the word.

One element is common to every hero's story, one that is nonnegotiable. Each one has seized an opportunity to make a difference in another person's life or the lives of many people, sometimes at great sacrifice to herself. As I've gotten to know the women whose lives are recorded in this book, either in person or by studying their accounts, the fidelity of this nonnegotiable element has proven itself time and again. Heroism is indeed an act based on a decision. When you take away the accolades and pomp surrounding history's heroes, what is left is a vast crowd of ordinary people who seized an opportunity. Captured a moment. Took a risk. Put their foot down. Or picked their foot up. Perhaps they weren't aware of it, but somewhere deep down they said to themselves, *"Who knows? Maybe I was born for such a time as this."*

Kay Arthur

(b. 1933 – d.—)

*"Beloved, How I wish I could talk with you face-to-face so I could
encourage you, challenge you, and support you—so that you can
discipline yourself for the goal of godliness. These are critical times,
and I know that only those 'who know their God will be strong
and do exploits for Him' (Daniel 11:32b). What an hour for
the church to hold forth the Word of life."*
—**Kay Arthur**, *How to Study Your Bible*

July 16, 1963 is a day etched in Kay Arthur's memory like the deep
carvings of a stone memorial.

A Southern belle living in Chattanooga, Tennessee, Kay and her
friends had gone to church all their lives. They knew the name of God
and had heard the name, Jesus, on many occasions. They called themselves Christian, but, according to Kay, they only "played church. We
really didn't *know* God."[1] And she had no foundation to handle what life
would soon throw at her.

Kay dreamed of someday marrying a loving man and being his wife
forever. Her first marriage to Tom seemed full of promise on her wedding

day, but the dream shattered two days later when Tom revealed the dark side of a depression that grew worse with time. After the birth of their two sons, Tom and Mark, Kay left her husband. She still wanted to be held, loved, nurtured, and protected. She wanted unconditional love. Thinking she would find what she was looking for in men, she dated many over the next several months, moving from one to the next in rapid succession. Before she was really aware of it, having found nothing of what she longed for, she had become something she never dreamed—an adulteress. To make matters worse, Tom called her frequently, threatening to commit suicide. One day, she responded flippantly, "Just make sure you do a good job of it."

At a party one night, she was complaining about her histrionic life to an acquaintance named Jim. Listening patiently, he replied, "Why don't you quit telling God what you want and tell him that Jesus Christ is all you need?"[2]

In disgust Kay snapped back, "Jesus Christ is not all I need." She went on to enumerate a litany of things that she felt were critical to her happiness. Yet Jim's words stuck with her through the night. "My sins were obvious. Even I could not excuse them. For the first time in my life, I had seen my poverty of spirit."[3]

The next day, Friday, July 16, 1963, Kay was so grieved over her sin that she called in sick to the doctor's office where she worked as a nurse. She tried to put on her best face for her two small sons, but midmorning she excused herself and ran upstairs, throwing herself to the floor beside her bed. "Oh, God, I don't care what you do to me. . . . Will You just give me peace?"[4] God gave her more than peace; he gave her the Prince of Peace, Jesus Christ. That weekend she opened the Bible that had been gathering dust on a shelf and began reading. What she found was like buried treasure, the keys to life itself.

Kay has been reading the Bible voraciously ever since, sharing what she finds with people around the globe. Relating her story, she reminds her audiences that although she'd been going to church all her life, she does not believe she was a true Christian until the day she called on the name of Jesus for salvation. From that day forward, she lived life anew, forsaking her old lifestyle. While she still had the same desires, she knew that only Christ could truly fulfill all her needs. As she prayed about her future, her eyes opened to her own irresponsibility toward her broken marriage. Perhaps if they worked together, with the Lord's help, Tom could overcome his depression and their relationship could be healed. Just when she was about to call him to discuss reconciliation, she learned that he had committed suicide. The combined guilt over her failed marriage, sinful lifestyle, and Tom's death was excruciating. This time she knew what she must do. Kneeling beside her bed, she placed everything in the hands of God. Only in him would she find forgiveness and peace.

Within a year she met Jack Arthur, a missionary who had served with Pocket Testament League in Africa and Latin America for over thirty years. The couple married in 1965. Together with Kay's two boys, they went to Guadalajara, where Kay gave birth to her third son. Sharing the gospel in Mexico was like a dream come true for the woman whose primary purpose in life was to share the Word of God, but it was short-lived. Four years later she was diagnosed with pericarditis, and they returned home to Tennessee permanently. Kay could not understand what had happened. They had been serving the Lord in a needy place; why would that be taken away? But she chose to trust the Lord. While Jack supported the family by working as station manager of a local Christian radio station, Kay was leading a Bible study in her living room. She had developed an extensive, systematic method for studying the Bible and was using her new system, which she called inductive Bible study, to teach.[5] The crowd, mostly teenagers and an increasing number of adults, soon outgrew her home. In 1970, Kay and Jack bought a barn sitting on thirty-two acres of land just outside the Chattanooga city limits. When the burgeoning crowd outgrew the barn, they knew something bigger was happening. At that time, a group of 250 women in Atlanta, Georgia was looking for a Bible study teacher. They heard about Kay's teaching method and invited her to lead them. "My heart's cry to God during those years was, 'Lord, when you call me to leave Atlanta and these two hundred and fifty people, will they be able to [spiritually] feed themselves?'"[6] The group grew to seventeen hundred people and became the beginning of a nondenominational organization dedicated to preparing in-depth Bible study materials, comprising study guides by topic or book of the Bible and a videotaped teaching series by Kay. Jack joined her in leading the work, which they called Precept Ministries.[7]

At any given time well over one hundred thousand people across the United States are involved in Kay's Precept Upon Precept Bible study courses, with tens of thousands more studying throughout the world in fourteen languages. Since its humble beginnings, the ministry has expanded to include radio and television programs. A large staff handles publication of the study guides, correspondence, sales, and a training center for study leaders, who then take the inductive study courses to their own corner of the world. Aside from the Bible study courses, Kay has written more than thirty-five books in forty-eight languages, with more than four million copies in print. She also designed the Inductive Study Bible, which uses the New American Standard translation of the Bible and adds annotations, maps, charts, profiles, and hefty margins for writing personal study notes.

What sets Precept Ministries apart from other organizations that produce Bible study materials is its heavy emphasis on biblical scholarship and in-depth training for leaders. "The Bible was written so that anyone who wants to know who God is and how they are to live in a way that pleases him can read it and find out," Kay says in her videotapes. "The Bible tells us everything we need to know about life. That, my friend, is why you need to study it for yourself."

Questions/Thoughts for Reflection: Kay Arthur's trademark when talking to any audience, whether in public, print, on audio, or before a camera, is to look the crowd in the eye, as it were, and address each one as *Beloved*. What she wants to say is personal because life is at stake.

Beloved, do you know how much God really loves you? Do you know he has a plan for your life and wants to help you achieve it? If you have never given your heart to Jesus Christ, will you consider it now?

Prayer Focus: Dear Jesus, I confess that I am a sinner in need of forgiveness. I want to give up control of my life to you. Please take away my sins and make me a new person. I welcome you into my heart to live forever.

Mary Kay Ash

(b. "unavailable" – d. 2001)

"Some might consider the Golden Rule corny and old-fashioned, but no one can deny its simple truth. Imagine how much better our world would be if everyone lived by this creed. . . . Life is too short to live without the Golden Rule. It's as simple as that."

—Mary Kay Ash, www.marykay.com

Mary Kathlyn Wagner slumped down in a chair at the kitchen table of her parents' modest home in Houston, Texas. With her gravely ill father asleep in the other room, the house clean, laundry folded, and dinner prepared, she finally had a few quiet minutes to finish her homework before her mother came home from a fourteen-hour shift at a downtown diner. As she pondered the schoolwork on the table before her, the door opened and her mother walked in. Noting the forlorn look on her daughter's face, the woman set down her purse and slid into a chair beside her.

"Having a tough time? I know you can do it, Mary Kay!" She tousled her elementary-age daughter's hair and went into the bedroom to change for dinner.

In fact, Mary Kay always brought home straight-A report cards. She also took trophies in typing and debate, and outsold every other child at Girl Scout cookie sales and school fund-raisers. In spite of difficult childhood years growing up during the Great Depression, or perhaps because of them, Mary Kay excelled in almost everything she did. These life experiences prepared her well for the events that would later unfold.

When she was a young woman, a failed marriage to Ben Rogers left her with three young children to support—Ben, Marylyn, and Richard. Believing the old adage that when God closes a door, he always opens a window, she dreamed of making something of herself someday and felt she could succeed if she worked hard. She took a part-time job and began studying to be a doctor, until the results of an aptitude test confirmed her childhood experience. She had a gift for sales. She quit school and threw herself full-time into a sales position at Stanley Home Products, where she skyrocketed to the top of the sales force. To keep herself motivated, she wrote weekly goals in soap on her bathroom mirror. But being a successful businesswoman in the days when most women were housewives had its bitter side. Later, as national sales director of World Gift, she saw men whom she had hired and trained being promoted to higher positions with twice the salary. In 1963, she'd had enough and retired from corporate sales.

Success as a saleswoman stayed in the forefront of Mary Kay's mind. With more and more women entering the workforce, perhaps she could teach them something from her experience. What began as a how-to women's career book became an outline of the perfect company. "Before long," Mary Kay has since said, "I began asking myself, 'Why are you theorizing about a dream company? Why don't you just start one?'" Within a month of retirement, she decided to turn her fictional company into a reality, with a single imperative governing all subsequent decisions: God first, family second, career third. No venture would ever be worth its success if she lost track of this guiding principle. Another foundational tenet for Mary Kay was the Golden Rule: Do unto others as you would have them do unto you. "Some might consider the Golden Rule corny and old-fashioned, but no one can deny its simple truth. Imagine how much better our world would be if everyone lived by this creed. . . . Life is too short to live without the Golden Rule. It's as simple as that."[1] She planned the company so that employees would be rewarded for their efforts through expert training, vacations, bonuses, and a salary that grew proportionately with their sales.

With her company's structure firmly set in her mind, Mary Kay set about to find the right product. She bought a skin cream formulation and enlisted her second husband, George Hallenbeck, to handle operations. Believing that every person has God-given talents waiting to be brought to fruition, she hired and trained nine friends to become sales consultants for her new company, Beauty by Mary Kay. But the new venture seemed doomed before it ever left the ground. One month before the official launch date of September 13, 1963, George suffered a massive heart attack, killing him instantly. In her grief Mary Kay considered giving up her vision of a woman-owned, woman-run company. Ben, Marylyn, and Richard thought otherwise, suggesting to their mother that she might never have another chance to put her dream into action. Although her own mother had passed away years before, Mary Kay once again heard her voice ringing strong and true, "You can do it, Mary Kay!" Recruiting her youngest son, Richard, to run operations, the company opened its doors on target.

In its first year earnings exceeded $198,000. True to her word, Mary Kay rewarded her sales force with incentives beyond compare by any other direct sales organization. In 1969, she decided to reward her own efforts with a new car. She took one of her pink compacts to a Dallas Cadillac dealership and asked that a sedan be specially painted to match. Then the idea struck her, why not reward all her top sales associates the same way? To date, more than eighty thousand Mary Kay beauty consultants have earned the right to drive a signature Mary Kay pink Cadillac.

Mary Kay Inc. has grown to become a multibillion-dollar global company, with more than two hundred of its sales associates earning career commissions in excess of one million dollars. But simply rewarding her beauty consultants has never been enough for Mary Kay, nor was it ever her sole objective. Her greatest impact on the thousands of women who joined the Mary Kay team over the decades was opening doors to women who lacked opportunity; building self-esteem, self-confidence, and self-respect; and teaching them that the more you give, the more you receive. To reinforce this principle, in 1996, she augmented her own personal charitable giving by starting the Mary Kay Ash

Charitable Foundation. After seeing her third husband, Mel Ash, suffer from a lingering bout with cancer (he died in 1980), the foundation initially supported scientific research to help find a cure for breast, uterine, cervical, and ovarian cancers. In 2000, having spoken to hundreds of women experiencing domestic violence, the foundation expanded its outreach to include grants to women's shelters and other community outreach programs that focus on women's issues.

Mary Kay died at home surrounded by her family on Thanksgiving Day, November 22, 2001. Yet her legacy lives on. Since 1963, she personally, her foundation, and her company have won dozens of awards, ranging from the Direct Selling Association's Hall of Fame Award for top sales (1976) to her most recent (2004) achievements: Greatest Female Entrepreneur in American History (Baylor Graduate School of Business) and being listed in the Top 25 Leaders of the Past 25 Years (Wharton School of Business). Scores of articles have been written about her, and her own three books have been best sellers.[2] But her greatest gift was the changed lives of the women who have joined the Mary Kay team. "The extraordinary thing," says Richard Rogers, who continues to serve as the organization's president and CEO, "is the way Mary Kay caused people to believe in themselves."

Questions/Thoughts for Reflection: Everyone understands the power of words. A cutting remark, spoken decades ago, can have the same destructive impact on a person's life as if it had been said only yesterday, resulting in poor self-esteem and low achievement. To the contrary, Mrs. Wagner's words, *"You can do it!"* not only stuck with her daughter Mary Kay, it also gave her strength and enabled her to pass along the same kind of encouragement and self-confidence to thousands of others.

What kind of legacy will your words leave?

Prayer Focus: Lord, may my words always reflect your love for the men and women you have created, whose paths cross mine throughout each day.

Jill Briscoe

(b. 1935 – d.—)

"Give my words wings, Lord.
May they alight gently on the branches of men's minds
bending them to the winds of Your will.
May they fly high enough to touch the lofty,
low enough to breathe the breath
of sweet encouragement upon the downcast soul.
Give my words wings, Lord.
May they fly swift and far,
winning the race with the words of the worldly wise
to the hearts of men.
Give my words wings, Lord.
See them now
nesting down at Thy feet.
Silenced into ecstasy—home at last."
—Jill Briscoe, "Wings"

When God calls a married couple to service, there is only one thing to do: join hands and follow. Together, that is. No one knows this better than Jill Briscoe—pastor's wife, author, and inspirational speaker.

A native of Liverpool, England, Jill never stepped foot into a church until after a trip to the hospital while attending Homerton College in Cambridge, England, where a nurse introduced her to Jesus Christ. The year was 1953; she was eighteen years old. At Homerton her fledgling faith was nurtured by Intervarsity Christian Fellowship. After graduation she returned to her hometown and began teaching in a rough section of the city. Several of her students, street kids who were involved with Liverpool gangs, challenged her at every turn. How could she ever hope to reach these children under the circumstances? One day she went to their neighborhood and sought them out, sharing Jesus' love with them as well as her own dreams for their futures. To her surprise they were receptive. A relative newcomer to the church, she invited the boys and girls to join her at Sunday services. But when she and her young ragamuffin friends entered the sanctuary, people turned their heads as if to say, *"How dare you bring those wild young people in here?"* The experience haunted her for many years to come.

In 1958, Jill married Stuart Briscoe, a banker who gave his spare time to an outreach called Torchbearers, a branch of Capernwray Missionary Fellowship.[1] In 1960, Stuart joined the Capernwray staff, traveling as much as nine months of the year. Over the next ten years, three children were born to the Briscoes. As the 1970s approached, God began speaking to them about the amount of time Stuart was away from home and how the children were growing up without much time spent with their father. They agreed to an invitation to pastor a small church called Elmbrook in Brookfield, just outside of Milwaukee, Wisconsin. Now, at least, Stuart would come home every night to his wife and children. But having never before experienced a pastorate, both Stuart and Jill were apprehensive. When moving day arrived in 1970, they had no idea what to expect. Amid the flurry of thoughts and feelings, Jill knew one thing for sure. Remembering her experience with the street children years before, she wanted a mission-minded church that was open to the poor and needy.

The first congregational meeting held after the Briscoes settled in at Elmbrook turned into a heated debate about baptism. As tempers rose and insinuations were made against the new pastor, the deacon seated next to Jill began muttering, "He's new, doesn't know what he's doing, and already he's destroying this church."

Fuming quietly, Jill did not know what to say but found herself rising at last to defend her husband. Blurting out a few incoherent sentences, she burst into tears and ran out the back door. More clashes followed in the ensuing months. All the while, Jill wondered if they had made a mistake. Had God really called them to Elmbrook? As she and Stuart looked back at the benchmark events leading up to their decision to move, there was no mistaking God's hand leading them down the path they had taken. Praying together, they realized the circumstances of God's calling are secondary to the calling itself. That things were not rosy did not mean they were in the wrong place. Now all they needed to find out was where God wanted to take them next. As the months passed they began to see themselves as two rugby players who moved in unison and complemented each other but who had not yet learned how to work with the rest of their team. They must discover how to appreciate the members of their church in all their diversity, nurture their strengths, and mobilize them toward common goals.

Unbeknownst to Jill, throughout this difficult time God was showing her how to be an encourager. Looking back years later, she states, "The whole experience taught me that my greatest joy in ministry is helping people put their gifts to work, multiplying ministry. I cherish giving the ministry away, discerning women who have gifts and pushing them off the deep end, swimming with them."

As the Briscoes and their congregation grew into a cohesive whole and began to work in tandem in ministry to the surrounding community, Elmbrook's population multiplied exponentially. Jill began to receive invitations to speak to women's groups, pastors' wives retreats, conventions, missionary conferences, and evangelical crusades. Growing increasingly intuitive to the needs of each audience and God's heart for each individual in attendance, she thrived on the challenge of tailoring her speeches to the needs of the group. Once, having been invited to address a crowd of graduating beauticians and their guests at a nearby cosmetology school, she spoke from Isaiah 64 about the potter and the clay. "While the clay itself may appear pleasing to the eye, the structure of the vessel is what the potter must focus his attention on, or the piece will not survive the fire of the kiln." After her speech the president of the school called Jill backstage. Hoping that she had not overstepped her bounds as keynote speaker to the primarily secular group, she was delighted to hear he wanted to accept Jesus Christ as his Savior.

After thirty years at Elmbrook, Stuart stepped down from his responsibilities as head of staff. During his tenure the church grew from a congregation of four hundred to seven thousand, plus eight satellite churches throughout the greater Milwaukee area. Other ministries also naturally fell into place. Through Telling the Truth, a service offered via Elmbrook's media department, all of the tapes, books, radio broadcasts, and TV shows the couple created over the years became available to the public. As this service blossomed, the demand for both Jill and Stuart as evangelists, teachers, and inspirational speakers grew.

The group Jill has consistently felt most drawn to over the years has been pastors' wives. Having seen in her thirty years at Elmbrook the devastating effects of mounting social, cultural, and economic pressures on these women, with an ever-increasing number of failed marriages and destroyed ministries, she feels a strong responsibility to help support and encourage pastors' wives around the country and throughout the world. "When I speak to groups of pastors' wives, I ask, 'How many of you feel called to marriage?' Everyone raises a hand. Then I ask, 'How many of you feel called to ministry?' Only half raise their hands. . . . They ask, 'How can I limit ministry's intrusion into our marriage?' . . . But ministry is not the rival of marriage; rather, marriage is the vehicle of ministry."[2]

In response to what she considers a traditional lack of support for pastors' wives and other women serving in ministry roles, Jill started writing a newsletter in 1990 to address the special needs of these women. *Just Between Us* is now a quarterly magazine with subscribers in all fifty states and in more than seventy-five countries. "Ministry wives and missionary wives, seminary students, Bible study leaders, and women in ministry all face special challenges and pressures that warrant peer help and encouragement," says Jill, who is the magazine's executive editor. "*Just Between Us* wants to be the friend you need to inspire and challenge you to discover that ministry in the power of the Spirit is a privilege!"

Both Stuart and Jill now serve as ministers-at-large for Elmbrook. Most of their time is devoted to traveling and speaking where their special gifts and talents are most needed. At age sixty-nine, Jill keeps a schedule that would rattle the most seasoned travel veteran, being home all of six weeks in 2003. As long as the Lord grants her health and stamina, she will continue to go where called through 2005. She serves on two boards, World Relief and Christianity Today, Inc., and works closely with other organizations, such as Wycliffe Bible Translators and the U.S. Armed Forces, as well as with Anne Graham Lotz (daughter of Ruth and Billy Graham), speaking at arena events around the country. To date she has written untold articles and more than forty books, including study guides, devotional material, poetry, and children's stories.[3]

Questions/Thoughts for Reflection: Marriages are constantly under siege from pressures and temptations beyond their control. When husbands and wives are involved in ministry, these destructive elements can be doubly troublesome and even more deadly because the victim is not just the marriage, but the ministry as well. As the divorce rate climbs among couples serving the Lord in some capacity, there is an increasing inclination to withdraw, isolate the marriage, in an attempt to preserve it. In so doing, the art and joy of doing ministry *through* marriage and family are lost. In the end the family suffers the most harm, as the children—no longer exposed to the example of service once exhibited through their parents—grow up without a sense of responsibility to a community.

Are you a single person hoping to marry one day? Pray that God will give you discernment to recognize the right marriage partner, so that your lives will not only complement each other but also the service to which God will one day call you.

Are you already married? Pray that God will strengthen your marriage as you personally commit to giving yourself away to the areas of ministry in which you feel he is calling you to serve.

Prayer Focus: Dear heavenly Father, I realize I am not an island; you have not called me to Christian service in a vacuum. Help me to entrust my relationships to you, knowing that it is within the context of those relationships that you will help me grow and do my best for you.

Amy Carmichael

(b. 1867 – d. 1951)

*"Talk of beasts in human shape! It is
slandering good animals to compare bad
men to beasts. . . . He is a temple saint—
earthly, sensual, devilish. Now put beside
him a little girl—your own little girl—
and leave her there—yes, leave her there in his hand."*
—Amy Carmichael, *Things As They Are*

A my Carmichael's eyes flew open just in time to see the hills outside
her Millisle, Ireland home turn emerald green with the rising sun.
Her mother's words from the night before still ringing in her ears, she
leaped out of bed, ran to the mirror, then began to wail.

"What in heaven's name is the matter?" Mrs. Carmichael cried as she
entered Amy's room.

"You told me that if I prayed, God would answer," Amy said between sobs. "But my eyes are still brown; they did not turn blue!"

Mrs. Carmichael drew her precocious young daughter into her arms.

"No is an answer, too," she soothed. "There must be a good reason God wants you to have brown eyes."

That was the early 1870s. Amy continued to long for blue eyes until one day, years later, she looked in a different mirror in the far-off land of India. Reflecting back was the image of a woman dressed in a sari, her skin darkened with stain so that no one would suspect her of being anything but Indian. She wanted to confirm the practice of temple prostitution involving children, which had been repeatedly denied by Indians and summarily dismissed by the English. Draping the end of her sari over her head, the fabric fell around her face, framing her brown eyes. *Brown eyes!* she thought suddenly. Had her eyes been blue, her ruse would have been discovered immediately. *So this was the reason for God's no those many years before!* So disguised, she entered the Hindu temple and saw for herself what no one was willing to admit—little girls and young teenagers, sold by family members into slavery as temple prostitutes for the pleasure of Brahmin priests and other temple patrons.

From an early age Amy knew God was calling her to overseas missions work. Always the daredevil, she longed for excitement and adventure. What could be better than traveling to distant lands, doing God's work? Later, as a young woman living with her family in Belfast, where they had moved after her father's death, her childhood energy blossomed into a graceful vigor bridled by Christian love. On Sunday mornings she noticed scores of factory women sitting in the back of the church with their heads covered by shawls, belittled by the other women in the church who came each week in stylish hats. Speaking to the parish pastor, she organized a separate Bible study for the women whom she called "shawlies." Soon hundreds of these women were coming to learn about God. The experience further fueled her desire for missionary work.

During much of her time in Belfast, Amy lived in the household of a close family friend, Robert Wilson, as a companion to his two motherless sons. As founder of the annual Keswick Convention, an event intended to encourage godliness throughout the Northern Ireland area, Robert introduced Amy to many famous preachers and missionaries. Eventually convention leaders formed their own missions committee, commissioning Amy as their first emissary. On March 3, 1893, she set sale for Japan. Immediately upon landing, she experienced the alienation common to foreign missionaries, as she struggled to learn the language and fit into society. Visiting her first communal bathhouse, the customary place to wash, she was aghast as the Japanese women took turns poking her and commenting on her wavy brown hair and the size of her bosom. Against the recommendations of her interpreter and guide, she stubbornly held fast to her Western diet and dress until one winter day, while attempting to share the gospel with an elderly woman, she was interrupted by the woman's inquisitive handling of her fur-lined hand muffs, which turned the conversation in a completely different direction. From then on, Amy vowed to wear kimonos and eat the same food as her hosts.

But her time in Japan was short-lived. Suffering from a nervous condition that rendered her useless with pain, fever, headache, and fatigue, she left after fifteen months of service to see a specialist in China, who advised her to find a dryer climate. Unsure of where to go, she returned home on December 15, 1894, the day before her twenty-seventh birthday. She spent another winter in the home of Robert Wilson, nursing him after a stroke and seeking God for guidance after what she considered a failed missionary trip. During this time she received a letter from a friend living in Bangalore, India, to whom she had written earlier about her distressing poor health. "The climate here is healthy; delightful, in fact. It might be possible to live here even if China and Japan are taboo," the letter stated.[1] Amy immediately wrote to the Church of England Zenana Mission Society, under whose auspices her friend was working. Would they accept her as a missionary?

On October 11, 1895, Amy set sail for India, where she fell in love with the destitute women and children. While she had begun to dress and eat like the people she wished to serve, she struggled to master the Tamil language and to understand the Hindu religion with its many gods. She also struck some of her fellow missionaries as disrespectful and controlling, as she openly criticized their priority of protecting British interests over ministering to the Indians and opening the gospel to them.

After months of language learning in Bangalore, she traveled on to Pannaivilai, a small village along the Tambaravarni River. By 1898, she had won three village women to Christ. Two years later the "Starry Cluster," as the band of women was called, moved once more, to an enclave of Christian natives in the town of Dohnavur. From there they traveled around the countryside, sharing their faith with anyone who would listen. As young boys and girls began converting to Christianity, they cried out to Amy for sanctuary after Hindu laws evicted them from their homes because of their newfound beliefs. Sometimes bruised from beatings and filthy from living on the streets, these children were not at all lovely to behold. Amy looked past their exterior and saw the beautiful children of God they could become. She gave refuge to as many as she could in an orphanage built in Dohnavur; soon the number reached into the hundreds.

In March 1901, Amy was visiting new converts in the village of Pannaivilai when a woman approached her with a seven-year-old girl in tow. "Preena came to me last night in desperation," the woman said. "She just escaped the Hindu temple in Perungulam. They were training her to be a *devadasis,* a woman of the temple."

Amy had heard vague rumors of temple prostitutes, a secret practice that had allegedly been going on for centuries, but neither the Indian nor British authorities seemed interested in verifying the facts. The next day the facts presented themselves, as a mob of angry temple officials came demanding that Preena be handed over to them. When Amy refused, they dispersed—too afraid, Amy decided, to expose an activity they desired to keep secret. The incident fueled her courage and imagination. After disguising herself as a Hindu and seeing with her own eyes the children who were being sold into slavery as temple prostitutes, she understood why God had called her to India. The evil must somehow be exposed; in the meantime she would rescue and shelter as many temple girls as possible.

In the following weeks Preena led the Starry Cluster to other *devadasis,* all of whom desperately wanted to leave the temple. Entering the orphanage, they received food, shelter, an education, and Christian love. In an effort to inform the world of the evil practice of temple prostitution, Amy wrote a book titled *Things As They Are,* which was published in England in 1903. A scathing rebuke of the practice of child prostitution in the Hindu temples and the Brahmin priests who secured the girls, the book spurred a great controversy over the practice's historical place in an ancient society and whether missionaries should interfere with such native rituals. Many people, including fellow missionaries, accused Amy of exacerbating the problem and creating tension with the local authorities. Their complaints fell on deaf ears. Each time Amy saw a spark of new life in the eyes of one of the *devadasis,* where there once had been a dull apathy and pain, she knew she was doing the right thing.

Amy eventually resigned from the mission organization that supported her and began her own work, called the Dohnavur Fellowship. Over the ensuing years she rescued and sheltered more than a thousand children, dispossessed converts to Christianity as well as temple girls seeking sanctuary. She was known as *Amma,* or "mother," to all. At one time she was threatened with imprisonment and death because of her activities, but a telegram arriving on February 7, 1914, stated that all charges had been dropped and the case was dismissed.

Amy's involvement with the Fellowship slowed after a crippling accident in 1931. Having written a handful of books to date, she used the time in bed to write many others, more than thirty-five in all. In 1948, temple prostitution was finally outlawed, due in large part to her tireless efforts. She died on January 18, 1951, having served over fifty-six years in India without furlough. The work of the Dohnavur Fellowship—a compound comprising a hospital, sixteen nurseries, and numerous other buildings on over four hundred acres of land—continues to this day.

Questions/Thoughts for Reflection: Amy Carmichael's work with street children and temple prostitutes earned her the reputation of being a lover of the unlovely. Looking around at our own unlovable people— the homeless, the prostitutes, the drunks, the drug addicts, the criminals, the foreigners whose ways we do not understand—it is difficult to imagine having a heart large enough to exhibit some show of respect, let alone love. Frankly, it's easy not even to want to try. But God wants to break through our apathy, to help us recognize that even the unlovely in our society are his creation, having the divine spark embedded in their souls, waiting to experience a rebirth. Perhaps that spark is meant to be lit by you.

Prayer Focus: Lord Creator of heaven and earth, enlarge my heart to appreciate the whole of your creation, all my fellow sojourners on earth—not just the ones who are appealing to the eye or with whom I can agree and whose company I enjoy.

Edith Cavell

(b. 1865 – d. 1915)

"I do not want to be remembered as a martyr or a heroine,
but simply as a nurse who tried to do her duty."
—Edith Cavell, *Belgium Under the German Occupation, A Personal Narrative*

Edith Louisa Cavell declined the offer. No, she would not turn toward the stone wall; she would face the firing squad as she had faced life—head on. Within seconds after her refusal, her delicate figure, gray hair still tucked in a bun atop her head, lay lifeless on the ground.

What horrible crime had this woman committed that led to her demise at the prison of St. Gilles in Brussels, Belgium, in the early morning hours of October 12, 1915?

Edith's story began on the other side of the English Channel in 1865. The first of four children born to Reverend and Mrs. Frederick Cavell, Edith grew up in the vicarage her father had built next to his church in Swardeston, England. High spirited, nothing could keep Edith from her favorite pastimes of tennis, ice skating and painting, or an occasional forbidden game of cards with her siblings in the vicarage while their puritanical father led services in the chapel.

23

In spite of what some considered frivolous pursuits, Edith grew up with a deep love and respect for God and the church. As a girl of ten, she saw the need for a church room to hold the growing Sunday school services for village children. She wrote to the bishop of Norwich requesting his assistance. Would he take on the building project? Yes, he wrote back, he would help, provided the village, poor as it was, raise a sizable portion of the needed money. Edith rose to the challenge and encouraged villagers to find ways of funding the project. When the necessary amount was raised (three hundred British pounds), she boldly wrote to the bishop again, reminding him of his promise. In just a few years, the building she had envisioned was complete.

Edith spent the final years of her formal education at Laurel Court, Peterborough, where she learned French and trained to become a teacher. Noticing the bright, vivacious young woman from Swardeston, who took to her second language with such flair, the schoolmaster decided Edith would be perfect for a private teaching position in Brussels, Belgium.

Before taking the position in 1890, Edith used part of a small inheritance to tour the Continent, where she visited a hospital run by a doctor with a staff of female nurses. The idea of using ordinary women in the nursing field, an area dominated historically by Catholic nuns, intrigued her. But why not? However well-intentioned the nuns were, they had no medical expertise. What wonders could women perform when they combined their natural compassion and capacity to nurture with a trained hand? Edith was so impressed that she endowed the hospital with a portion of her legacy. She arrived at her post in Brussels with a growing interest in nursing.

For the next five years, Edith perfected her French while teaching in a private home. In 1895, she returned to Swardeston to care for her father through a brief illness. She enjoyed giving him the personal attention he needed and thrilled to see him recover so quickly. She decided to test her budding nursing skills as a volunteer at Fountains Fever Hospital in nearby Tooting. Convinced after several months that nursing was her life's calling, she applied for training at London Hospital.

The following summer, a typhoid fever epidemic broke out in Maidstone. Edith was among six nurses sent to care for the victims. By the time she arrived, hundreds of people had already contracted the fever; a few had died. The days seemed endless with mopping feverish foreheads, bathing patients to keep their bodies free from the effects of intestinal distress, and helping to make them comfortable as the disease exacted its toll. Her hard work and that of the other nurses paid off. Of the seventeen hundred people who contracted the fever, only 132 died.

For the next several years, Edith practiced nursing in both private and public settings. As assistant matron at Shoreditch Infirmary, she pioneered a new concept: follow-up home visits to patients after their discharge. In 1907, a letter arrived from an acquaintance in Belgium, Dr. Antoine Depage, requesting that Edith assist him in caring for a child with special needs. Recognizing Edith's aptitude for nursing, the doctor shared with her his vision to train nurses in Belgium along the lines of Florence Nightingale in England. Would Edith, now in her forties, consider helping him open the first women's nursing school in Belgium? Edith responded with an unequivocal yes.

Initially the school, called the Berkendael Institute, was not well accepted, especially by the middle and upper classes. "The old idea that it is a disgrace for women to work is still held in Belgium," Edith wrote home during the school's infancy, "and women of good birth and education still think they lose caste by earning their own living." But when the queen of Belgium broke her arm and sent to the school for a nurse, its status soared. By 1912, the institute provided nurses to three hospitals, twenty-four communal schools, and thirteen kindergartens, with Edith lecturing to doctors and nurses alike.

Throughout this time Edith often returned to England to visit her mother who now lived alone in Norwich after her father's death. In 1914 she was weeding her mother's garden when news arrived that Germany had invaded Belgium. Mrs. Cavell pleaded with her daughter, who would turn fifty within a year, not to return. But Edith would not be dissuaded. "At a time like this, I am more needed than ever," she replied. By August she was back at her post.

Edith understood fully the risks of working in a war zone and the likelihood that soldiers from both sides would be brought to the school. She impressed on the nurses in her charge that their first duty was to care for the wounded irrespective of nationality. The institute became a Red Cross hospital, with German soldiers receiving the same treatment as the Belgian, French, and British. Soon Belgium fell to Germany. All but two of the sixty British nurses were sent home; only Edith as first matron and her chief assistant remained to assist their Belgian counterparts.

In the fall of 1914, advancing German troops cut off the retreating British and French. For days the stranded soldiers lived like hunted animals, finding shelter in haystacks and barn lofts. Most were found and shot. Two British soldiers found their way to the institute, where they were hidden for two weeks before being escorted by friendly hands into neutral Holland. Others followed, and an underground lifeline was established with the aid of a Belgian named Philippe Baucq. The operation was dangerous, especially for Edith. To safeguard the nurses under her charge, she alone assumed the responsibility of sheltering Allied soldiers—in her home if she must—and organizing their transport between the school and a chateau in Mons owned by Prince and Princess de Croy. To Edith, sheltering and smuggling these hunted men was just as humane as tending to the sick and wounded.

By the summer of 1915, about two hundred men had passed through the underground operation, including a Belgian spy. Within days the institute was searched. Two members of the escape route team were arrested, including Philippe Baucq. On August 5, Edith was also detained. Hearings for the prisoners began on October 7; on October 9, Edith was brought before her accusers. During questioning, her German interrogators tricked her into believing the other members of the escape team had confessed to aiding the enemy. "Had I not helped," she admitted, "the men would have been shot."

While helping English, French, and Belgian soldiers escape into the Belgian countryside, even to neutral Holland, was an offense against the German occupation, it did not merit execution. But during Edith's examination and subsequent trial, her interrogators discovered she had done far worse.

"Did you aid English soldiers left behind after the early battles last autumn in the area about Mons?"

"Yes."

"How many soldiers did you aid? Twenty?"

"More than twenty; two hundred." Edith pressed her lips together into a slight smile.

"English?"

"Yes, English, but French and Belgians too."

"Too bad the English are so ungrateful."

"No," Edith countered, "the English are not ungrateful."

"How do you know this?"

"Because some of them have written to me from England, to thank me."

"From England? They have written from England?" her inquisitor snapped.[1]

The room fell silent. With this admission Edith had violated paragraph 68 of the German Code, which states: "Whoever, with the intention of helping the hostile Power, or of injuring the German or allied troops, is guilty of one of the crimes of paragraph 90 of the German Military Penal Code, will be sentenced to death for treason." The particular crime referenced, of which she was found guilty, was "conducting soldiers to the enemy." To have helped her countrymen find their way back to their native England, German enemy territory, was indeed a capital offense.

Edith was one of twenty-seven people condemned that day. Of these, two were singled out for immediate execution before a firing squad, Edith and Philippe Baucq. The Germans likely wanted to make an example of Edith of what would happen to anyone—young or old, male or female—attempting to assist the enemy back to his homeland.

On October 11, Edith and Philippe were transported to the *Tir Nationale* (the National Firing Range). A kind German Lutheran prison chaplain obtained permission for the British chaplain at Brussels and rector of the English church, Stirling Gahan, to visit Edith in her cell during the hours before her death. The two talked and sang, and Edith took the Sacraments. Her life recently had been hurried and not always happy, she admitted, and she was grateful for the ten weeks of rest since being taken into custody. During those weeks she had read from the Bible and the Book of Prayer and had written letters to her mother, her colleagues, even to a young woman fighting addiction to morphine. Her correspondence complete, she was glad to be dying for her country. With her own execution only days away, Edith's letters revealed no bitterness toward her captors.

In the early morning hours of October 12, Edith and Philippe were escorted outside. Two firing squads, each consisting of eight men firing at six paces, faced their respective victims, who were asked to turn and face a rear wall. Edith refused. Tradition has it that her executioners fired wide, reticent to kill the frail, gray-haired nurse. When one soldier, a Private Rimmel, threw down his rifle in objection, a German officer shot him on the spot for refusing to obey orders. Edith fainted and was shot by the officer before having the chance to recover.[2]

After the war Edith's body was found in a grave marked only by a plain wooden cross. It was exhumed and escorted to Dover, where a great procession accompanied the coffin through Westminster Abbey and then on to Norwich Cathedral.

At her burial service on May 15, 1919, Bishop Pollock described Edith as alive in God and as someone who, quoting Edith from Mr. Gahon's notes of their final hours together, has taught us a valuable lesson: "Standing as I do in view of God and eternity, I realize that patriotism is not enough; I must have no hatred or bitterness towards anyone."

Every year, on the Saturday nearest the anniversary of her death, a memorial is held at Norwich Cathedral in Edith Cavell's honor.

Questions/Thoughts for Reflection: Edith Cavell's story is a vivid reminder that there is honor and personal contentment to be found in placing the needs of others above our own. It helps us to recognize that human life is valuable, whether that life belongs to a fellow American or someone living in Iraq, a friend or a foe.

Describe the picture painted by Edith's actions of the biblical mandate to love one's enemy. In what ways did she put a face on her enemy, and how do you think that might have helped her treat every soldier, regardless of nationality, with human dignity?

Prayer Focus: Dear God, it is hard enough to pray for my enemies, much less provide for their needs in some tangible way. I don't want to do either, yet ignoring your commands would be like ignoring your own precious gift of salvation to me; for I was once your enemy, but you invited me to be your friend. You have graciously given me what I don't deserve and mercifully forgiven me my every transgression. Help me to remember that I *can* love because you first loved me.

Jerrie Cobb

(b. 1931 – d.—)

*"I have this feeling that life is a spiritual adventure,
and I want to make mine in the sky."*
—Jerrie Cobb, www.jerrie-cobb-foundation.org

Six-year-old Geraldyn "Jerrie" Cobb lay flat on her back under the clear Oklahoma night sky. She was already familiar with the seasonal constellations. Her young heart leapt at the sight of the full moon, a large brilliant disk rising above the horizon. With a childlike faith that God had a purpose for every human being, she knew she was destined to live her life "up there."

Daughter of Lieutenant Colonel William H. Cobb and Helena Butler Stone Cobb, Jerrie was born on March 5, 1931 in Norman, Oklahoma. Her father being a military pilot, she grew up with aviation in her blood. She longed to fly as he did; as a twelve-year-old she got her wish. Soon she was sharing the cockpit of his 1936 Waco biwing airplane. So great was her desire to fly that by age sixteen she was barnstorming around the Great Plains in a Piper J-3 Cub, announcing the arrival of an elephant circus. On the side she gave rides—anything to practice flying.

On her eighteenth birthday Jerrie received her commercial pilot's license and began looking for a flying job. But with the recent return of male pilots from WWII, Jerrie's expertise went unnoticed by major employers. To pay for additional schooling, she flew crop-dusting and pipeline patrol routes.[1] Within a year she was teaching men how to fly. At age twenty-one she was delivering U.S.-built military fighters and four-engine bombers to foreign Air Forces around the world. Over the ensuing years, she broke three world records for speed, distance, and absolute altitude, and received numerous awards, including the Amelia Earhart Gold Medal of Achievement and Pilot of the Year.

Shortly after flying in the world's largest air exposition, the *Salon Aeronautique Internationale* in France, and receiving that organization's coveted Gold Wings for being its first woman pilot, Jerrie was contacted by Dr. Randolph Lovelace, chairman of NASA's Life Sciences Committee. The Russians were planning to send their first woman cosmonaut into orbit; would she be interested in training for space flight? On February 7, 1959, Jerrie reported to the Lovelace Clinic in Albuquerque, New Mexico, confident she could match her fellow applicants' (all male) scores in the clinic's rigorous physical and psychological testing. For weeks machines designed to simulate space travel spun, plunged, jerked, and tumbled each applicant. Among a myriad of psychiatric tests, Jerrie endured long periods of isolation, even the freezing of her inner ears, to see how she would respond. She passed all phases of testing in the top 2 percent. In August 1960, she became the United States' first woman astronaut trainee.

Impressed with Jerrie's exceptional scores, Dr. Lovelace asked her to help NASA select other women for testing. Twelve others passed the Lovelace Clinic's rigorous testing program and entered the space training program along with Jerrie, forming what became known as the Mercury 13. After completing her training, Jerrie was named consultant to NASA administrator James Webb and eagerly awaited her flight into space.

But some NASA officials were not ready to accept a female astronaut. During secret candidate screening, NASA added one more rule to the candidates' checklist. An astronaut must also be a jet pilot, a role only a military pilot could fulfill. To date women had not been allowed to fly in the military. The Mercury 13 astronauts were permanently grounded. Regardless of the fact that Jerrie had logged more than double the number of flight hours as most of the other candidates, flying a wider variety of planes, she was suddenly disqualified from space travel.

In 1962, Jerrie and one other member of the Mercury 13, Jane Hart, testified in House Space Subcommittee hearings on flying women into space. They pointed out that due to their smaller stature and lighter weight, women were perfect candidates for the crowded conditions of a space capsule and the current-day rockets with their lighter payloads. But their testimony was overshadowed by that of astronaut John Glenn, who had flown in the *Mercury 7* space mission. "The fact that women are not in this field is a fact of our social order," Glenn announced. "[Using women astronauts] may be undesirable."[2] It would take twenty years before gender space travel restrictions were lifted. In June 1963, Cosmonaut Valentina Tereshkova became the first woman to fly into space.

Jerrie was devastated as her dream quickly evaporated. After months of prayer, she concluded that if she could not be of service to the United States and the American public as an astronaut, she would find some other way to live a useful life serving humanity. During her days flying pipeline patrol, she became aware of the desperate needs of indigenous people living in the Amazon basin, the largest tropical rain forest in the world, where malnutrition and disease run rampant.[3] She quit NASA, packed up *The Bird*, her twin-engine bush plane, and flew to South America. There she took on a task that few other pilots wanted, flying over uncharted jungle and landing in terrain no more hospitable than the moon itself to bring medicine to the sick and rice for planting to the hungry. Aside from transporting doctors and other humanitarian workers, she learned how to give inoculations, pull rotting teeth, deliver babies, and harvest rice. Most rewarding of all was learning Indian dialects so she could share the love of God with a people fearful of evil spirits and of their own spirits being eaten by snakes and destined to roam alone in the jungles forever.

After hundreds of trips to the Amazon, a group of friends in Oklahoma formed a foundation to help support Jerrie's ongoing work.[4] Remembering one incident, Jerrie wrote in her foundation newsletter, "Last night I sat with the chief of this Indian village as he lay dying from meningitis. My medicines could not help him. He was a fine young leader of his people. Through our efforts here, his tribe has learned to grow crops to feed themselves, trading rice with neighboring tribes for wild game. . . . Every time he could find the strength, he would ask me about God. I assured him that God loved him, cared for him, and would receive him into his heavenly kingdom. He died peacefully."

Jerrie refuses to use money from the foundation for herself. "Every penny, nickel, dime and dollar from the foundation goes toward buying seeds and medicines for the primitive Indians," she explains in her foundation's newsletter. "I have always believed in supporting myself, and I insist *The Bird* does the same. When we go broke, we fly aerial surveys for the countries that encompass the Amazon, or we go to Rio, Bogotá, or Miami and do some aviation consulting. Knowing how badly these people need help, I could never use a cent of the foundation's money for me or *The Bird*."

The work can be discouraging as well as rewarding. "Sometimes when I'm lying in my hammock at night in some Indian communal *maloca*, I get down and out. But the next day the sun does shine, *The Bird* and I take off on another jungle flight, and yes, I realize that many are dying, many are suffering, but some are living because we are here."

Some of Jerrie's flights over the years have included transporting missionaries whose work brought them to the dense Amazon jungle. In the mid-1990s, she took another step in her spiritual journey when she heard of Wycliffe missionary Ray Rising's abduction by FARC,[5] a Colombian guerrilla group. On October 26, 1995, she wrote the following to the crisis committee negotiating for Ray's release: "I would like to offer myself to FARC in exchange for Ray. Please discuss it with your committee, and let me know. I would need about two weeks to get my affairs in order. I assure you this is a serious offer, made in love."[6] While the crisis committee declined her offer, it proved what so many have felt about Jerrie for decades. She is a courageous, selfless woman and a true American hero.

To date Jerrie has been giving humanitarian aid to the indigenous people of Amazonia for over forty years. Meanwhile her list of honors and awards for her work and aviation activities has continued to grow, the pinnacle being a nomination for the Nobel Peace Prize in 1981. But despite all of her accomplishments, she still longs to fulfill her lifelong dream of space flight. "I have this feeling that life is a spiritual adventure, and I want to make mine in the sky."

Questions/Thoughts for Reflection: It is easy to assume that if we attend church regularly, do our best to follow the Ten Commandments and the Golden Rule, we are living a life pleasing to God. Then along come Jesus' words in John 15:13, "Greater love has no one than this, than to lay down one's life for his friends," and we realize that what we thought was the end-all to the Christian life is really only the headwaters to a deeper spiritual commitment, not only to God but also to our fellow-man. But the truth is, few of us will ever dedicate our entire lives to humanity much less have the opportunity to make the ultimate sacrifice for another human being as Jerrie Cobb did. If that is true, what relevance do Jesus' words have for us today?

Take a few moments to meditate on John 15:13. Read the verse aloud, listening carefully to each word as you articulate it. Pause, then repeat the verse, speaking slowly and thoughtfully. Did any word or portion of the phrase claim your interest? Repeat the verse once more, letting your mind interact with the word or portion of phrase that seems significant. What does it mean in relation to the entire verse? What might it mean in the context of your life? Allow any feelings you have in response to the word or phrase rise to the surface. Acknowledge your feelings, then release them. Finally, ask God to reveal what he would like to impart to you through your meditation.

Prayer Focus: "Speak Lord in the stillness, while I wait on thee; hushed my heart to listen in expectancy."

Deborah, Judge of Israel

(b. "unavailable – d. "unavailable")

"So may all your enemies perish, O LORD! But may they who love you
be like the sun when it rises in its strength."
—Deborah, Judge of Israel (Judg. 5:31 NIV)

Deborah awoke with a start. For weeks a feeling had been nagging at her, and she had been unable to shake it.

Like every good Hebrew wife, she took care of her husband Lapidoth's needs, kept their clothes clean and their home comfortable. "She's a good woman," Lapidoth would boast to his friends. "Who else could concoct such lavish meals on such a miserable budget?" For with Ehud dead and no judge to take his place, bedlam prevailed among the children of Israel.[1] Taking advantage of the mayhem, Jabin, king of the Canaanites, had attacked the area south of his stronghold in Hazor, taking control of the trade routes and nearby farmland.[2] Times were harder than ever.

"And you wouldn't believe the people who line up at our door to talk to her about their problems!" Lapidoth would crow, throwing up his hands in complaint. "Some man wanting judgment against an employer that cheated him out of wages, a pair of brothers fighting over their inheritance, a mother wanting my wife's opinion about a suitor for their daughter. Ridiculous!"

For all his grumbling, Lapidoth was secretly proud of the respect his wife commanded among men and women alike in their little town in the hill country of Ephraim. And why not? God had granted to a woman an uncommon wisdom that surpassed even that of the town elders.

This morning, as Deborah stretched in her bed, the same indescribable feeling gnawed at her like never before. Yes, she was a good wife, and the community esteemed her. But God wanted something more of her, something bigger than she could possibly imagine. *But what?*

After dressing and sending Lapidoth off to work, she tossed the hood of her *kesut* over her black hair and set off down a steep trail. She had decided to visit her childhood playground, a cluster of palm trees that grew in a valley between the villages of Ramah and Bethel. There, under the shady fronds of one particularly lush tree, she had spent many hours as a young girl thinking and praying and pondering what life as an adult woman would be like. It was a peaceful place, full of good memories. Perhaps, if she took her usual spot under the tree, these mysterious feelings would crystallize into a coherent thought.

As often occurs when we are filled with expectation, nothing much happened to Deborah as she sat under the tree except for the occasional breeze that blew through her hair. While she felt at one with God, her feelings of anticipation went unabated. Yet the spot drew her back day after day, and the visitors who once made their way to her home now found her under the palm tree. Their numbers were not great at first, yet each guest seemed to leave with a lighter heart and greater sense of purpose. As her fame spread, the lush tree under which she sat became known as the Palm Tree of Deborah.

Twenty years passed. As Jabin's oppression increased, so did the stream of people—Israelites coming from all over the promised land—leading to Deborah's shady haven. Many began calling her a prophetess[3] and judge over all Israel. The terms bothered her at first, but soon the Lord quelled her trepidations. This is what he had been calling her to; this was her God-given destiny. Still she sensed there was something more.

One day during prayer, a thought took shape in Deborah's mind, a thought she attributed to God: The Lord had instructed Barak, son of

Abinoam, commander of the Hebrew army, to gather ten thousand troops at Mount Tabor to wage war against Sisera, the commander of Jabin's armed forces. Victory belonged to Israel if Barak would obey God's command and fight. But Barak had failed to carry out God's directive. Was he fearful of Sisera's epic reputation for cruelty? Perhaps he was afraid of the nine hundred iron chariots at the enemy's command? Truly the Hebrew army was no match for such machines of war. Still God's decree was not to be ignored. She must find out.

Deborah sent a messenger to the town of Kedesh in Naphtali with a request for Barak to come to her immediately. Respecting Deborah's reputation as a judge, Barak came without delay.

"Has not the God of Israel commanded you to deploy troops, ten thousand men from the tribes of Naphtali and Zebulun, to Mount Tabor?" Deborah asked the commander. "Has he not promised you victory over Sisera, with his nine hundred chariots and his army of thousands, as you engage him in battle at the River Kishon? Why do you delay?"

Barak bowed his head in deference to Deborah. "If you will go with me, then I will go; I will not go without you!"

Deborah tried to size up the Hebrew commander. Surely he did not rise to his position of authority by cowardice. No, he was a brave man with nerves of steel. Sometimes such men's spiritual aptitude is not as sharp as their spears; perhaps he did not trust the inner voice speaking softly within.

"I will go with you to fight against Sisera," Deborah replied to the man of war. "But you should know that because you hesitated, there will be no glory for you in battle. The Lord will sell Sisera into the hands of a woman."

Barak returned to Kedesh with Deborah by his side. He sent messengers to the sons of Naphtali and Zebulun, ten thousand men in all, calling them to gather for battle on the slopes of Mount Tabor where the chariots of Sisera could not reach. Sisera learned of the pending attack and gathered his own army of chariots and foot soldiers on the plains of the Kishon River. There he waited for Barak.

The appointed day for the advance dawned. Deborah, who came to represent God's voice to the Israeli army, gave the battle cry, "Up! For this is the day in which the Lord has delivered Sisera into your hand!" Following their commanding officer, Barak's men ran down the mountainside into the plains, where Sisera and his mighty militia awaited.

How could an army of ten thousand foot soldiers, trained more in the use of the shepherd's staff than in the sword, defeat an expertly trained army, including the most advanced military weaponry of its day? With the Lord's help anything is possible. Barak and his men met Sisera's chariots and foot soldiers with a clash of steel. Miraculously, they drove the Canaanites north through the Kishon River valley to the cities of Harosheth and Hagoyim. By the time Barak reached these northern cities, nearly the entire Canaanite army had been slain. Only one man had survived, Sisera himself.

Seeing that his army was nearly destroyed, Sisera dismounted from his chariot and fled on foot toward the town of Zaanaim near Kedesh. On the outskirts of the village, a woman named Jael saw the commander and called to him from her tent, "Come inside; I'll hide you. Don't be afraid." Because Jael's husband, Heber the Kenite, was a friend of Jabin king of Canaan, Sisera trusted her and entered her tent, where no man was welcome except her husband. Surely his enemy would not look for him there!

"Lie down here, and I'll cover you with a blanket," Jael said.

"Thank you. But first, can you spare me something to drink? I've been running for hours."

"Here, have a little milk. Now hurry, before anyone comes."

Sisera lay down on his side on the ground. Jael threw a blanket over the commander's legs, then began pulling it up toward his face. Before she could finish, Sisera stopped her hand.

"I must ask one more favor. Stand in the doorway and keep watch. If any man comes and asks whether a man is here, you must tell him no. Do you understand?"

"Of course. I will take care of everything," Jael replied.

Sisera lay still under the blanket. Even so, he did not hear Jael as she left the tent, then reentered moments later with a stake in one hand and a hammer in the other. Quietly she knelt down beside Sisera. She surmised the crown of his head, the jaw, the ear, then aligned the point of the stake with the Canaanite commander's temple. She raised the hammer and gathered her strength for a firm blow. She was used to driving the heavy tent stakes into the hard ground. This job would require strength of a different kind.[4]

In the annals of ancient history, it is recorded that Sisera, commander of the Canaanite army, was killed by a woman, just as Deborah predicted. With his army destroyed Jabin king of Canaan, along with his guards, was also killed by Barak and his men. From that day and for the next forty years, Israel lived peaceably in the land with Deborah as its judge.

Questions/Thoughts for Reflection: As people living in the twenty-first century, it is hard for us to understand that someone could be so attune to God's voice as to proclaim a direct, detailed inquiry to another person, such as the one Deborah addressed to Barak. Nor can we easily fathom a loving and merciful God orchestrating the destruction of thousands of people. But like a camera lens that can zoom in and out of a panoramic scene, we must try to broaden our thinking to include the entire picture. The nation of Israel was intended to be an example to the rest of the world of what it was like to be in a dynamic relationship with the true and living God. A God who nurtured, chastened, and protected Israel as a parent would a beloved child. For a span of forty years, God used Deborah to help accomplish this purpose.

As powerful as God is, he still chooses to use ordinary women and men to represent him to the world he created and the people in it. Just as he gave Deborah skills and abilities to help her carry out his will, God gives to each of us certain skills and abilities to do the same. Take a few moments to draw up a list of your strengths. Ask your family and friends for their input. Then pray over your list, asking God to lead you to the special task he wants you to perform using the skills he has given you.

Prayer Focus: Heavenly Father, I want you to use me. Help me to know what you want me to do and what skills I have that can help get the job done.

Shirley Dobson

(b. "unavailable" – d.—)

"I see [the National Day of Prayer] in this country as believers all across this nation standing in the gap for America. . . . And my heart's cry is through the prayers of God's people, that He will stretch out His hand and return to us in the way of a revival or spiritual renewal in this land, that foundation that this country was birthed in."
—Shirley Dobson, www.backtothebible.org

How does a self-described private person who would have preferred a quiet life end up as the highly visible chairman of the Task Force for the National Day of Prayer? Shirley Dobson can tell you that it does not happen overnight but rather after many years of preparation.

Shirley found prayer essential from an early age. Her mother, sensing that she needed help raising little Shirley and her brother in a household with an alcoholic husband, carted her children off to a neighborhood church in their hometown of Torrance, California each Sunday. There in Sunday school Shirley first heard that "God loves all of us and knows each of our names."[1] What a comforting thought, that she could talk to God! Before long she invited Jesus to come into her heart. When her father went on alcoholic binges, she would fall to her knees beside her bed, begging her heavenly Father to protect her and her family. When her parents divorced, Shirley's prayers changed to an innocent request for a new father who would make her mother happy. A year later her mother met a nice man who became Shirley's stepfather. Encouraged by the answered prayer, as Shirley entered the teenage years, she began to pray a second specific prayer, for a Christian husband who would provide her with the kind of loving, stable home she had missed in her youth.

At Pasadena College where she received a BA degree in education, Shirley met a tall gregarious Texan named Jim Dobson. Shirley fell in love with this determined man with a rock-solid faith. Three years later they married. Once again it became apparent that God had answered her prayers in a way that exceeded her expectations. The Dobsons raised two children and Shirley brought them up in the tradition of prayer that had sustained her since childhood.

In 1967, Jim earned a Ph.D. in child development and expanded his work to include a thriving family therapy practice. The next decade was a dream come true for Shirley. While her husband taught as an associate clinical professor of pediatrics at the University of Southern California, School of Medicine, and served on the attending staff of Children's Hospital of Los Angeles, she stayed home and raised her children in their quiet Arcadia neighborhood. Eventually Jim began to publish his theories about early childhood development and raising children, eventually producing a series of films on the subject, to be viewed in churches and home gatherings. It was seen by more than eighty million people over the next few years. As his popularity exploded and demand raged for more resources, Focus on the Family, a nonprofit organization dedicated to the preservation of the family, was born.

Being "Mrs. Dobson," Shirley was sucked into an uncomfortable limelight. Yet as a deeply committed Christian bathed in the grace of God, she has accepted her new, ever-challenging public role with humble charm. She soon discovered a delightful benefit that she had not anticipated; as Focus on the Family became ingrained in American society and well-known around the world, she gained inroads to pray for and with individuals of high profile who otherwise would never have crossed her path, including celebrities, government officials, even U.S. presidents.

Meanwhile, Vonette Bright, wife and cofounder of Campus Crusade for Christ, had formed a national prayer committee devoted to motivating Christians nationwide to pray for their country and its leaders. As chairman of the committee, she introduced legislation that was unanimously passed by Congress and signed by President Ronald Reagan in 1988, making the first Thursday of May the annual National Day of Prayer. Shortly thereafter a task force was created to give structure to the new prayer effort, which Vonette led as chairman until 1990. When it came time to pass the torch to a new leader, she tapped her friend Shirley Dobson's shoulder. "[Praying for our country and its leaders] is where my heart is," says Shirley. "I feel that prayer is the hope of our nation."[2] She has been the chairman of the National Day of Prayer ever since.

"This country was founded on the God of the Bible and on his values and principles. So as long as we stay in line with these, he will bless this land. But in recent decades, we have strayed from that moral foundation and we're reaping the consequences in our churches, our families, and our nation. My heart's cry is that through the prayers of God's people that he will stretch out his hand and rekindle a revival that will bring us back to our spiritual roots."[3]

Although the National Day of Prayer was created by congress for people of all faiths, our Task Force is a Judeo-Christian expression of this prayer movement.

Besides leading the National Day of Prayer effort, Shirley is a much sought-after speaker and author of numerous articles and several books. She coauthored three books with Gloria Gaither, two about building lasting childhood memories and the other about infusing the home with Scripture so that children grow up hearing the Word of God. She and Jim together wrote a devotional book, *Night Light*, about building intimacy in marriage. Her latest book, *Certain Peace in Uncertain Times*, leads readers down a path of prayer. No matter what your external circumstances might be, God wants you to experience inner peace. Shirley wants to show you how.

Questions/Thoughts for Reflection: Revelation 8:3–4 tells us that in heaven, the prayers of the saints are collected and mixed with incense in a golden vessel; together they rise like a vapor to the throne of God as a sweet-smelling perfume. How great is the fragrance of that perfume when the people of God raise their hearts and minds with one accord in prayer! If you have never participated in a National Day of Prayer gathering in your hometown, make a commitment to do so the first Thursday of May.

Prayer Focus: Dear God, like the disciples of old, I ask of you, teach me to pray.

Elizabeth Hanford Dole

(b. 1936 – d.—)

*"Life is not just a few years to spend on self-indulgence and career
advancements. It's a privilege, a responsibility, a stewardship to
be lived according to a much higher calling—God's calling.
This alone gives true meaning to life."*
—Elizabeth Hanford Dole, *100 Christian Women Who Changed the 20th Century*

The sultry Sunday afternoon was no different from any other in
Salisbury, North Carolina in the mid 1940s. It had rained all morning, but by early afternoon the sun was bright and hot, evaporating rain-
drops from the lush landscape. After attending the local Methodist
church, ten-year-old Mary Elizabeth Hanford wended her way along
steamy sidewalks to her Grandmother Cathey's house for an afternoon of
cookies, Bible stories, and games with the other neighborhood children.

Thus, the first tiny seeds of faith were planted for the daughter of a
wealthy wholesale florist. Elizabeth had few concerns in those days. Now
much has changed but not her lifelong pursuit of God.

All Christians struggle at times to balance faith with daily living, striving to keep God in the forefront. For Elizabeth the conflict has been intensified by her ambitious nature. She got her first taste of leadership in the third grade when she was elected president of the Bird Club at her school. Then in the seventh grade she started the Junior Book Club and made *herself* president. Since then she has rarely missed an opportunity to be in the spotlight. That meant doing everything perfectly because the public eye was watching. Voted Most Likely to Succeed in her senior year in high school, she went on to run for almost every imaginable office at Duke University, achieving highest honors as student body president and May Queen. She graduated Phi Beta Kappa with a degree in political science. After a brief stint at the University of Oxford, she earned master's degrees in education and government from Harvard in 1960. When she entered Harvard Law School in 1962, she was one of only twenty-four women in a class of 550. She graduated among the top of her class with a degree in law in 1965.

While working in the Office of Consumer Affairs under the Nixon administration, Elizabeth met then-Senator Robert Dole of Kansas, who was the Republican National Committee chairman at the time. In 1975, after being appointed by the president to the Federal Trade Commission (FTC), Elizabeth and Bob married. Elizabeth resigned from the FTC in 1979 to campaign for her husband in his short, unsuccessful bid against Ronald Reagan for the Republican presidential nomination. Reagan's first appointment as president–elect was Elizabeth as assistant to the president for public liaison, a key White House position in which she thrived. "I have always loved to talk," she jests. Jokes aside, she took the job seriously. During an interview with *The New York Times* in 1982, Reagan's chief of staff, James Baker, said of her, "Elizabeth has one of the toughest jobs here. She has excellent political judgment, and she's extremely bright."

As the years passed and she climbed up the political ladder, working in a number of capacities under Johnson (as a Democrat), Nixon and Reagan (as a Republican), Elizabeth also worked on her public persona, creating a sleek, flawless image. By her own admission, however, perfectionism and success were the dominoes that led to a spiritual confrontation in her life. There was no great epiphany or revelation, only solace in a theological insight: *The restless heart can find peace only in God, not in personal achievements.* "There came a time when I had to face what commitment to God is all about," Elizabeth told a crowd of fifty-three thousand who had gathered for an Anaheim, California Harvest Crusade in 1996. "I thought I had to do everything 100 percent perfect, but I finally realized that meant putting myself first and God second. Although I was raised a Christian, I had not found salvation."

Elizabeth accepted Jesus Christ as her Savior through the guidance of a pastor in the 1980s and began attending the National Presbyterian Church in Washington, D.C. Since then, instead of spending her Sundays poring over notes and agendas for the upcoming week, she goes to morning services, passes leisurely time in quiet reflection, and enjoys her husband, family, and friends.

In February 1983, Elizabeth took a new post within Reagan's cabinet as secretary of transportation, the first woman ever to hold that position. During her tenure she led in the initiation of random drug testing to protect public highways and the crusade to raise the drinking age to twenty-one, and she directed the overhaul of the aviation safety inspection system. In the fall of 1987, she again quit her job to campaign for her husband in the Republican race for the presidency. Once again Bob was defeated, this time by George H. W. Bush, who went on to win the election. When he took office, Bush immediately appointed Elizabeth as secretary of labor, saying she understood the changing workforce, including vast numbers of women. In her new position Elizabeth worked to increase public safety and health in the workplace and improve relations between labor and management. She also played a key role in resolving the bitter eleven-month Pittston Coal Strike in Southwestern Virginia.

After only twenty-two months in office, Elizabeth resigned from the Labor Department in 1990 to become the first woman since founder Clara Barton to hold the office of president of the American Red Cross. As the largest charitable organization in the United States, larger than many companies on the Fortune 500 list, the Red Cross has a current (2004) budget of nearly two billion dollars, with approximately one and a half million employees and volunteers. As president of the organization, she traveled around the world, offering hope in the midst of enormous suffering and need in places such as the African continent, Eastern Europe, even on American soil, in the aftermath of the Oklahoma City bombing. "It was a mission field for me working with city and federal officials, right down to people who had lost loved ones and the survivors themselves. I knew I was making a difference."

Once more, in October 1995, Elizabeth announced her decision to leave her job and campaign for her husband in his run for the presidency against Bill Clinton. This time, she made clear that regardless of the outcome of the election, she would return to her post at the Red Cross in 1996. There was more work to be done, she said, inspiring people to give of their time, their financial resources, and their blood to aid the hurting and the dispossessed across America and around the world. Elizabeth remained with the Red Cross until January 1999, when she herself sought the Republican presidential nomination. She became the first viable woman candidate for the presidency from any major political party, attracting thousands of first-time voters into the democratic process. After losing the nomination to George W. Bush, she went on to serve the people of her home state of North Carolina in the United States Senate, winning 54 percent of the vote in the November 2002 ballot. As senator she is focusing on growing the economy, improving education, and lowering the costs and accessibility of quality health care.

Elizabeth has received numerous awards and honorary degrees over the years, but her greatest reward remains the fruits of her civil service career. "With clear heads, open eyes, and full hearts, we can choose a new future for our nation. But I have to say, that will come only if we all continue to work hard and prayerfully in the mission fields where God has placed us. . . . Be encouraged to press on, to continue to proclaim the good news, the only news that can save us as individuals and truly strengthen this nation we love so well."[1]

Questions/Thoughts for Reflection: When asked about her biggest flaw, Elizabeth Dole responds with, "I am a recovering perfectionist." Hosts of Christians, striving to respond to God's mandate to "be holy, as I am holy," can relate to Elizabeth's struggle. Where is the line between excellence—doing our utmost best—and perfection, which cannot possibly be achieved? Thank God for Jesus Christ, who was given to us as a gift from the God who knew we could never measure up to his standard of holiness.

Prayer Focus: Jesus, thank you for relieving me of the responsibility to be perfect. By your grace, help me to do my utmost best in service to you and the world you created, then prayerfully hand the rest over to your trustworthy care.

Elisabeth Elliot

(b. 1926 – d.—)

*"When I have the opportunity to speak to prospective missionaries,
I want to emphasize an encounter with the cross. I think it takes
a deep, spiritual encounter with the cross before we're really
qualified to call ourselves missionaries."*
—**Elisabeth Elliot, as told to Mission Frontiers**

Four-thirty on Sunday afternoon, January 8, 1956, was slow in coming for Elisabeth Elliot and four other anxious missionary wives. Five days earlier their husbands had taken off in a Piper Cruiser to prepare a field base and hopefully meet with representatives from the Auca, a tribe of native Indians who lived in the forests of northern Ecuador. So far all had gone well. In fact, the men were expecting to make their first official contact with the Auca earlier that day. Waiting for 4:30 to arrive, the time the couples had agreed to talk again by radio, Elisabeth reviewed her life leading up to what she anticipated would be a victorious moment.

She was born of missionary parents serving in Belgium after World War I. Shortly after her birth her parents returned to the United States where they raised six children in Pennsylvania, then New Jersey.

Elisabeth's was a true missionary home, a never-ending stream of guests. As a child she delighted in procuring the family guestbook, inviting each newcomer to sign in. At any given time she knew exactly how many visitors had passed through their doors and from what part of the world. In time hundreds of signatures from forty-two different countries were gathered in the book. Most were missionaries, either home on furlough or just passing through. Each had a unique story with which to regale Elisabeth and her siblings, of some hardship borne or miracle experienced.

Looking back to this time of her life, Elisabeth acknowledged how being surrounded by missionaries and their stories affected her ideas and opinions about what being a Christian means. These were the life stories of *everyday Christians,* she concluded, not believers who had been tagged or set aside by God for some special assignment. She knew at a young age that if she desired to be a follower of Jesus, she, too, could expect to endure difficulties and sorrows interspersed with the joys of discipleship. "Of course," Elisabeth has since told audiences, "I didn't know what the nature of my difficulties might be. . . . [As Christians] we are to be totally at God's disposal. There is no other way except the way of the cross."

At Wheaton College in Illinois, Elisabeth met a man who shared her deep spiritual convictions—Jim Elliot. Having grown up in a Christian home in Portland, Oregon, he, too, had heard thrilling missionary tales that made him yearn for the adventure of distant lands. Although the couple felt an attraction to each other, their drive to follow God's will and purpose for their lives was stronger. Both felt called to missions but to different parts of the world, Elisabeth to Africa and Jim to South America. If God wanted them together, he would have to work out the details, they decided.

God did just that. After graduation Elisabeth's plans for Africa did not work out, and she accepted an assignment in Quito, Ecuador to work with the Quichua Indians who did not have a written language. A year later Jim arrived at the same location. They married in 1953; two years later they gave birth to their only child, Valerie. As they worked among the Quichua, a dream evolved within both Elisabeth and Jim to find a tribe that had been untouched by the outside world. They learned about the Auca Indians, also known as the Huaorani. Over the years

Ecuadorian natives as well as representatives from Shell Oil Company had tried to penetrate the tribe, with disastrous results. Auca tribesmen had killed everyone who had ever ventured into their territory.

With language training complete, the Elliots and four other couples—Nate Saint, Pete Fleming, Ed McCulley, Roger Youderian, and their wives—decided to attempt making contact with the dreaded Auca tribe. After locating the village on September 19, 1955, they devised a strategy to demonstrate to the tribe their peaceful intentions. Filling a parcel with food and gifts, they secured it with a rope. With a portable loudspeaker in hand, they flew over the Auca village on numerous occasions, dropping the packages and repeating the phrase *Biti miti punimupa*, "I like you; I want to be your friend," as they slowly flew overhead. For several weeks they repeated the process. Finally the day came when the villagers tied a gift of their own to the rope, to be hauled away by the missionaries, a beautiful feathered headdress.

On the morning of January 3, 1956, Nate flew his male companions, a prefabricated tree house, and supplies to a landing strip that consisted of a narrow stretch of beach along the Curaray River, just outside the forest that concealed the Auca village. For the next three days, the men set up a field base, shouting friendly words intermittently into the forest. On the fourth day an Auca tribesman and two women appeared. Understanding only fragments of the Auca dialect, the men determined that the following day they would be met by a delegation of some sort. That night they excitedly told their wives about their anticipated meeting. All their hopes, prayers, and efforts to that point were about to be realized. The couples agreed to talk again at 4:30 the following evening.

On January 8, the prearranged time for radio contact came and went in silence. For the five women eager to hear a word from their husbands, the silence was deafening. The next morning a pilot flew over Palm Beach[1] and saw Nate's plane. Two days later he returned for a closer look. Lying on the beach were four bodies, all pierced through with spears. A crew of men returned once more to find the body of the fifth missionary downstream, where a current had carried it.

When Elisabeth heard that all five men had been killed, the words of a nineteenth-century missionary, Amy Carmichael, leapt to mind: *In acceptance lieth peace.* God had given Jim to her and their ten-month-old daughter for a short time; she would cherish the moments they had together and accept God's sovereign decision. "What else can you do except turn to Christ and say, 'Lord, you are in charge, I accept this.' Following means one step at a time, one day at a time."[2]

Sensing that her life's purpose in Ecuador had not yet been fulfilled, Elisabeth packed up little Valerie and returned to Quito and the work she had been doing with the Quichua Indians. In 1957, through a remarkable set of circumstances, two Auca Indian women came to live with her. During the ensuing months the three women grew to understand and trust each other. As she became more competent with the Auca language, Elisabeth spent long hours talking with the women about the missionaries' purpose in the country and why she and her friends had gone to the Auca village. The tribeswomen responded by explaining that after initial contact had been made with the five men on the beach, the village grew afraid that their peaceful gestures were an evil ploy to seduce them into opening up their village, that the men were really cannibals intent on killing them. The women became fast friends. When the tribeswomen returned to their village a year later, they invited Elisabeth to come with them. For two years mother and daughter lived among the Aucas, sharing the love and forgiveness of Christ among the villagers. When Elisabeth left the tribe, she said good-bye to lifelong friends, many of whom had become Christians ready to spread Christ's way of peace with the rest of the village.

Elisabeth returned to Quito once more, where she stayed until 1963. Then, sensing her work in Ecuador complete, she came home to the United States. In 1969, she married Addison Leitch, a professor of theology at Gordon Conwell Seminary in Massachusetts. After only four years of marriage, she again became a widow when Gordon died of cancer. To help make financial ends meet, she took in two boarders. Soon, her life filled with speaking engagements, writing *The Elisabeth Elliot Newsletter*,[3] hosting a popular daily radio talk show called "Gateway to Joy,"[4] and writing more than twenty books.[5] Eventually she married one of her boarders, Lars Gren. Her daughter Valerie married the other boarder and gave Elisabeth eight grandchildren.

Elisabeth's favorite topic when speaking to prospective missionaries is the cost of discipleship for every Christian:

[Jesus] says to each of us, "Do you want to be my disciple?" If the answer is yes, then there can be no question about the willingness to fulfill the three conditions of discipleship, which is to give up your right to yourself—and that flies in the face of everything that the world is saying. When the world is saying, "Be good to yourself, work on yourself, do your own thing," that is the absolute opposite of giving up your right to yourself. You can't take up the cross until you've given up your right to yourself. The second condition is "take up your cross," and that certainly means suffering of one sort or another. And the third thing, of course, is "to follow." And that means a determined obedience, from here to eternity.[6]

Questions/Thoughts for Reflection: Among the many quotes taken from Jim Elliot's diary, which Elisabeth included in her biography of her husband's life, one stands alone as representative of Jim's sacrifice and Elisabeth's life: "He is no fool who gives what he cannot keep to gain that which he cannot lose." Take a few moments to meditate on what these words mean. Do they shed any new light on your life?

Prayer Focus: Holy Spirit, help me daily to shed more of myself so that I may look more like Christ.

Esther, Queen of Persia

(b. "unavailable" – d. "unavailable")

"Go, gather all the Jews who are present in Shushan, and fast for me; neither eat nor drink for three days, night or day. My maids and I will fast likewise. And so I will go to the king, which is against the law; and if I perish, I perish!"
—Queen Esther (Esth. 4:16)

During the time of the Hebrew captivity, in the reign of King Ahasuerus of Persia (presumed to be Xerxes the Great, 486–465 BC), a beautiful young Jewish woman named Esther found herself in the unlikely circumstance of becoming queen.[1] The prior queen, Queen Vashti, was cherished, as were all women of her era, for her beauty alone; she had no rights whatever except for those the king bestowed upon her. So on the day she chose to disobey her husband, she lost her position if not her head. Following a beauty contest that spanned the entire Persian kingdom, the crown passed to Esther.

After five years in this position, the new queen learned from her cousin Mordecai that an official in the empire, Haman, had written a decree that every Jew living in the king's realm should be slaughtered on a certain day. Making matters worse, he had poisoned King Ahasuerus's mind against the Jews, who lived peaceably in the land. Listening to Haman's lies, the king sealed the decree with his own signet ring, creating an irrevocable document according to Persian law. By the time Queen Esther heard of the decree, the Jewish people were already doomed.

King Ahasuerus did not know that Esther, who had become the love of his life, was Jewish. If she exposed her background now, she, along with the other millions of Jews living in the empire, would be killed. But that is exactly what Mordecai asked her to do: plead before the king for the lives of the Jewish people, her people.

Esther was no different than the rest of us would be in her situation. Her heart filled with doubt and fear. She even made excuses, saying, "Everyone knows that any man or woman who goes unsolicited into the inner court of the king will be put to death unless the king holds out the golden scepter. Even me."

To this Esther's wise cousin replied, "Who knows whether you have come to the kingdom for such a time as this?" (Esth. 4:14).

Esther, you're the one. God put you in the king's palace for a reason. You are the hero here, if you'll just take the risk. You are the one.

Finally, after asking Mordecai and the rest of the Jews in the city to fast, Esther agreed to go before the king, uninvited and very much alone. Three days later she put on her royal robes and nervously stood in the inner court of the king's palace. Looking through an opening, the king saw his lovely queen and raised his scepter toward her. Relieved, she entered the chamber and touched the top of the scepter. She did not divulge her request immediately. Instead, she followed a well-devised plan intended to prepare the king's heart. When the time was right, she revealed her heritage and begged for the lives of her people somehow to be spared from Haman's death trap, including Mordecai, whose life Haman plotted to extinguish.

Wrath smoldered within the king as he began to understand Haman's evil plot against an innocent people. Before Haman could finish his plea for mercy, King Ahasuerus ordered him to be hanged on the gallows Haman had built for Mordecai.

Nevertheless, it was too late to reverse the decree against the Jews, which the king himself had unwittingly signed. All he could do was try to offset the damage. With this in mind, he signed a new decree giving the Jews the legal right to defend themselves against their enemies, whoever they may be, in whatever way necessary. For two days Jews throughout the entire realm fought and overpowered their attackers. On the third day peace reigned in the land, and Mordecai was named second in command in place of Haman. Ever since, this historic event has been celebrated as the Feast of Purim.

All because of the courage of one young woman who responded to the call: *Who knows but that you have come to the kingdom for such a time as this?*

Questions/Thoughts for Reflection: It might be easy to think we would be willing to die for Christ, but the truth is that kind of courage is usually borne out of many small decisions to make a stand for God even when there is little at stake.

Have you ever been afraid to tell someone you are a Christian? If so, what were the ramifications of your decision to either share your faith or keep quiet? Looking back, would you like to change your decision?

Prayer Focus: Dear Father, please help me to share my story of transformation with those around me. Help me to tell how your life-giving message has changed my life in great and small ways. Help me to share how your unfailing love has brought me hope and peace in a disconcerting world. And through my words, imperfect though they are, may you be glorified.

Elizabeth Fry

(b. 1780 – d. 1845)

"I have just returned from a most melancholy visit to Newgate, where I have been at the request of Elizabeth Fricker, previous to her execution tomorrow morning at eight o'clock. I found her much hurried, distressed and tormented in mind. Her hands cold and covered with something like the perspiration preceding death and in a universal tremor. The women with her said she had been so outrageous before our going [to meet her] that they thought a man must be sent for to manage her. However, after a serious time with her, her troubled soul became calmed."
—**Elizabeth Fry,** *Memoir of Elizabeth Fry*

Eighteen-year-old Elizabeth Gurney left home in Norwich, England on February 4, 1798, for the Meeting for Worship in which an American preacher named William Savery would be speaking. Being an unorthodox Quaker in her colorful dress and purple boots with scarlet laces, she did not much like going to Meetings but was intrigued to hear her first American. The message was so inspiring, Elizabeth wrote in her diary that night: "Today, I have felt there is a God." The following year she went to London to hear again the American pastor preach, in addition to a new "plain Friend," as most Quakers of the time were called, acquaintance, Deborah Darby. Because opportunities for women to voice their opinions outside the home were so rare, Elizabeth was excited to hear what Deborah had to say. As the Meeting wound down, Deborah walked up to Elizabeth, proclaiming, "You are born to be a light to the blind, speech to the dumb and feet to the lame!" Elizabeth thought Deborah had made a mistake. She loved the fine clothes and opportunities to visit the theater and the opera that her wealthy father afforded her; a life of service was not the future she looked forward to.

But as Elizabeth grew in her faith, she began to realize that inner beauty mattered more than outward appearance. She forsook her silk gowns and colorful shoes to don the simple no-frills dresses common to plain Friends. As she studied her Bible and prayed, she found herself drawn to the children of factory workers who were left to their own devices while their parents were at work. At her family's country home in Earlham, she began a Sunday school for these children, known as "Betsy's imps" by Elizabeth's sisters, feeding and clothing them, and reading to them from the Scriptures.

In the summer of 1799, a family friend named Joseph Fry visited the Gurney estate, casting a favorable eye on Elizabeth. Joseph also came from a wealthy family whose fortune had been made through importing tea, spices, and other luxuries, as well as a new bank, of which Joseph was then in charge. He asked Elizabeth to marry him, but she refused. "He is dull," she complained to her diary. But Joseph persisted, and with time Elizabeth came to love him. Besides, with her heart set more and more on helping the destitute and needy, she felt fortunate to find a man who was open to a wife who wanted to work outside the home in service to others. They were married the following year.

Over the next twenty years, twelve children were born to Elizabeth and Joseph. Concerned that the ongoing responsibilities of a large family would cause her to become a careworn and oppressed mother who neglected her civil duties to the community, Elizabeth visited the nearby Islington Workhouse, a shelter for the destitute, as often as possible. There she gained a reputation for sound teaching and great compassion. In 1812, a French aristocrat came to her for help. He had been touring British prisons for several weeks and had found the women's prison in nearby Newgate especially atrocious, with women lying on stone slab floors in misery with typhoid fever and babies left to die after their mothers were hanged or shipped off to Australia for their crimes. Hearing of Elizabeth's work at Islington Workhouse, he thought she might be able to help. The following day Elizabeth visited the prison. The conditions were even more horrific than the Frenchman had described. In one cell she watched as two women stripped the clothes off a dead baby to give to another child. Elizabeth handed out the clothing she had brought with her, promising to return with more. During subsequent visits she distributed clothes and fresh straw for the sick to lie on. She talked and prayed with the prisoners, assuring them that in God's eyes they had worth.

But the death of one of her own children and financial difficulties within her husband's bank kept Elizabeth from returning to Newgate until 1817, when her brother-in-law, a member of Parliament, pleaded with her to go back. Crime was on the rise; the women's prison was overcrowded and susceptible to riots. Something must be done. Elizabeth arrived just as a fight broke out among several of the women. The turnkeys hesitated letting her in for fear she would be assaulted. But Elizabeth insisted. Picking up a crying infant from the floor, she appealed to the prisoners' motherly instincts, saying, "Is there not something we can do for these innocent little children?" Enchanted by Elizabeth's concern for their welfare, the inmates quieted down.

"How can we do anything for them in here?" one prisoner asked.

In response Elizabeth returned with various materials so the prisoners could sew and knit small handicrafts that could be sold for food, clothing, and fresh straw. She suggested that the women form a prison school, assigning the more educated and capable inmates as teachers and administrators. But she could not go on supporting the reform effort by herself for long. Selecting eleven Quaker women and the wife of a clergyman, they formed the Association for the Improvement of the Female Prisoners in Newgate. The governor of the prison was so impressed with the behavior of the prisoners that he agreed to allow a matron to come supervise the school and the other work projects. When Elizabeth appealed to the Lord Mayor of London for funds to pay part of the matron's wages, he granted her request.

Elizabeth was also especially concerned about the treatment of prisoners who were about to receive the death penalty or be shipped to Australia, where England dispatched many of its convicted criminals. Finding that many of these prisoners suffered tremendous anxiety the night before their sentence was to be carried out, inciting riots and inflicting harm on others, Elizabeth made a point to visit with the prisoners hours before their death or deportation, sharing with them psalms from Scripture and holding their hands in prayer. She also pressed to have the mode of prisoner transportation changed from an open cart to a closed carriage in which the shackled occupant would not be exposed to the jeering public. Finally, to those who were to be shipped overseas, she provided bags of materials to create handcrafted projects, giving the prisoners something productive to do onboard ship as well as a product that could be sold for food upon arrival in Australia.

In 1818, Elizabeth was invited to the Committee of the House of Commons on London Prisons to give a report on her prison reform activities. In it she stressed the importance of education and useful employment in a prison rehabilitation strategy. The report spread throughout much of England and Europe, where she was invited to come before officials and royalty and share her ideas. Soon Ladies Committees sprouted up all over the continent, following the model Elizabeth had initiated. In 1823, The Prison Act was passed by British Parliament, incorporating many of Elizabeth's ideas.

The next twenty years proved difficult ones for Elizabeth. After the Fry Bank failed in 1828, the public cast a suspect eye on Joseph Fry and his wife, as did the Quaker Church. Believing that God materially blessed those living faithful lives, rumors flew about why the financial calamity occurred, followed by doubts as to Elizabeth's competency and calling. Had she absconded funds from the bank to subsidize her prison work? The Society of Friends also became critical of her role as a mother, faulting her for the fact that many of her children had married non-Quakers. Her husband was disowned from the Society, something tantamount to becoming a social outcast. In her final plea for prison reform before another House of Commons Committee in 1832, Elizabeth's thoughts about the detrimental effects of solitary confinement and the death penalty were virtually ignored.

Although Elizabeth had fallen into disrepute among her own countrymen, from which she never recovered, she is hailed to this day as the leading proponent of prison reform in Britain. She spent the last fifteen years of her life promoting her ideas in France, Belgium, the Netherlands, and Prussia. While she never visited Germany, a young pastor became so intrigued by her work that he carried her ideas to that country and set the wheels of prison reform in motion. Elizabeth died on October 12, 1845.

Questions / Thoughts for Reflection: Prison reform and the death penalty will never be popular topics of discussion. While some feel the death penalty is just punishment for certain crimes, others believe it only exaserbates a vicious cycle of violence, and that no matter what the offense, everyone deserves a chance to reform. Still others settle for some quiet act of awareness raising, such as a group of monks at a California monastery who ring the bells in their tower each time a death sentence is carried out at a nearby federal penitentiary. Lest we try to avoid the issue altogether, Jesus' haunting words ring out from Scripture, creating a dilemma for his followers: "The Spirit of the Lord GOD is upon Me, because the LORD has anointed Me to . . . proclaim liberty to the captives, and the opening of the prison to those who are bound" (Isa. 61:1; see also Luke 4:18).

Prayer Focus: Jesus, in this life there are many prisons, from the steel doors that snap shut behind their captives to prisons of the heart and mind, rendering their owners powerless in the midst of physical freedom. Make me sensitive to each kind of imprisonment, and empower me to proclaim liberty in a way that brings glory to your name.

Gloria Gaither

(b. 1942 – d.—)

"Because He lives, I can face tomorrow.
Because He lives, all fear is gone.
Because I know He holds the future,
My life is worth the living just because He lives."
—Gloria Gaither, "Because He Lives"

The entertainment industry has created more than its share of drug addicts and alcoholics, narcissists and cynics. Few have emerged from its grips with their lives enriched. One such woman is Gloria Gaither.

As a minister's daughter growing up in Michigan, Gloria Sickal wrote poems and journaled voraciously about everything from nature to faith to the ups and downs of life. She knew she wanted a future in full-time Christian work, but with opportunities for women limited to teaching and missions, she never dreamed God could use her penchant for words to forge a career. Instead she thought she would someday marry a missionary and serve in Africa. In preparation for a lifetime of field-work, she enrolled in Anderson College[1] in Anderson, Indiana, majoring in French and sociology. Unable to escape her love for language, she added a third major, English.

While Gloria was studying at Anderson and teaching at a nearby high school, a teaching colleague, Bill Gaither, dropped a pencil in front of her to get her attention. At first the pair snatched a few minutes here and there in the school hallways, talking about their mutual interests in faith, politics, and literature. Bill had already formed his first musical group, the Bill Gaither Trio; soon they were sharing song lyrics as well. "I began 'fixing' the lyrics to Bill's songs—giving him a line here, a phrase there, an ending or an opener. Eventually we began to develop a system that almost always involved us both searching for the right way to express—Bill in music, I in words—a great idea that would not be silenced."[2] During Christmas break of 1962, the couple married. The following spring Gloria graduated cum laude with degrees in English, French, and sociology.

Settling down in nearby Alexandria, Gloria and Bill continued to write and share their songs with anyone who would listen. As a lyricist, Gloria's own insecurities and struggles became fodder for some of her poetic lines. A self-proclaimed thinker and doubter, she learned to open herself up and allow God to turn her thoughts and doubts into verbal expressions of faith to which others could relate. Experiences with people, difficult situations, lessons that tested her faith and strengthened her hope, biblical insights, a sermon, even prayer—all became seeds that eventually germinated and blossomed into some combination of Gloria's lyrical talents and Bill's musical ability, conveying in song deep issues of the heart and of faith. Even then, however, music was a passionate pastime, not something Gloria aspired to turn into a forty-year career. But God had other plans. Before long, word spread about the Indiana couple who churned out Southern Gospel music from their garage. Church choir directors and evangelistic singers began stopping by each week, curious about the Gaithers' latest creation. Sometimes the calls turned into lingering visits, with Gloria offering guests a meal served up with a healthy dose of conversation.

Over the next two decades, Gloria balanced her time between raising the couple's three children, writing, and performing (weekends only) hundreds of gospel songs, including classics such as "Because He Lives" and "There's Something about That Name." In 1974, amid their many ongoing projects, she and Bill embarked on an undertaking they called a "Praise Gathering," a weekend getaway for Christian believers from all backgrounds and walks of life to come and enjoy being one family.[3]

The 1980s brought Gloria face-to-face with a whole new set of challenges, with a successful TV show, the *Gaither Gospel Hour*, a strenuous touring schedule, and studies for her master's degree in literature.[4] While her marriage has always been rock solid, it has also been a journey, filled with fiery personal tests, mountain top highs and valley lows, and above all, God's faithfulness. "Bill and I have always been going in the same direction, and that has kept us together over the years," Gloria says, looking back on her now-forty-year marriage. "Of course, we haven't always agreed on how to get there."[5] Gloria's recipe for marital happiness has been a commitment to a purpose larger than herself or her musical career and to that which is lasting, family bonds and the kingdom of God.

As the 1990s came into view, Gloria began dreaming of a place where seekers like herself, looking for spiritual truth, could come, enjoy a warm cup of coffee, listen to enriching music, and browse through Christian resources, all in a beautiful environment. She remembered the early days of creating music in the garage and sharing it with friends at her dining room table and the living room piano and wanted to recreate the ambience of those golden moments. In 1996, her dream was realized with the opening of Gaither Family Resources, which shares grounds with the Gaither Music Company and Gaither Studios. Complete with a latté bar, "Gaither Family Resources is a place of creative solitude and real community while providing an incredible array of books, gifts, art, home décor, creative toys and Homecoming music to visitors traveling to Alexandria from all over the world."[6] In March 2003, another dream became reality with the publication of the first issue of *Homecoming* magazine. Still going strong, the magazine's purpose is to inform and inspire Christians all over the globe.[7]

The pilgrim road Gloria has traveled, trying to maintain a simple faith amid the complexities of the entertainment business, has not been easy. But the rewards of dedication to her marriage and her God have been great: over six hundred songs, sixty recordings, a dozen musicals,[8] numerous Grammy and Dove awards; dozens of award-winning "Homecoming" videos, several business ventures geared toward building up the church and enhancing the Christian music industry, and a collection of books for adults and children.

But for Gloria none of these successes match the wonder of being a mother, and grandmother to her five grandchildren. A recent recipient, along with Bill, of the "Songwriters of the Century" award,[9] her main concern is still family, and her prayers reflect this priority. "I pray for [my grandchildren], that they will know God for themselves, that they will develop all of the unique abilities that God has put in them, and that they will have healthy relationships that are eternal. I pray . . . for Bill and me, and for my children at every stage, that God will protect us from cynicism. I pray that God will keep us simple and childlike in our faith so that we don't miss the wonder of it all."[10]

Questions/Thoughts for Reflection: God has blessed many of us with wonderfully creative talents and abilities. As we learn to expand and express these innate talents, we are faced—whether knowingly or unwittingly—with the decision of whether to use our gifts to enrich life or exploit it. Pressures are great, from peers to teachers to the industries served by each creative venue, to press the moral limits to new levels of depravity. The unfortunate truth is that this downward slide can happen unbeknownst to the artist/creator, simply by being unaware or by not making deliberate choices to use her creativity for godly purposes.

Has God given you special creative talents? Choose this day to surrender your abilities to the service of God.

Prayer Focus: Heavenly Father, thank you for the creative gifts you have given me. Help me to use them to build up your kingdom and lead people to your son, Jesus Christ.

Lakita Garth

(b. "unavailable" – d.—)

*"Is everyone going to wait until marriage [to have sex]? No.
But that doesn't mean we shouldn't set a standard."*
—Lakita Garth, Congressional Speech, 1998

Have I ever been naked in bed with a guy? No. I'm not having sex until I say 'I do,' which means I do you, you do me, and we don't do anybody else. No ringy, no dingy."[1]

The high school audience laughs. It's a play on words, but that is where the play stops. The topic is serious, and the teens know it. Adding dynamite to the speaker's discourse is the fact that she is no prim librarian-type, trying to hide a woeful life of failure to attract a man behind her message. This is Lakita Garth, 1995 Miss Black California and second runner-up in that year's Miss Black America pageant. She's a real beauty queen with a real message that she hopes will spur a new kind of sexual revolution, one that adds the word *abstinence* back into the vocabularies of teenagers and young adults the world over.

Lakita grew up in a project community in San Bernardino, California, which *Money* magazine designated in the late 1980s as one of the most dangerous places to live in America. Her father died of cancer after serving in both Korea and Vietnam, leaving her mother to raise Lakita and her four older brothers alone. Even with an absent father, Lakita always knew she was loved and what was expected of her, abstinence being high on the list. But that did not just mean abstaining from premarital sex. It was a lifestyle Lakita's parents encouraged that encompassed self-control, self-discipline, and practicing delayed gratification. "Abstinence is not just about shaking one's finger at a generation and telling them to 'just say no' to sex," Lakita now tells her audiences. "Self-control, self-discipline, and delayed gratification are essential to every individual who wants to achieve success in life, whether it be a satisfying relationship or a career."[2]

Speaking to city, state, and federal government officials, as well as school districts and church groups, she counters snickering remarks that abstinence education does not work with a quick retort: "The proof is in the pudding." Of all their contemporaries who grew up in that San Bernardino suburb, only the Garth children made it out unscathed by drugs, prison time, or single parenthood. Lakita's brothers grew up to become a doctor, a lawyer, an engineer, and a career naval serviceman. Lakita graduated from USC and currently works as a media commentator, professional entertainer, and CEO of her own company, a role in which she advocates abstinence and warns against the dangers of premarital sex (including teenage pregnancy and STDs), especially among African-Americans. According to a 2000 report by the Centers for Disease Control and Prevention, AIDS is the number one killer of African-American males ages fifteen to forty-four; African-American females do not fare much better.[3] A 1997 study found that 45 percent of African-American adults had herpes.[4] "Sex isn't evil. Sex is wonderful, and we should teach our children to respect it," Lakita frequently tells large groups of parents. "But we must be consistent. We don't say, 'Don't do drugs, but if you do, use a clean needle.'"

Lakita credits this kind of common-sense wisdom and her personal drive to wait for sex until marriage not only to her parents but also to her maternal grandparents, Walter and Louise Long. Every summer the Garth family would drive to Alabama to visit the Longs. After Louise died, Walter, then in his nineties, would rise early each morning and disappear for a few hours. One day, as an inquisitive eleven-year-old, Lakita asked him where he went. "I go [to the cemetery] to talk to my best friend, your grandmother," he replied. "I don't know anything else about any other woman, and I don't want to. Louise was the stuff."

Lakita has found the vast majority of teenagers and young adults want that kind of intimacy. She wants to show them how to wait for it. Talking to junior high, high school, and college students across the nation, she asks if they are being taught the three ideals that make up abstinence as presented in her message. The answer is the same. "Abstinence is always mentioned in class as the best thing, but the rest of the period is used to show us how to put on condoms. . . . No one is showing us how to [abstain]."[5]

Not a natural political activist, Lakita believes that in this situation change must come from the top down. Case in point: After President Bill Clinton's statement under oath that he did not have sex with Monica Lewinsky, insinuating that oral sex was not really sex, the incidents of oral sex among teenagers skyrocketed, along with the number of reported cases of oral herpes and other related STDs. So when Lakita was invited to share her thoughts about abstinence, and the high cost of premarital sex and teen pregnancy, with a U.S. Congressional Subcommittee, she jumped at the opportunity. For nearly an hour on July 16, 1998, she delivered powerful testimony dispelling ten myths surrounding teen sexuality. "Discouraging sexual activity among teens, not accommodating it as we have, should be the priority. Permissiveness and an undisciplined lifestyle have never, and never will, produce sustained excellence or success. . . . Abstinence can and should be taught not only as the cornerstone of sex education but as a lifestyle to be mastered."[6]

The battle to promote abstinence is an unpopular one, which smacks in the face of American culture as it is exhibited in TV shows and films. Surprisingly, the ones offering the most resistance to Lakita's message are not her young audiences but adults who either have yet to make the connection between the lie of "safe sex" and teen pregnancy and STDs or are more concerned about personal freedom at any cost. To these skeptics she extends the challenge to educate themselves and see if the latest statistics coming out of the National Institute of Health and the Centers for Disease Control and Prevention do not substantiate her claims. She concludes her challenge by adding, "One of the most frequently asked questions I get [from students] is, 'Why haven't I heard this before?' I need you to help me answer this generation."[7]

Questions/Thoughts for Reflection: No matter what the topic, it is never easy to voice an unpopular viewpoint. "Everybody is entitled to their own opinion" works fine when it comes to spaghetti sauce, but when the choice involves biblical, moral, or ethical issues of right and wrong, especially when people's lives are at stake, it is time to take another look at the problem. Is there some issue you feel strongly about, on which you have been reluctant to make a stand?

Prayer Focus: Almighty God, give me the resolve to stand up and be counted for what is right, the courage to raise my voice, and the strength to make a difference.

Helena, Mother of Constantine the Great

(b. Circa 248 – d. Circa 330)

"[Helena] became . . . such a devout servant of God, that one might believe her to have been from her very childhood a disciple of the Redeemer of mankind."
—**Eusebius, early church historian, www.gospelnet.com**

Helena's excitement grew as her eyes fell on a piece of wood buried in the hard ground outside of Jerusalem. She ordered the workers to slow their digging to procure intact whatever lay below. As hours turned to long days of meticulous digging, three crosses emerged. But on which one had her beloved Savior, Jesus Christ, been crucified?

Much of Helena's early life is shrouded in uncertainty. The exact date of her birth is unknown, though believed to be around AD 248. According to some historians she was the daughter of King Coel Godhebog of England, where her future husband, Emperor Constantius Chlorus of Rome, spent some time putting down a rebellion. But it is more likely that she was born in Drepanum[1] near the Black Sea in Asia

Minor. Unclear also is when Helena converted to Christianity from worshipping the Roman gods of the time.

What is certain is that at some point in her life, Helena married Constantius Chlorus and they had one son, Constantine. Around 292, Constantius was named Caesar of Gaul,[2] Spain, and England under the western Roman emperor, Maximian. To gain political favor he divorced Helena and married the emperor's stepdaughter Flavia Maximiana Theodora. The move succeeded; Maximian named Constantius Chlorus as his successor. In 305 Maximian died, and Constantius began his rule as emperor of the western region of the Roman Empire.[3] Helena lived in obscurity from the time of her divorce until 306, when Constantius died and Constantine took his place. Immediately Constantine summoned his mother to the imperial court, conferring on her the title of Augusta and ordering that all should honor her as mother of the sovereign.

For the next several years Helena gave her time and wealth to charities benefiting the poor. In 313 Constantine initiated the Edict of Milan, ending the persecution of Christians and legalizing the Christian faith. According to the church historian Eusebius, Helena was baptized at the age of sixty-three, shortly before the time of this edict. Is it possible her faith could have influenced her son's judicial decision, which affected thousands of Christians throughout the empire? For the next ten years, she lavished her riches on destitute Christian churches from England to the borders of Palestine.

In 324, when Constantine's enemies were finally defeated and he became sole emperor of the entire Roman Empire, Helena entered Palestine itself. There she began a pursuit that would last the rest of her life. *Where exactly in Bethlehem was Jesus born?* she wondered. *Of the many tombs cut out of the rocky hillsides, in which had he actually been buried? From what mount had he ascended into heaven?* These and other holy sites that had long since been buried with the passing of time consumed her thoughts.

Through interviews with Jews and Christians in the area, research of local historical documents, and excavations, Helena located the supposed sites of Jesus' birth in Bethlehem and his ascension to heaven on Mount Olivet outside of Jerusalem. She set to work supervising the construction of ornate basilicas at both sites,[4] at Constantine's expense. She also allegedly located the site of the holy sepulcher where Jesus' body was laid to rest, beneath a temple dedicated to Venus. She ordered the temple to be demolished and a church erected in its place. But where was Golgotha, the place where Jesus had been crucified? And where was his cross?

According to tradition,[5] in about 328, when she was eighty years old, Helena enlisted Judas, bishop of Cyriacus, to help her find the holy site. At the designated location was another heathen temple, which Helena ordered destroyed. For days Judas and his workers dug in the parched ground. At a depth of twenty feet, they struck upon a piece of wood. The digging slowed as they carefully unearthed three crosses. Surely these were the same ones used by the Romans to kill Jesus and the two thieves! But with no inscription attached to any of the three, how was Helena to know which one bore her Savior? She carried the three crosses to a woman afflicted with an incurable disease. One by one the woman touched the crosses. Upon brushing her fingertips across the rough wood of one, she was instantly cured of her illness. Helena built a church on the spot where the crosses were found. She shipped the true cross of Christ to Constantinople,[6] sending portions of it to the church in Rome and many other basilicas across the empire.

Around this time Constantine sent a message to his mother that he had rebuilt the town of Drepanum, renaming it Helenopolis. Her search for the holy sites of Jesus' life and death complete, Helena left Palestine to repose in her namesake city. It is not known exactly where she died, but the year is believed to be AD 330.[7] Her remains are now held inside the Vatican Museum in Rome.

Questions/Thoughts for Reflection: Are you at a place in life where you are trying to make career decisions? Do you want to donate some free time to a charitable organization but are unsure which one is the best fit for you? Most people have a better chance at succeeding in a career path or lay ministry that is aligned with their own unique talents, abilities, and interests. Certainly Helena's inquisitive mind coupled with her interest in archaeology (before the word was even defined) produced remarkable achievements for a woman of her day.

Take some time to write out which career paths and life areas interest you. Consider taking an aptitude test, the Myers-Briggs Type Indicator or the Strong Interest Inventory instrument to help discern your innate talents and interests. Then boldly step forward in the direction of your desired goal, prayerfully expectant that God will lead you.

Prayer Focus: God, guide my thoughts as I ponder and write; direct my heart as I search for your will for my life.

Roberta Hestenes

(b. 1939 – d.—)

"If God gives you a vision, take the risk. There will always be people who don't see it until it starts to happen. Start by building a team with those who do see the possibilities, and move forward as you see responsiveness and openness. Be bold and obedient, keep going."
—Roberta Hestenes, personal interview

As an educator, pastor, and world Christian, Roberta Hestenes has been loved and hated but never ignored.

Roberta grew up in a California home hostile to the Christian faith. Her parents, being Southern Baptist and Roman Catholic, had come to blows over differences in their beliefs and decided long before Roberta was born to leave religion by the wayside. Yet as a teenager Roberta felt a spiritual hunger. Having seen and experienced abuse in her family, she yearned for a goodness that transcended her everyday circumstances. Against the wishes of her parents, she was baptized and confirmed in the Lutheran Church, Missouri Synod at the age of sixteen.

Entering Whittier College in 1957, Roberta heard for the first time in her life that she could know God personally; immediately she invited

Christ into her heart. Three weeks later she went to a workshop led by InterVarsity Christian Fellowship where she learned how to lead a dorm room evangelistic Bible study. Within a few weeks students from her dorm were coming to faith, who then began similar studies in the surrounding dorms. Meanwhile Roberta became a mainstay in the Campus Fellowship group, InterVarsity activities, and at a little Quaker Church in nearby La Mirada. While Christian women in the 1950s were not given many influential roles, Roberta was an exception. As her mentors got to know her, they recognized in her unusual leadership qualities and gave her opportunities not afforded to most women of the time. Spending time in the presence of missionaries who shared their stories of spreading the gospel in remote places around the world, a passion grew within Roberta to serve in the mission field.

At an InterVarsity conference on campus, Roberta met John Hestenes, a physicist who also felt God's calling to the mission field. In 1959, the couple married and left Whittier College for Fuller Theological Seminary in Pasadena. Although Roberta had not yet received a college degree, because of a Fuller policy allowing wives to take classes free of charge, she found herself surrounded by some of the best Christian thinkers of the time. After two years at Fuller, they transferred to UC Santa Barbara so that John could get his master's degree in nuclear physics. Believing they were eventually headed for the mission fields of South America, Roberta earned her bachelor's degree from UCSB in Hispanic studies. In 1964, with their degrees completed, the Hestenes applied to the Latin American Mission as missionary candidates. To their surprise the mission board turned them down. "We believe your calling is to work in a university setting," the board explained. Roberta was taken aback. She felt certain she had been called to full-time Christian work; what could that be if not the foreign mission field? Little did she know at the time that God would call her to mission work of a different kind.

The next few years were spent giving birth to three children and following John as he pursued his doctorate, first to California Lutheran College in Thousand Oaks, California, then to the University of Washington, where Roberta took numerous graduate courses in rhetoric and public address. She also began teaching Bible studies and leading small groups at University Presbyterian Church in Seattle. In 1967, the pastor, Rev. Robert Munger, recognized Roberta's gift for Bible teaching and asked her to join his staff as director of adult education and small groups. "At that time most conservative Christian leaders were against women in ministry unless they really knew the woman well. That was true in my case," remembers Roberta. Pastor Munger was especially impressed by people like Henrietta Mears, director of Christian education at Hollywood Presbyterian Church and a leader behind Billy Graham's ministry, and Vonette Bright, cofounder of Campus Crusade for Christ. He saw in Roberta the same qualities he had seen in these other women and encouraged her to pursue full-time Christian ministry.

Times were tumultuous for women in any kind of leadership role in ministry. While Roberta's pastor, husband, and a few other men supported her efforts as a church staff member, others—including the mentor who had initially led her to faith and continued to influence her life—did not believe in what she was doing. It was a roller-coaster journey full of joy, uncertainty, and sometimes heartache. Daily she spent personal time praying and searching the Scriptures for answers. Weekly she met with a small group of women who prayed for one another's needs; time and time again her prayer requests focused on much-needed guidance from God.

Late in 1974, Fuller Theological Seminary asked Roberta if she would spearhead a new program on Christian formation and discipleship. By this time John had received his doctorate in physics. Believing that he was employable wherever there was a major university, he decided to support his wife's dream of teaching at Fuller, which had become a world-renowned evangelical seminary. In January 1975 the couple moved back to Pasadena, California, where Roberta became the first tenured female instructor at Fuller's School of Theology. She continued teaching at Fuller for twelve years, during which she completed her own education.[1]

In 1979, along with raising three children, volunteering to serve on World Vision's board, and facing ongoing animosity over her increasingly public role in Christian leadership, Roberta learned she had endometrial cancer. For three months she endured heavy radiation treatment and wrestled with questions about her faith and potential death. She began journaling daily to deal with her emotions and found that writing about what she was thankful for helped her keep life in perspective. She soon learned that her search for a grateful heart in the midst of a life-threatening illness had far-reaching effects. "During the long radiation treatments, I would sing hymns, thinking nobody was listening. At the end of my last treatment, the radiation technician, who had been monitoring each of my sessions from the next room, told me she was deeply touched by the hymns I had sung." Looking back on that most difficult time of life, Roberta says it added depth to her faith and gave her compassion for the troubles of others. It also taught her another lesson: "*Now* is the time to pursue what the Lord puts in front of you. Don't wait until it's too late."

In 1987, healed from cancer, Roberta had the opportunity to follow her own advice. She was invited by Eastern College,[2] a small Baptist liberal arts college in St. Davids, Pennsylvania, to lead the school as its president—an unheard of honor for any woman, especially one with a Presbyterian background. Moving to the small town outside Philadelphia, she became the first woman college president among the Coalition of Christian Colleges and Universities.[3] Along with teaching classes in Christian spirituality and founding the Center for Christian Women in Leadership, she was expected to raise funds for the college, increase the student population, and rejuvenate a faculty that initially harbored some distrust for the woman coming from the West Coast. In time she accomplished each of her goals, as the student body grew from eight hundred to over three thousand, and she and the faculty grew to love and respect each other. "I never aspired to the presidency of a college or any of the positions I have held. It was the Holy Spirit who called me to that position and the Holy Spirit who helped me do the job. It was not easy; there was quite a learning curve."

All the while Roberta faced continual opposition to her leadership. Like spiritual growth in the midst of persecution, she learned to be bold in following her calling. "If you let the doubters in your life rule—those who don't believe in your life mission—you'll never go anywhere. It's what I call the tyranny of the uncommitted. To overcome this tyranny, consult with others to glean God's wisdom; build a team to work with what you have and where you are; then as doors open, walk through them."

The toughest part of Roberta's job was fund-raising. Believing that a Christian college should have a strong music program, she lined up a team of consultants who could guide her through the process of creating and launching her idea. But the school had a tight budget with no excess to fund a new venture. Sensing a strong calling to proceed, she prayed. A few months later a supporter of the college passed away. In his private safe was found a Mozart manuscript, Variation in C Minor, that had been lost to the world for over one hundred years. The manuscript was sold to the Salzburg Festival in Austria for one and a half million dollars, the amount needed to fund the new music program.

While working at Eastern, Roberta held a part-time post as parish associate at Wayne Presbyterian Church. During her tenure there, she was drawn into a growing controversy about the ordination of homosexuals within the Presbyterian Church. As the years passed, she became a prominent figure in the discussion. While God had given her a tremendous love for the homosexuals she knew, she remained convinced Scripture teaches that practicing homosexuals should not be ordained. In 1996, she was asked to chair the general assembly committee regarding ordination and human sexuality. At the assembly, the issue exploded into a volatile debate. As chair of the committee, she helped to pen the constitutional provision regarding "Fidelity and Chastity," which confirmed her personal stance on the issue. "It was the toughest public issue I have ever had to deal with," Roberta has since disclosed. "I wanted to be compassionate toward those who were struggling with the issue of homosexuality, but I had to remain faithful to Scripture. The church cannot shift with the dominant culture, nor can it try to straddle the fence." For her staunch public posture, Roberta became the target of a great deal of hostility, including threats of personal harm. While attitudes have since softened toward her, she is still not welcomed in some circles and considered a hero in others.

One month after the 1996 general assembly, Roberta was called to the head pastor position at Solana Beach Presbyterian Church in Southern California. She felt she had done all she had set out to accomplish at Eastern. Meanwhile the pastor at Wayne had been stricken with cancer, leaving her to preach on Sunday mornings. Unexpectedly her passion for working within a church setting was rekindled. When the call from Solana Beach came, she was ready. Soon a vision for the affluent congregation of Solana Beach to minister to the surrounding poor Hispanic community blossomed into a dream that extended beyond the boundaries of the church's immediate neighborhoods into the heart of Africa, as the congregation adopted the Afar Tribe in Ethiopia. The new relationship provided the tribe with resources for education and opportunities to hear the gospel, as well as a continual stream of volunteers to help dig wells and teach new methods of food production.

Eventually, Roberta's pioneering work in Ethiopia caught the attention of World Vision, on whose board she had been serving since 1979. The organization asked her to come on board as a full-time staff member, ministering to the spiritual needs of World Vision's thirty thousand missionaries. In early 2000, Roberta accepted the position. She spent over half of the next four years on the road as World Vision's international minister. Finally, in 2004, she cut back her work for World Vision to part-time and accepted a part-time parish associate position at Community Presbyterian Church in Danville, California, near two of her children and their families. She also teaches classes at Fuller Theological Seminary. In her spare time, she is a corresponding editor for *Christianity Today* magazine, writing numerous feature articles and news stories. She is also the author of seven books. She has been a speaker in Africa, Asia, Latin America, and Europe, as well as all over the United States.

Summing up her career, Roberta says, "I'm an educator, a pastor, and a world Christian. Not everyone accepts my career path as from God, but if he calls us and gives us the gifts we have, then it is up to him to work out the details. I have believed in faith that God would work things out. He has not disappointed."

Questions/Thoughts for Reflection: One of the hardest things to do in life is relinquish control of our own destiny. Like being on a rollercoaster ride with nothing to do but hold on for dear life, giving up the reins of control is unsettling if not down-right frightening! In actuality, however, the Bible teaches that the aura of control is just an illusion. We have never had control of our destiny; rather, our lives are in the hands of God, subject to his mercy and grace. Isn't it time to recognize this fact and consciously hand over the reins of our lives to God?

Prayer Focus: Dear God, rather than fight with you over control of my life, which is rightfully yours to begin with, I want to cooperate with you in accomplishing whatever you desire to achieve in me. Give me a willing spirit and the ability to recognize your guidance and follow you.

Hildegard of Bingen

(b. 1098 – d. 1179)

"There was once a king sitting on his throne. Around him stood great and wonderfully beautiful columns ornamented with ivory, bearing the banners of the king with great honor. Then it pleased the king to raise a small feather from the ground, and he commanded it to fly. The feather flew, not because of anything in itself but because the air bore it along. Thus am I, a feather on the breath of God."
—**Hildegard of Bingen, "Gothic Voices"**

Today the mystics of old are little understood men and women from the Middle Ages who saw visions, dreamed dreams, experienced other-worldly encounters, and received special revelations. They are—to our modern mind—the figures of fantasy or perhaps science fiction, not ordinary life. Yet no scholarly account of Christian church history would be complete without significant attention being given to the Christian mystics, including Hildegard of Bingen. To her contemporaries Hildegard was a down-to-earth woman whose writings, pictures, and visions, appreciated by popes and paupers alike, paved the way for much-needed church and social reform. For today's Christians, her unusual story continues to be a source of inspiration that the Christian life can be lived on all levels of human existence, integrating all our senses and abilities with the world around us as we seek God in our daily lives.

Hildegard was born the daughter of a knight in AD 1098, in Bermersheim, Germany. Little is known about her early life except that she was a sickly child who began seeing what she called visions at an early age. According to legend, as a five year old, she described for her nurse an unborn calf still growing inside its mother as white with spots on its brow, its feet, and on its back. When the calf was born weeks later, it was exactly as Hildegard had described it. Realizing that others did not share her ability to see anything but the physical world, she soon learned to keep her visions to herself for fear of embarrassment or ridicule.

At eight, according to custom, her parents offered her, the tenth child, as a tithe to God. She entered the Benedictine monastery at Mount Saint Disibodenberg and began studying with Jutta, a recluse who had committed herself to a lifelong existence of isolation, self-deprivation, and prayer in a small room attached to the Disibodenberg monastery. For years Hildegard's daily life revolved around hours spent in prayer, song, and reading Scripture in Jutta's small room. Because of her teacher's radical ideas, Hildegard's education was rudimentary at best. Yet the two gained a reputation for holiness that spread throughout the Rhine Valley. Before long, more girls from noble families joined the two hermits, forming a small convent. At age fifteen Hildegard took the vows of a Benedictine nun, her life following the same pattern for the next two decades.

When Jutta died, thirty-eight-year-old Hildegard became the new head of the small convent. Unlike her mentor she believed in a balanced life and left the isolation of her cell to interact with her nuns, teaching them what little she had learned through books about science, medicine, and health care. Believing their days on earth should be a celebration rather than the dirge Jutta exhibited, Hildegard encouraged her nuns to wear floor-length white silken veils with golden tiaras over unbound hair to the Eucharist in anticipation of their union to Christ as the heavenly bridegroom.

Hildegard guarded the secret of her visions until 1140, when at the age of forty-two, she saw a vision that changed her life: "A fiery light, flashing intensely, came from the open vault of heaven and poured through my whole brain. Like a flame that is hot without burning it kindled all my heart and all my breast, just as the sun warms anything on which its rays fall. And suddenly I could understand what such books as the Psalter, the Gospel and other catholic volumes both of the Old and New Testaments actually set forth."[1] All at once, it seemed, she could understand Scripture and interpret theology in a way previously blocked to her. And, the vision continued, she was to abandon her reticence about sharing what she saw with others.

Thus began a series of spiritually significant visions. Present-day scholars have proposed that they were not true revelations from God at all, rather auras and other visual effects brought on by migraine headaches. Hildegard's own description of sickness, blindness, and temporary paralysis following her visions suggests this to be a possibility. Her writings also reveal her agonizing efforts and lengthy prayers to decipher them and their accompanying illnesses, much as a person might strive to understand a lingering, debilitating illness today. While Hildegard's conclusions about her visions may not satisfy everyone, the impact they had on her life and their far-reaching effects on Europe and the Church in Rome cannot be overstated.

In spite of the directive to share what many have since considered her heavenly gift, Hildegard struggled with feelings of inadequacy. Why God would use a "poor little figure of a woman" to do his work on earth was beyond her comprehension. She keenly sensed her lack of a formal education, recognizing especially her poor grasp of Latin grammar. How could one as unlearned as herself even begin to understand, much less write about, theology to a religious world dominated by well-educated men? To do so would be considered presumptuous and improper. Yet without the approval of these religious leaders, she would be dubbed a heretic.

Setting her qualms aside, Hildegard devoted the next few years to capturing her visions on paper. Her first book, *Scivias* (a contraction for *Sci Vias Domini*[2]) contained in-depth description and interpretation of her visions, as well as illuminations[3] depicting what she had seen. It also included biblical commentary and advice on how practicing Christians with secular as well as religious vocations could live in order to reach the heavenly city.

Hildegard respected Church hierarchy and was loyal to papal authority. If her visions were to gain an audience, it would be through the Church's official channels. She sent part of the work to a friend and leading churchman, Bernard of Clairvaux, requesting that he bless it and confirm her calling. Not only did he bless it, he also passed it along to Pope Eugenius III, who was known for maintaining a hard line against controversial theology. The pope sent a papal commission to investigate the orthodoxy of Hildegard's work more fully, then gave it his resounding approval by reading it aloud at the Synod of Trier in 1147. With Pope Eugenius's blessing, she became known as a prophet of God, a title almost unheard of in connection to a woman. Freed from conventional female roles, she could now write and act within the Church in whatever way she saw fit. In response to the pope's endorsement, Hildegard wrote back urging him to work harder at Church reform.

As Hildegard's fame increased, the little convent at Disibodenberg reached its capacity. In 1150, she and eighteen nuns moved to another convent, Rupertsberg at Bingen, on the banks of the Rhine River.[4] In Bingen, with the help of an assistant, she wrote prolifically. Her entire works consist of approximately seventy poems, seventy-seven chants, and dozens of antiphons.[5] Her nine books include three books of theology, two commentaries, two biographies, and two books related to science and medicine[6]—the only medical works written in Germany during the twelfth century. She also wrote a musical drama, *Ordo Virtutum*,[7] the first in recorded history. Permeating her many works is the idea of wholeness in Christ in contrast to the brokenness of the world. To describe this wholeness Hildegard used agricultural terms that her contemporaries could understand. She longed for the world to be fertile with the "greening power" or *viriditas* of God. Whereas the world was like parched soil that would eventually shrivel up the people dependent upon it, *viriditas* was like a nurturing rain, bringing moisture to the soul and causing it to grow. Like a kernel of wheat that, under the right conditions, issues forth fruit, the potential for *viriditas* exists in the womb of all humanity. Along with God's "moisture" (the Holy Spirit) comes growth, manifesting in creativity to serve God through music, poetry and prose, and art.

More than one hundred of Hildegard's letters have survived the centuries—scathing rebukes written to emperors, popes, bishops, and nobility about their God-given responsibility to ensure that every individual under their jurisdiction is treated fairly, protected from injustice, and realizes his full potential. Describing the people of God as *Ecclesia*, a woman battered and defiled through the excesses and corruption of Church clergy, Hildegard warned that if Church officials did not reform their ways, God would judge them much as he did the Hebrew kings of the Old Testament. In a letter to an aging pope about the abuse of power by those under his authority, she wrote, "You have to realize that your powers of perception have grown weak and you are too worn out to curb the arrogant boastful behavior of those in your charge. Why do you not stop these destructive men?"[8] To the German king and Roman emperor Friedrich Barbarossa, she wrote, "Be on your guard, lest the Sovereign King cast you down to the ground as a consequence of the blindness of your eyes that do not see rightly as you hold in your hand the scepter of your reign. Let not, then, the grace of God be lacking in you."[9] Most men, even in positions of power, would never have dared write such letters for fear of retribution. However, all respected Hildegard, and her letters were well received.

Wanting to remain faithful to her call to bring *viriditas* to the world, at age sixty and in chronic poor health, Hildegard began preaching in convents and cathedrals, before popes and emperors, even in marketplace squares. Her first public sermon is thought to have taken place in the cathedral in Trier, the oldest church in Germany. Explaining what the Living Light had shown her through her visions, she went on to describe God's never-ending love and kindness, calling on people to overcome their spiritual lethargy and experience the *viriditas* that would come if they turned their lives over to God. To anyone who dared challenge her authority, she would respond that if men had not abdicated or abused their God-given leadership, there would be no need for God to choose a frail, poorly educated woman to serve as a prophet.

"Listen," she would frequently tell her audiences. "There was once a king sitting on his throne. Around him stood great and wonderfully beautiful columns ornamented with ivory, bearing the banners of the king with great honor. Then it pleased the king to raise a small feather from the ground, and he commanded it to fly. The feather flew not because of anything in itself but because the air bore it along. Thus am I, a feather on the breath of God."

Hildegard died on September 17, 1179. Because her musical compositions, chants, and antiphons were written in notation that can be understood today, they are currently experiencing unprecedented revival.

Questions/Thoughts for Reflection: Have you ever felt that God could not use you because of a physical, emotional or mental limitation, or some social handicap? Remember Hildegard, through whom God did mighty things in spite of her poor education and visions that some authorities today would consider questionable. Remember also the words of Christ to the apostle Paul in 2 Corinthians 12:9, "My grace is sufficient for you, for my power is made perfect in weakness" (NIV).

Prayer Focus: Heavenly Christ, help me to accept myself with all my imperfections and weaknesses, knowing that through them your power can rest upon me.

Kay Coles James

(b. 1949 – d.—)

"In order to honor the legacy of those who have come before you, it is your responsibility as a citizen to reject cynicism and apathy and get involved in the public policy and political processes. You owe it to your family, community, and nation to make certain that liberty, freedom, and economic opportunity are secured and protected."
—**Kay Coles James, "Strong Men and Women"**

Imagine a housing project with backdoor alleyways overrun with discarded couches and other refuse and front-door access to drug trafficking and crime, where the word *neighborhood* refers not to a safe place for children to play but a stomping ground where gang members and dealers draw boundaries across which other gang members and dealers may not cross without consequences. Now imagine an African-American child growing up in such a housing project, a child whose fledgling spirit of adventure is crushed by an alcoholic father that cannot hold a job, whose sole emotional support comes from a mother struggling to raise six children on welfare.

For Kay Coles James such an existence does not require much imagination. She was the child, and the neighborhood was Creighton Court in Richmond, Virginia, a government-subsidized housing project that had long since gone the way of similar housing developments in big cities across the country. In this environment little Kay Coles got her first taste of poverty, her first peek at violence. Her little girl dreams aside, she sometimes wondered if her life could ever be any different from what she saw looking beyond the drapes of her living room window.

Born in Portsmouth, Virginia in 1949, Kay moved with her family to Creighton Court in Richmond when she was a toddler. Despite the fact that Mrs. Cole's own dreams had melted away years before, she was determined to help her children attain a better life. To that end she insisted they practice good posture and eloquent speech that belied their poverty-stricken situation. Although her welfare checks did not allow for the purchase of fancy clothes, she maintained a strict dress code of neatly washed and pressed garments. Above all, she demanded good scholarship in school. But as her children got older, Mrs. Coles found there was only so much she could do for them. She sent her only daughter to live with her sister in another part of Richmond, where she hoped Kay would have more opportunities. Although Kay now lived in a better neighborhood, she was still vulnerable to the racial slurs and demeaning conduct commonly perpetuated against blacks living in the South. A sense of self-worth was hard to come by.

Kay first learned she could have a personal relationship with Jesus Christ in high school. Then, attending Hampton University—under the nurturing guidance of several mentors along with InterVarsity Christian Fellowship—her faith came into full bloom. For the first time she felt valued for her own personhood regardless of the color of her skin. Able to put her country's Christian heritage and her own ethnic inheritance into perspective for the first time, she absorbed American history, government, and public administration classes. She graduated in 1973 with a strong sense of civil responsibility and calling to help others.

Kay's first job out of college was working in an administrative position at the phone company in Roanoke, where she met her future husband, Charles James. Having been raised in a home with an alcoholic, she had definite ideas about what a family should, and should not, look like. Charles had all the right qualities; the couple married soon after. Three children soon followed, Chuck, Elizabeth and Robert. As a stay-at-home mother for many years, Kay found raising her three children her biggest delight and her greatest responsibility. "Families who are based in faith are fortresses. You can go out and conquer the world when you know you have a support base back home. I think the first family value should be to value faith and family. If this didn't influence all decisions I make, I'd be in trouble. Our nation desperately needs a generation with such a legacy."[1]

One day one of her sons came home and showed Kay some pictures he'd found of aborted babies. He wanted to know who would do such a thing and why. The incident prompted a family discussion, with Kay trying delicately to explain that while Scripture states that every human life from the moment of conception has worth in God's eyes, some women feel they have no other option but to have an abortion, and they seek out doctors who will help them. After deep thought her son responded, "Can't you do something to make [the abortionists] stop killing the babies?"

"If I'm given the opportunity, I'll try," Kay responded. She went to bed with her son's question lingering in her mind.

Not long after this conversation, having returned to work in the private sector and gained a reputation as a leader with strong opinions about abortion, Kay received a call from the National Right to Life Committee in Washington, D.C. asking if she would debate the abortion issue on television. Eventually she went to work full-time for the committee as their director of public affairs, promoting the dignity and sanctity of all human life. Working with crisis pregnancy centers across the nation as they offered hope and practical assistance to women experiencing an unplanned pregnancy, she knew she had fulfilled her promise to her son. She also knew she was on the road to something bigger. Eventually her work led to state and federal government posts where she could actually help create public policy and make a difference in a number of areas of personal interest.

Today Kay's resume of public service is impressive as well as demonstrative of her heart's concern for the nation. After serving minor appointments under former President Ronald Reagan, including the White House Task Force on the Black Family, she was appointed by former President George H. W. Bush as assistant secretary for public affairs at the U.S. Department of Health and Human Services and as associate director for the White House Office of National Drug Control Policy. In the 1990s she served as secretary of the Republican National Convention and a member of the Platform Committee. She became secretary of Health and Human Resources for the Commonwealth of Virginia, a member of the Virginia State Board of Education, and chairperson for the National Gambling Impact Study Commission, under appointment by House Speaker Newt Gingrich. In March 1996 she was hired as dean of the Robertson School of Government at Regent University.

Seeing a national trend toward nonparticipation in civil duties by the American public, Kay left Regent University in 1999 to pursue a passion—the Citizen Project of the Heritage Foundation in Washington, D.C., an organization dedicated to restoring a strong ethic of citizenship and civic responsibility in America. "When this nation began, it was clearly an experiment. The Founding Fathers knew success depended on an informed citizenry who would participate in the process. We would not survive if people were apathetic, disengaged, and cynical. Yet, today, each election cycle shows plainly that a few people are making the decisions that shape the culture for the rest of us."[2] As senior fellow of the project, she became its director in 1999, a post she held for two years.

After President George W. Bush's election to the presidency in 2000, Kay was nominated as the director of the U.S. Office of Personnel Management. On July 11, 2001 the appointment was confirmed by the U.S. Senate. As director she is directly responsible for thirty-six hundred federal employees, an annual budget of nearly three hundred million dollars, and trust funds exceeding twenty-nine billion dollars. She advises President Bush on matters of personnel administration for the nearly two million members of the Federal civil service workforce and helps federal agencies across the country meet their strategic objectives, improve their human resources management, and plan for the future. Most recently she helped create the Department of Homeland Security and is partnering with the Department of Defense to reform and modernize its civilian personnel system. "With our nation under attack, to know I have the ability to do something is a *tremendous* feeling. I couldn't be happier or more fulfilled knowing I'm serving God and, in my own way, keeping the hope of America alive."[3]

Kay has served on a number of boards, including Focus on the Family, and has received several honorary degrees and awards. She continues actively to express her passion for the sanctity of life and the importance of the American public fulfilling its civil responsibilities. "A heated debate now rages about whether Christians should be involved in government," Kay states.

Some Christians want to back off and disengage; I think this is inexcusable. . . . We're in this predicament because too many good people have thrown up their hands and walked away. If we truly want to turn the tide back, we must recognize our responsibility and become involved. The challenge for every Christian today is to ask what we can do for our country, our communities, and our families. Instead of waiting for political change to occur in Washington and our state capitols, we must renew the individual's obligation in a just society. Only by embracing our core beliefs and working for change in each of our lives can we truly see regeneration.[4]

Questions/Thoughts for Reflection: Bringing about change is not easy and requires perseverance. While lasting change is sometimes measurable only by the passing of generations, it can be done. Kay Coles James suggests the following steps: (1) vote regularly; (2) talk to your family, especially your children, about what it means to be an American; (3) hold elected officials accountable after election; (4) stay informed; (5) get involved; (6) pick an issue that you are passionate about and become an activist; (7) get on mailing lists; (8) volunteer your time; (9) give financially to organizations you believe in; (10) encourage others to do the same.

Prayer Focus: God, as I look at society today, help me not to lose heart but to recognize my own civil duties to bring renewal to the country I so dearly love.

Madeleine L'Engle

(b. 1918 – d.—)

*"How can anyone even begin to have an incarnational view of the
universe without an incredible leap of the imagination?
That God cares for us, every single one of us, so deeply that all power
is willing to come to us, to be with us, takes all the imagination
with which we have been endowed."*
—Madeleine L'Engle, *Two-Part Invention*

Five-year-old Madeleine Camp set her book of George MacDonald fantasies aside and gazed out a window into the lives of other New York City dwellers living in the unshaded apartments across the street from her bedroom. After a few minutes she took a piece of lined paper and a pencil and began to write a story about a "grul" ("girl" in her childhood scrawl) not unlike herself. Her first accomplishment in a long career of writing short stories, poems, nonfiction works, and novels, the youthful tale foreshadowed the same imagination and feminine spunk that readers and critics the world over have both praised and denounced throughout six decades of publishing.

Writing success did not come easily to Madeleine, who began using the name L'Engle (a maternal surname) after quitting a brief acting career to pursue writing full-time. She grew up on the fringes of Bohemian society prominent in 1920s Manhattan, where her writer/journalist father and pianist mother hosted many parties and artistic gatherings that Madeleine enjoyed from the doorjamb of her bedroom. Even from that vantage point, she basked in the creative energy that continually flowed through her home. In 1930, the family moved to Europe in hopes that the clean Alpine air would cure her father's lung disease, brought on by exposure to mustard gas during WWI. The sudden move plunged twelve-year-old Madeleine into another world entirely. A shy, precocious "nonachiever" in grade school, she now spent each school year at a boarding school where she blossomed into a happy, productive student. Even after returning to the United States a few years later, taking up residence in her deceased grandmother's beachfront home in Jacksonville, Florida, Madeleine thrived at Ashley Hall in Charleston, North Carolina.

Following high school, Madeleine enrolled at Smith College in Northampton, Massachusetts, studying both writing and the theater. But Manhattan still ran through her veins. After graduating from Smith in 1941, she headed straight for Greenwich Village in New York City, where she believed the theater would give her the finishing touch she needed to be a published writer. By selling war bonds in theater lobbies, she was able to attend dozens of plays for free and eventually meet the producers and directors who would grant her bit parts and understudy roles. While earning equity minimum wage of sixty-five dollars a week during theater runs, selling war bonds, and working part-time at a local hospital, she spent every spare moment writing.

The Greenwich Village years were tough on Madeleine. Isolated once again by her desire to write, she had few friends outside the theater and even fewer dates. One young man, whose company she both enjoyed and found disturbing, committed suicide within a year of their meeting. Another, a cultivated Hungarian refugee who took her to fine restaurants and the opera, wanted her as his mistress. A third proposed marriage more out of the need for a mother to his children than mutual love. Badly shaken and confused by these events, Madeleine sought solace and clarity almost nightly at Ascension Episcopal Church, the only church in the area that stayed open after the theaters closed. Rejecting her Anglican heritage with its emphasis on stoicism, she needed a place where she could express years' of pent-up feelings through prayer, find peace, and just be. "My father died when I was seventeen and no one told me that it was all right to cry, to hurt. True to my tradition, I carried on, did all the brave things, and repressed my grief. . . . Ascension Church was a special place for me, part of my deepening, along with the piano, the books, and the typewriter, which had once been my father's."[1]

After seeing a number of her short stories in print, Madeleine's first book, a coming-of-age novel titled *The Small Rain*,[2] was published in 1945. The story of a young woman seeking fame, fortune, and love in Bohemian society of Europe and then Greenwich Village, it followed the pattern of Madeleine's own life to that point, complete with its emotional highs and lows. Later that same year she was cast in Chekhov's *The Cherry Orchard*, where she met her future husband, a dark-haired, blue-eyed actor named Hugh Franklin.[3] The pair hit it off immediately; they were married the following year. She spent the next decade and a half in their new home, a rustic farmhouse called Crosswicks in rural Connecticut, raising their children—daughter Josephine, born in 1946, son Bion, born in 1951, plus a goddaughter named Maria—writing, and helping Hugh run the country store they had taken over to get away from the stresses of theater life. Although she experienced a few more publishing successes, mostly children's stories about family life and growing up, none captured the essence of the writer future generations would come to know and love so well.

Even in their new pastoral surroundings, it was hard to avoid the furious debate over Communism that was sweeping the nation like fire in a wind tunnel. Articles depicting the USSR as a menacing evil threatening American democracy battled against the voice of communist sympathizers rising above small talk at dinner parties for the attention of audiences across the country. For Madeleine the debate sparked thoughts about the greater struggle of good and evil human beings face within themselves. More to her liking were articles in science journals about new discoveries in the fields of particle physics and quantum mechanics. In one such article she stumbled across the concept of a "tesseract," the fourth dimension of a cube. Soon her imagination began to whir as she postulated how tesseracts might enable time travel. In a heartbeat the idea for a new book was born in which a young female protagonist must search through time and space to find and rescue her scientist father from evil. The resulting novel, *A Wrinkle in Time*,[4] helped to crack open the genres of science fiction and fantasy to a waiting audience. After eighteen rejections the book was published in 1962 and became an overnight success. The following year it won the coveted Newbery Medal Award.

While the book quickly went to reprint to meet demand, a growing number of critics arose to protest its "theology." How can a Christian write a book that contains no mention of God? One that rubs against the evangelically correct language of the time? Above all, how can a Christian promote the imagination, that tool of the mind so often twisted and perverted for evil? To Madeleine's dismay, ministers preached sermons warning against her book; librarians refused to stock it on their shelves; in some cities, officials banned it altogether. All of which fueled the book's popularity even more.

"How can anyone even begin to have an incarnational view of the universe without an incredible leap of the imagination?" Madeleine asks in her memoir, *Two-Part Invention*. "That God cares for us, every single one of us, so deeply that all power is willing to come to us, to be with us, takes all the imagination with which we have been endowed."[5] Discarding views that her work is un-Christian, she explains, "A Christian writer should create good art. Bach's music is totally Christian, and yet how can you find anything in it to proclaim it as such?"[6] About her so-called non-Christian characters, she writes, "Sometimes the characters are technically not religious, not believers, but people who simply live their faith."[7]

Besides, Madeleine has never contended to be a Christian writer, just a writer who struggles to be a Christian, whose beliefs are "subject to change," echoing Paul's command in Philippians 2:12 to "work out your own salvation with fear and trembling," an assertion that further maddens her critics but is quietly understood by her legions of readers.

Once the general store began paying for itself, the challenge was gone and so was the appeal. Hugh longed for the theater again. The family moved back to New York, spending most of their time in the city and visiting Crosswicks on holidays. Madeleine's pattern remained unchanged after Hugh's death in the fall of 1986. As writer-in-residence and librarian at the Cathedral of St. John the Divine in New York City, a volunteer role she has filled since 1965, her days are consumed with library work, research, manuscript review, and correspondence, when she is not traveling to speaking engagements or with family at Crosswicks. And, of course, writing. "Since I started writing when I was five, it's hard for me to understand anything else. At its best it is like Michelangelo seeing a discarded piece of stone, looking at it, and having his heart's expression chip it into the form of David."[8] At any given moment, she says, she has more book ideas in her head than there are hours in the day.

Over the last half century, Madeleine has stubbornly remained true to her craft and her literary voice, as is reflected in more than fifty books and untold numbers of stories and articles. As a practicing Episcopalian who attends the Eucharist, prays, reads Scripture and holds private devotions daily, she no longer worries that her fiction strikes some as being too worldly simply because her characters do not blatantly appear Christian. Her greater concern is whether her stories inspire others to live more courageously and creatively. "I think if we speak the truth and are not afraid to be disagreed with, we can make big changes."[9]

Critics aside, millions of fans agree that Madeleine's body of work has changed the world for good. Her *Wrinkle in Time* series has inspired young and old alike to love science. Her spunky female protagonists have encouraged girls and women of all ages to accept that it is OK to use their brains, to view themselves as capable, to imagine a better future. Her nonfiction helps her enduring audience to face their own end-of-life challenges with courage as they read how Madeleine's experiences with family, aging, and death tested and strengthened her. Above all, her writing encourages us to hold on to our preconceptions of how God should act in our lives a bit more lightly, allowing his sovereignty to reign supreme.

Questions/Thoughts for Reflection: Oftentimes Christians working in creative fields are painfully stretched by critics and evolving market demands as they try to express their art while staying within acceptable industry standards. At the heart of many debates is an attempt to define boundaries for the imagination in Christian art forms, indeed, whether there is a place for it in the Christian life at all. Crashing into this discussion like a wrecking ball are Madeleine L'Engle's prophetic words:

"How can anyone even begin to have an incarnational view of the universe without an incredible leap of the imagination? That God cares for us, every single one of us, so deeply that all power is willing to come to us, to be with us, takes all the imagination with which we have been endowed."

Do you enjoy using your creative talents to express your love for God, his world, and his people? Dare to use your imagination to envision the possibilities God may have in store for your life!

Prayer Focus: Breathe on me, breath of God. Help me to live as one victorious in Christ, reflecting to a barren world all the wonderful possibilities that walking with you by my side brings.

Mary of Bethany

(b. "unavailable" – d. "unavailable")

*"Why do you trouble this woman? For she has done a good work
for Me. For you have the poor with you always, but Me you do not
have always. Assuredly, I say to you, wherever this gospel is
preached in the whole world, what this woman has done
will also be told as a memorial to her."*
—Jesus, regarding Mary of Bethany

Over the years scholars have had a heyday describing Jesus' disciples
and followers: faithful, fickle, cocky, insecure, zealous, comical,
fearful, flighty. However, one follower in particular has remained a stead-
fast reminder of what it meant in Jesus' day, as well as our own, to be a
true friend of God. A simple woman, Mary of Bethany proved to be fer-
vent in spirit to the one she chose to call Lord and loyal beyond compare
in her understanding of his mission.

Scripture does not tell us how Mary met Jesus. Perhaps she saw him
teaching in the temple in Jerusalem. She might have witnessed his rage
at the money changers when he flipped over their tables during Passover.
But it was her sister Martha who offered the first dinner invitation. Soon

Mary, Martha, their brother Lazarus, and Jesus were close friends. Whenever Jesus came to the area, he likely stayed in their home, a pattern developing with each visit. Mary, who normally worked alongside Martha, would set aside her duties to sit at Jesus' feet, soaking up every word he said. She saw greatness in him and did not want to miss even one opportunity to be in his presence. Eventually Martha became perturbed not only at Mary but also at Jesus for allowing her sister's behavior to persist. It wasn't right, and she told him so.

"Master, don't you care that my sister has relinquished all her chores? Tell her to give me a hand!" she cried (Luke 10:38–42).

Much of living out the Christian life is learning a different set of values and priorities. Whereas there is nothing wrong with maintaining a home or catering to a houseguest, Jesus knew Martha had become distracted with these activities and had neglected the most important pursuit of all—spending time with him.

"Martha, dear Martha," Jesus scolded gently. "You're making too much fuss about this. Only one thing is truly essential, and Mary has chosen it. I won't take that away from her."

Eventually Lazarus, the breadwinner of the family, became gravely ill. His death would spell disaster for Mary and Martha. How could they keep their home and still put food on the table? Where would they go? Knowing that Jesus would want to hear about his dying friend, Mary and Martha sent a messenger to Jesus, across the Jordan River several miles away. But by the time he arrived, Lazarus was already dead, wrapped in spices and buried in a stone tomb sealed with a large boulder. The sisters were consumed with sorrow. "Lord, if you had been here, our brother would not have died," Martha said. While Mary made the same observation, she seemed less interested in a response than in simply wanting to share her grief with Jesus. Falling at his feet, she wept. As Jesus cried with her, their spirits joined in anguish.

It would not be the last time Mary and Jesus shared a moment of mutual understanding. Mary was in the habit of truly listening to every word Jesus spoke, including the numerous times he explained that he must die in order to fulfill his purpose, then rise from the dead. None of his other followers seemed to hear this, much less believe Jesus' prophecies of his own death. They were too preoccupied with thoughts of overthrowing the Roman occupation and reigning in their stead. Only Mary understood. She may even have believed that if Jesus himself could rise from the dead, so might he also bring her brother back to life.

And raise Lazarus he did. "Lazarus, come out!" Jesus shouted at the tomb, which had been opened. At the sound of his name, the dead man, bound hand and foot in grave clothes, came forth into the sunlight (see John 11:1–44).

From that day forward swarms of people flocked to see Jesus. He had become an instant celebrity, hated by the Pharisees now more than ever. What would happen if they could not control this man who stirred up the people? Might he rouse the Romans, who had the power to remove them from their places of authority? They must kill him, the Pharisees concluded. To avoid attention, Jesus spent the next several weeks in Ephraim, north of Jerusalem.

But the Passover was fast approaching; Jesus knew the time of his arrest drew near. On his way to Jerusalem, he took a detour to Bethany to visit his dear friends once more. As he sat visiting with his disciples and Lazarus in the home of Simon the leper, Martha busied herself with meal preparation while Mary was lost in thought. Sensing this might be the last time she would see her Lord, she wanted to impart some special gift that he could take away with him to whatever lay ahead in Jerusalem. But what, and how? She should help her sister serve the meal that night, and in the morning, Jesus would be gone.

Later that evening an idea came to Mary. Leaving Martha to serve alone, she dashed home where she kept an alabaster container of costly spikenard oil. The alabaster shone in the pale light of an oil lamp, a hint of translucent yellow and opaque white gypsum intricately carved into an exquisite flask. Hiding the flask beneath her cloak, she strode purposefully back to Simon's home. Finding Jesus seated at the table, she bent down and cracked the flask open on the ground, then poured its contents slowly over his head. She drained the last bit of oil onto his feet, anointing them little by little with her hair. She did all this in silence, as the fragrance of the pungent perfume rode on a slight breeze throughout the house.

The conversation around the table stopped abruptly as the men in the room gaped at Mary. Oblivious to their shock, Jesus sat in silence, eyes closed, savoring the tranquil sensation of oil dripping down his temples and being massaged into his tired feet. No one said a word for a long time. Finally, Judas Iscariot, who kept the money box for the group, broke the spell of the moment. "What in the world are you doing?" he shrieked. "That oil could have been sold for a year's wages and given to the poor. What a waste!"

Jesus opened his eyes as if waking from a pleasant dream. "Why do you trouble this woman? What she has done is a blessing to me, for knowing that my death is near, she has anointed my body for burial. The poor will be with you always, down through the ages. But I am here only for a short while longer" (see Matt. 26:6–13; Mark 14:3–9; John 12:1–11).

True to Jesus' prediction, within a few days he was arrested, beaten, and crucified. More than the hours of physical agony, the loneliness was excruciating. Nearly all his disciples and friends had abandoned him. Even his heavenly Father, who had been his constant companion throughout life, turned his back on him. And yet the fragrant oil of spikenard that Mary had poured over his head, saturating his hair and the skin on his face, lingered. The love of this one faithful woman lingered still.

Questions/Thoughts for Reflection: Have you ever heard someone tell of growing up in the days before indoor plumbing? For most of these people, the trouble of pumping and heating enough water for everyone in the family to bathe relegated that activity to once a week, usually on Saturday night. In Jesus' day even once a week would have been a luxury. It is easy to imagine that the potent fragrance of the spikenard oil stayed with Jesus for a long time, even to the day of his crucifixion. Each time he pushed up with his feet for a breath of air while hanging on the cross, his nostrils likely filled with the lingering fragrance of the savory perfume. What a powerful reminder of love and faithfulness the smell must have been to him, even if for a fleeting moment amidst the agony of death. All because one woman was daring enough to follow her heart.

You may feel that your faith is small or that you have little to offer to God. But are you willing to share what you do have in order to express your devotion to him?

Prayer Focus: Dear Jesus, thank you for Mary's example of devotion. Please give me courage that I might faithfully express and share my own dedication to you in tangible ways.

Mary of Magdala

(b. "unavailable" – d. "unavailable")

Mary Magdalene followed Joseph of Arimathea as he took Jesus' body down from the cross, observing the tomb where he laid it. There was no time before the Sabbath began to anoint the body properly for burial, but she could at least prepare the spices and fragrant oils before the sun went down. At dawn on the first day of the week, she took the embalming material to the tomb to anoint her Lord.
—**the Gospel writers, regarding Mary of Magdala**

The sun rose dusty and hot above the eastern mountains overlooking the calm Galilean sea, casting long shadows behind a group that had gathered on the western shore. In the middle of the crowd, a knot of curious onlookers encircled Jesus as he spoke to a young woman named Mary—"Mad Mary," as some from her hometown of Magdala called her, for she had lost her reason. "Too bad," tongues wagged as the villagers would catch sight of the pitiful beauty in the town square. "Such a fine family, and wealthy, too. What sin must she or her parents have committed to deserve such a shameful legacy?"

Jesus had heard the gossip but dismissed it as irrelevant. Evil spirits were responsible for her insanity; all that really mattered was that she stood before him now, longing with what little good judgment she had left to receive some touch and to be rid of her infirmity. True to his nature, though cultural mores would dictate that men never speak directly to women in public, Jesus gave her his full attention. With a single word he summoned the demons that had held her hostage for years to come forth and be gone. After a stubborn wrenching of the young woman's body, the spirits departed, leaving Mary in an unconscious heap on the ground. The crowd gasped. "Is she dead?" a few asked.

"Water, quick," Jesus commanded. One of Mary's friends leapt into action and ran into the village to fetch a bucket from the well. Waiting for the fresh water, he dipped a corner of his robe into the Galilean Sea and blotted Mary's face. After a few moments she revived. The crowd was awed in dumbfounded amazement.

"What? Why am I here?" Mary looked around, then fixing her gaze on Jesus' face.

"You do not remember, child?" Jesus said, offering her a sip from the bucket of water as it was passed into his hands.

Mary drank deeply. "No, I remember nothing," she said finally.

"You came to me to be healed. Your friends helped you." Jesus nodded to the handful of women and men who had guided Mary down to the water's edge.

"The voices?"

"They are gone."

Mary sat in silence, her face alert, listening intently. "They *are* gone!" Bending low, she pressed her lips against Jesus' dusty feet. "Thank you, Rabboni."[1]

Mary spent the next couple of years following Jesus wherever he went. As a girl she had wanted to learn under the rabbis at the synagogue as her brothers had done, but being female, she was forbidden. Jesus was different. He invited her to sit among the others as he taught under the palm trees, in grassy meadows, or on the sandy Galilean shore. Her head now clear, she was quick to understand the teachings of Moses and the prophets and thrived on the parables Jesus used to demonstrate spiritual truths. Only references to his pending death confused her. If he was truly the Messiah foretold of old, would he not reign as king? But there was plenty of time to comprehend everything. What she understood best of all was that he had freed her and deserved her unfailing loyalty, no matter what happened. In gratitude she used her personal means to supply the needs of Jesus and his disciples, buying food and shelter as surroundings allowed.

One day Jesus' predictions of his death intensified. Whereas before he made peripheral suggestions, now it was the focus of conversation. Then, like waking up to find that what you hoped was a bad dream is in fact a reality, it happened. Betrayed by one of his closest friends, temple guards arrested him. The rest of the disciples scattered. Within hours, Jesus faced false accusations from Caiaphas the high priest and stood trial before two judges, Herod and Pilot. He was sentenced to death. The next day Roman guards nailed him to a cross atop a hill outside Jerusalem.

Like the rest of Jesus' followers, Mary was devastated by the news. How could all this be, and what did it mean? Struggling to make sense of it all, one thing became clear. She could not leave him to die alone. Ignoring the humiliation of public acknowledgment that she knew the convicted criminal, she stood at the base of the cross beside Jesus' mother, two other faithful women, and John, the only disciple who had courage enough to stay by Jesus. Together, they mourned the suffering of their son, friend, and Lord.

At the ninth hour Jesus breathed his last breath. The crowds dispersed; John took Jesus' mother home. But Mary lingered behind. Who would take the body down? Who would give it a proper burial? Soon her questions were answered. Joseph of Arimathea, a member of the Jewish High Council, along with a Pharisee named Nicodemus, worked beside the Roman guards to remove Jesus' body from the cross. She watched as, with precious little time before sunset and the beginning of the Sabbath, the men packed the body with myrrh and other spices, wrapped it in linen strips of cloth, and laid it in a freshly hewn tomb on the side of a hill on the perimeter of a garden. With all their strength the men rolled a large stone before the entrance to the cave, then hurried home. Noting the location of the sepulcher, Mary herself rushed to where she was staying in Jerusalem. While she could not anoint the body before the Sabbath began, she could at least prepare her own mixture of embalming oils and spices as a sign of respect for her Lord. Jesus deserved much more, but under the circumstances it was the best she could do.

At dawn on the first day of the week, Mary took the embalming mixture and led a small band of Galilean women to the tomb where Jesus lay. She had no idea how they would roll away the massive stone that barred the entrance to the sepulcher, but she was determined to honor Jesus with due respect. They would find a way. When the women arrived at the garden, they were surprised to find that the stone had already been removed from the entrance to the tomb. Her knees knocking with fear, Mary entered the sepulcher. Jesus' body was gone! Beside the place where the linen clothes lay piled up stood two men in garments that shone like the sun on a brilliant day. Mary fell prostrate before them.

"You are seeking Jesus of Nazareth, but why do you seek the living among the dead? He is not here. Remember how he spoke to you when he was in Galilee, 'The Son of Man must be delivered into the hands of sinful men, and be crucified, and the third day rise again'? Indeed, he is risen!"

Terrified and confused, Mary was speechless. She scrambled out of the cave and, accompanied by the other women, ran toward the house where the eleven disciples were staying. She did not wait for the servant to allow her entrance but barged into their midst.

"Jesus' body is gone," she said, gasping to catch her breath.

"What do you mean, gone?" Peter demanded as the rest of the men stood at attention.

"We went to the tomb to anoint him," Mary answered. "When we got there, it was already open so we went in. The grave clothes were piled up to one side, but the body was not there. And there were two men. They talked about Jesus' being crucified and something happening three days later. I did not understand. They must have taken him away, but where?" She began to cry as the rest of the women nodded in agreement.

A handful of the disciples scowled. "Idle tales," they scoffed. "These women are imagining things."

"It's true! Jesus is gone!" Mary wailed.

Without warning, Peter bolted out the door. "I must see for myself!" he called back to the group. John and Mary followed while the rest of the men and women stood transfixed in uncertain debate over what had taken place.

Peter and John raced through the streets of Jerusalem. Mary, tired from her first sprint into the city to tell the disciples, slowed to a fast walk. As the men passed under the city gates toward the garden, John passed Peter and came to a stop before the open tomb. When Peter arrived, he immediately entered. The grave clothes lay in a mound to one side, just as Mary had said, and in another corner was the head shroud, neatly folded. As he gazed around, John entered behind him, followed by Mary.

"See, it is as I said," Mary whispered. "But now the men are gone too."

The trio stood staring into the empty tomb, trying to digest everything that had happened in the last three days. Jesus was gone; that much was certain. But where, and how? And would they ever see him again? "We will not figure this out standing here," Peter exclaimed. He and John left in silence, too bewildered to speak, leaving Mary to weep alone. Through her tears, she looked once more around into the crypt. The tomb, which had been empty moments ago, now held two brilliant figures, sitting where Jesus' body once lay. "Woman, why are you crying?" one said.

"Because someone has taken away my Lord, and I do not know where they have laid him." Mary heard a noise behind her in the garden. She turned to see a man who looked strikingly like Jesus, but of course he could not be, for Jesus was dead.

"Woman, why are you weeping?" the man said. "Are you looking for someone?"

"You must be the gardener," Mary said, drying her eyes with the sleeve of her garment. "I am looking for the body of Jesus, the man they laid in this tomb just before the Sabbath. If you have taken him, please tell me where so that I can pay my respects to him." Mary gestured toward the garden, her back turned momentarily away from the man. Suddenly she heard Jesus' warm, inviting voice.

"Mary!"

Mary turned around; her eyes opened to the truth. Jesus was not dead but *alive*. She ran to him and threw her arms around Jesus' neck. "Rabboni! Is it really you?"

"Yes," Jesus laughed, gently drawing Mary's arms away from his neck. "But do not cling to me, for there is much I have to do before ascending to my Father and your Father, my God and your God. Go now, tell the disciples that you have seen me. Tell them I shall meet them soon!"

Mary ran to the disciples like a gleeful child about to burst with a secret. As before, she broke into the house where they had continued to ponder the whereabouts of Jesus. "I have seen him. He is alive! Jesus is alive!"

Questions/Thoughts for Reflection: Over the years biblical scholars have speculated about why Mary Magdalene, a relatively insignificant character in the Gospel stories, was the first to see the risen Christ. Why not John, the "disciple whom Jesus loved," or Peter, who must have been brokenhearted after denying Jesus as he awaited trial? Why not Jesus' mother, who had suffered so much, or Mary of Bethany, whose heart was so closely aligned with Jesus' own? Or was it sheer coincidence, a matter of being in the right place at the right time? We cannot know for sure. What is inferred in the Gospel accounts is that Mary of Magdala lived each day with a pure heart and a grateful and willing spirit. Jesus never asks more from any one of us.

Prayer Focus: Dear Jesus, you taught that "blessed are the pure in heart, for they shall see God." May I live out each day with the same pure heart and grateful spirit. May I grow ever nearer each day to seeing God.

Mary, Mother of Jesus

(b. "unavailable" – d. "unavailable")

"My soul magnifies the Lord, and my spirit has rejoiced in God my Savior. For He has regarded the lowly state of His maidservant; for behold, henceforth all generations will call me blessed, for He who is mighty has done great things for me, and holy is His name."
—**Mary, mother of Jesus (Luke 1:46–49)**

Prior to Mary's birth, the Hebrew people had dwelt in great darkness, a deep hopelessness of the soul. They had already suffered hundreds of years of oppression under many rulers. Currently they were being ruled by the iron will of Rome and a power-hungry local king named Herod. Worse, God was silent. For centuries there had been no prophetic voice in the land.

In spite of this milieu, or perhaps because of it, we are told in Scripture (and it is confirmed by contemporaneous historians) that around the time of Mary's upbringing, a heightened sense of anticipation over the coming Messiah permeated each household. Young girls like Mary were raised with the idea that one of their own offspring might well be the child foretold by the prophets, who would save their people and bless their nation.

Some of Mary's childhood friends may have scoffed at the ancient prophecy but not Mary. Although we are told nothing of her personality or character during her early years, we can deduce much from the angel's greeting to the young virgin during that wondrous encounter spoken of in Luke 1, when Mary learned that she would indeed give birth to the long-awaited Christ child. "Rejoice, highly favored one, the Lord is with you; blessed are you among women! . . . For you have found favor with God," the angel declared (Luke 1:28, 30). Mary's reply also provides a glimpse of her character: "Behold, the maidservant of the Lord! Let it be to me according to your word" (Luke 1:38). Later in the chapter the words of the Magnificat (see Luke 1:46–55), a canticle of Mary's response to God's blessing on her life, further reveal a heart that knew God intimately and loved him deeply.

According to the Gospel accounts, Mary, as yet a virgin, did give birth to a male child. Eight days later Joseph, a devout man and legal father of the child, named the baby Jesus, meaning "the Lord saves." A miracle occurred, one of the first precious pearls in a long string.

The next wondrous event occurred forty days later. As ordained by Levitical law, the young couple took their newborn son to the temple in Jerusalem to be consecrated to God and to make an offering for Mary's purification after childbirth. There they met an old man named Simeon. Pious and full of the Holy Spirit, Simeon had heard God's voice one day, telling him that before he died he would see the Consolation of Israel, the Lord's Christ. From that day forward, he waited eagerly for the fulfillment of God's promise. Days, months, or perhaps years later, Joseph and Mary entered the temple, Joseph carrying a caged pair of turtledoves or pigeons for the ceremonial sacrifice and Mary with the baby Jesus in her arms. Spying the child, Simeon's heart leapt within him as if jolted by a bolt of electricity. There, just as God had promised, was the Christ!

Imagine Mary's amazement when Simeon reached for her newborn baby, the words of the *Nunc Dimittis*[1] on his lips. How her spirits must have soared, only to crash in a heap of confusion and foreboding upon hearing the words Simeon spoke to her directly following his expression of praise: "This child is destined to cause the falling and rising of many in Israel, and to be a sign that will be spoken against, so that the thoughts of many hearts will be revealed. *And a sword will pierce your own soul too*" (Luke 2:34–35 NIV).

A sword would pierce her soul? How could that be when by Simeon's own admission the child was destined to become the Savior of a nation and a light to the Gentiles! *Surely he's mistaken,* Mary must have thought. The man was old, after all, and these strange words seemingly had nothing to do with the rest of his prophecy. Still they cut her to the quick, and the dread they produced would stay with her for many years to come.

Perhaps on the verge of succumbing to despair, Mary soon heard another voice, the thin crooning of an ancient woman who dwelt night and day in the bosom of the temple, Anna the prophetess. Divine wisdom comes only to prepared hearts, and like Simeon, Anna was intimately attuned to God. Sensing Mary's distress, and perceiving that the child she cradled was none other than the Messiah, Anna shared a gift of encouragement with the young mother. With frail arms outstretched, the prophetess gave thanks to God for the Christ child and went about the temple proclaiming to everyone she met that the redemption of the Lord was at hand.

With Simeon's prophetic warning and Anna's parting words stamped in Mary's mind, the piercing of her soul soon began. After receiving visitors from the East, wise men bearing unusual gifts for the one born the King of the Jews, Joseph learned through a dream that King Herod would stop at nothing to find the child he perceived to be a threat to his throne, now a toddler, and kill him. They must flee Bethlehem! With little warning they had no time to pack; carrying not much more than the clothes on their backs, the young family left everything familiar and escaped by night into Egypt.

They stayed in that foreign country, probably in one of several Jewish settlements, until King Herod died. Once again God spoke to Joseph through a dream, telling him to return to Israel. However, to avoid Archelaus, Herod's wicked son who now ruled over the land of Judea, Joseph took his family north to their hometown of Nazareth in the district of Galilee.

Thus, in a very short period, in a culture in which most families spent their entire lives in a single village, Mary was forced to move a number of times, fearful for her son's life. The fear was well-founded, as the blood of dozens of male children still stained the memories of every family from the northern border of Galilee to the southern tip of the Dead Sea. The shadow hanging over Mary's heart was especially dark; none of the deaths would have happened, she knew, had it not been for her son Jesus.

Yet, just as she could not forget the Bethlehem massacre, neither could she ignore God's powerful hand of deliverance, another pearl in the string of miracles. A contemplative woman, she tucked everything that happened away in the precious storeroom of her memory.

Like so many miracles, however, thoughts of these events faded over the years for Mary and her husband, as the family laundry grew larger with the birth of each new child and Joseph's carpentry business ebbed and flowed with the economy. Before long the memories of supernatural visitors, prophecies fulfilled, and a nation to be saved became like soft breezes that blew on occasion through Mary's mind, each time bringing a strange yearning.

By the time Jesus was twelve years old, life had fallen into a fairly peaceful routine. That year, like every one before it, Mary and her family made the annual trek to Jerusalem for the Passover. When the feast was concluded, they headed home to Nazareth, part of a great caravan moving north along one of two main highways. Traveling along, Mary and Joseph noticed that Jesus was not by their side. He must be passing time with a relative or one of their many neighbors, they reasoned. It wasn't until nightfall that they began to worry. As twilight dwindled, they paced up and down the caravan calling out his name, to no avail.

The following morning Mary and Joseph left the caravan in a panic and headed south. They hoped they might find their son among the other caravans they passed, but entering the gates of Jerusalem that evening, they were empty-handed and beside themselves with worry. Had Jesus been waylaid by thieves along the road? Or had a shopkeeper in Jerusalem enticed the boy with his wares, and the lad was still in the city, scared but safe?

After searching the streets for three days, Mary and Joseph finally found Jesus sitting in the temple among the rabbis and students. To their amazement he was raising profound questions to the religious leaders; even more surprising, they were answering him and congratulating him on his perceptiveness! When it became clear to Mary that her son had intentionally stayed behind, her relief turned to irritation. "Son, why have you treated us like this? Your father and I have been anxiously searching for you."

Jesus' answer astonished his mother: "Why were you searching for me? Didn't you know I had to be in my Father's house?" (Luke 2:48–49 NIV).

This exchange reveals two truths: Even at the age of twelve, when most boys were just beginning to become "sons of the law," Jesus already had an uncanny knowledge of the books of the law and the prophets as well as a keen understanding of his unique relationship with God. For Mary this event was a jarring reminder that Jesus had a divine mission that superceded her hopes and expectations for her eldest son. Suddenly all the vague memories that had been relegated to the recesses of her mind leapt to the forefront, especially Simeon's disturbing prophecy. *Where would all this lead?* she must have wondered. And what would she give to keep the quiet, normal life she had experienced so far?

Eighteen years passed. Jesus grew up. According to Scripture, he remained in subjection to his parents and increased in wisdom and favor with God and men. He became a carpenter, working alongside Joseph, then became the head of the household after Joseph died. Life was not easy for Mary after Joseph's death, but Jesus was the ideal son and a good provider. She depended on him like never before. But after the incident in the temple eighteen years earlier, she never again forgot her son's destiny. With each passing day she knew the moment was coming when she would have to give him up to the purpose for which he was born.

The sun rose bright over the vineyards covering the Galilean hills one morning of Jesus' thirtieth year. He had just returned from a feast in Jerusalem in the district of Judea where he was baptized by his cousin John in the Jordan River, spent forty mystical days in the local wilderness, and met some new friends who had begun to suspect that Jesus was the long-awaited Messiah and accompanied him home to Galilee. Being fully human as well as divine, it could well be that his head was spinning from the recent events, and even now he was still processing what it all meant. But there was a wedding to attend in nearby Cana, to which he had been invited several weeks previously. He would sort things out after that. Freshening up in Nazareth from his long journey, he embarked on the short trip to Cana with his mother and newfound friends (see John 2:1–11).

The wedding feast was modest but inviting, and the families of the bride and groom were gracious to all, including Jesus' unexpected guests. Unfortunately, before the party was over, the wine ran out. Somehow, maybe by overhearing the groom's father speaking to the servants, Mary learned of the dilemma. The words rang like an alarm in her head; this was the moment she had been dreading—the moment when God would ask her to let her son go, to let him become all that he was meant to be, to let him perform miracles so that others might know what she had known all his life. But how?

Mary found Jesus and pulled him aside. "They have no more wine."

"What does that have to do with me?" Jesus replied. "My hour has not yet come."

Mary looked at her son in disbelief. *Of course your hour has come; don't you recognize it?*

Then the still small voice she had long associated with God began to mingle with her own thoughts. *Maybe he doesn't, Mary, but you do.*

At that moment two worlds came crashing together in Mary's mind. One was the world she had known for the past several years, a quiet world in which her son was always nearby, caring for her needs, a world in which he might some day marry and bring grandchildren into her life, a world of happiness. The other world was full of possibilities for her son of divine conception and birth. Surely it would contain inexplicable excitement and elation, but also—she knew from Simeon's prophecy—it would bring terrible sadness as well. The choice between the two, at that moment, was hers to make. Would she keep quiet, allow Jesus to forget his purpose for living? Or would she help him fulfill that purpose?

Her heart pounding, she turned to one of the servants who, at that moment, was passing by. She touched his elbow, causing him to pause and look at her. A bittersweet smile crossed her face. "Whatever my son says to you, do it," she said, then walked away leaving Jesus and the servant alone together in an awkward situation.

What went through Jesus' mind at that moment is unknown. What we can be certain of is that, sensing Mary's blessing on his mission or perhaps out of sheer respect for his mother, Jesus told the servant to fill several large containers with water, then bring a ladleful to the steward of the feast. When the steward tasted the water, which had miraculously turned into wine, he went to the bridegroom and exclaimed about the wine's fine quality. Would the guests, who had been drinking now for several hours, appreciate its full-bodied flavor? Why had he reserved the best for last? A murmur that began with the servants rushed like a torrent through the crowd. Soon everyone at the wedding feast knew what had happened: a little-known carpenter from Nazareth had just turned water into wine. Jesus' public ministry had begun.

Questions/Thoughts for Reflection: Life is full of difficult choices. Sometimes those choices seem to come directly from God, leaving us with nothing but empty whys. Have you, like Mary, ever been faced with giving up your dreams or ambitions? How did you feel at the time? Were you able to see how God might fill the void left in your heart, how the surrendering of your will to his could possibly have a positive outcome? What about now—has the passage of time allowed you to see things differently?

Prayer Focus: Dear Jesus, I want you to sit on the throne of my life—most of the time. But when I think about giving up my life's dreams, my career, my spouse, or my children, placing them under subjection to your purposes, I sometimes feel myself balk. Help me to understand in the deepest parts of my being that you have my best interest, and that of my loved ones, in mind. And help me be willing to give freely what I hold dearest to you.

Dayna Curry Masterson and Heather Mercer

(b. 1971 – d.— and b. 1977 – d.—)

"We were [in Afghanistan] to serve the poor through relief and development. That was our job, and we really were doing that. But because we love Jesus, as we related with Afghans, we shared where we found hope, where we found life. That came up in daily conversation, because in Afghanistan, faith is of the highest priority."
—**Dayna Curry Masterson and Heather Mercer, "A Higher Calling"**

They call themselves Prisoners of Hope because they went to prison for offering hope to the people of Afghanistan. What they discovered there reinforced their own hope in a God of sovereignty and miracles.

Dayna Curry was an unlikely missionary. While her parents were distracted with marital troubles, friends from her Nashville, Tennessee neighborhood exposed her to R-rated movies and pornography. She was in junior high school when her parents finally divorced. Searching for security and acceptance, she began experimenting with drugs, alcohol, shoplifting, and eventually promiscuity. She became pregnant at age seventeen. Fearing she would be expelled from school and rejected by her mother, she thought abortion was her only option. Sitting in the abortion clinic waiting room, her stomach turned somersaults as she waited her turn. Already feeling tremendous guilt from what she was about to do, she uncharacteristically closed her eyes and prayed silently, *Lord, let this baby go to heaven, and send me to hell.*[1]

After baring her mistake to her parents, Dayna began visiting the church where her mother was attending regularly. Slowly she began to feel loved and accepted. Peace replaced her desperate search for security. Even as she grew in her fledgling faith, however, there was the nagging draw of her old friends. When she graduated from high school, she chose Baylor University in Waco, Texas because of its good business program and because it allowed her to start her life all over again. In 1989 she headed for Texas.

A typical type-A teenager, Heather Mercer became even more driven when her parents divorced and her mother and a sister moved out of their home state of Virginia. Trying to bury her pain and confusion in her studies and school activities, she could never measure up to the new standards she set for herself. "I felt like a failure. I wondered, *Will I ever measure up?*"[2] Attending a church concert with a friend, the minister afterwards talked about Jesus' unconditional love and desire to have a personal relationship with each person in attendance. Having been a self-proclaimed holiday Christian, Heather had never before heard a message like this. She invited Jesus into her heart that night. After high school she decided to attend Baylor because she thought her faith would grow there. She began her classes in 1995.

Dayna and Heather never actually attended Baylor at the same time, yet from the moment they stepped foot onto the oldest university campus in Texas, their lives took on a kind of kinship. Both blossomed in the environment of Christian faith exhibited on the Baylor campus; both developed a heart for working in Third World countries that had little or no knowledge of the life-changing Jesus they had come to know and love. And both eventually became members of Antioch Community Church, a missions-minded offshoot of Highland Baptist Church. The day Heather started classes at Baylor, Dayna was in Uzbekistan, serving as a missionary for two years. She then returned to Waco, working as a social worker in a school for troubled youth.

As a sophomore Heather knew she wanted to try out the mission field. Timid about her youth and lack of experience, she prayed for guidance. "In prayer I felt God ask me if I could do three things: *Can you love your neighbor? Can you serve the poor? Can you weep as I weep for poor and broken people?* As I answered yes to all three questions, I realized God did not need someone with extraordinary gifts and achievements. He just needed someone who could love, share her life, and feel for others as he did."[3]

In November 1997, Dayna's and Heather's lives finally converged at Antioch Church, where they were both looking for an opportunity to serve the world's most destitute and hopeless on a short-term mission trip. That would be Afghanistan, they were counseled. At the orientation meeting they could hardly fathom the description of hardship and suffering under Taliban rule, which had been the law of the land since the fall of Communism the year before. All forms of entertainment were forbidden, all contact with the outside world cut off. Women were banned from working and girls from going to school. Consequences for social misconduct as determined by the Taliban, especially for women, were cruel or worse. No large gatherings, such as wedding or birthday parties. No balls for boys to play with or dolls for girls to dress up. Very little food. Virtually no heath care. What was allowed? Work and prayer.

Because Dayna and Heather were single, they were assigned as roommates for their stay in the capitol city of Kabul. During this trip they first encountered the women they later referred to as the "blue ghosts," Afghan women with their mysterious eyes veiled behind dark blue *burqas*.[4] Spending long hours with these women, listening to their tragic stories while supplying them with what little food, clothing, and medicine they could scrounge, the Americans vowed to return.

They did, under the auspices of German-based Shelter Now International (SNI)—Dayna in August 1999, and Heather in March 2001, over the objections of her mother, Deborah Oddy. Deborah's youngest daughter, Hannah, had died suddenly the year before. She did not feel Heather had taken enough time to grieve or that she was thinking clearly in her decision to travel to a dangerous country. When Deborah's pleas to her daughter went unheeded, she wrote several letters to members of Congress asking for their intervention. There was no reply.

The goal in Afghanistan under SNI was twofold: meet the immediate, practical needs of the people, including food, clothing, and medicine; and create jobs that would enable them in the long term to take care of themselves, such as helping women—especially widows—market home-based skills like sewing and embroidery. As opportunities arose out of their daily interactions to share personally about matters of faith, SNI workers were simply instructed to use caution and good judgment. It was the latter objective that landed Dayna and Heather in trouble five months after Heather's arrival.

During their work and travels, the pair made many acquaintances. Having been subjected to intense suffering for many years, first under Communist rule and then under the Taliban, Afghans had long since dispensed with small talk. Life was simply too difficult and sometimes too short. Even more surprising, they were generally receptive to matters of faith and curious about Dayna's and Heather's beliefs in particular. What would drive the two women away from their homes in the land of comfort to help needy people in the land of the forsaken? Within minutes of meeting, Afghan women would pour out their hearts to Dayna and Heather. Heartsick for their plight, the two Americans often shared about their personal source of strength and hope. As they talked about Jesus to the Afghans, first through prayer and simple story books they had used during literacy training, then through radio broadcasts (they supplied the forbidden radios) coming from outside Afghanistan, they knew they needed to be careful for fear of falling under Taliban scrutiny.[5] But they weren't really proselytizing, they reasoned; they were merely answering the Afghans' questions. When asked on a couple of occasions for a more in-depth description about Jesus' life, teachings, death, and resurrection, the women found their rudimentary language skills lacking. Then they secretly popped a DVD into a laptop computer and played the *Jesus* film, which had been translated into the Pashto and Dari languages commonly used in Afghanistan. While Dayna and Heather still thought this practice fell within the range of routine conversation, the Taliban felt otherwise.

On August 3, 2001, Dayna and Heather, along with six other SNI aid workers—four Germans and two Australians—were arrested. During many hours of grueling interrogation, they were repeatedly ordered to sign statements they could not readily read. The women refused. Finally an interpreter was provided, and they devised a system of communication both sides found acceptable: The interpreter would write down the Talibs'[6] questions in English; Dayna and Heather would write out their responses in English, signing beside each response; the interpreter would translate the women's response back into Pashto. *What comprised their work in the country? What was the extent of their work? What occasion did they have to visit Afghans in their homes? What did they talk about there?* The list seemed endless, but it did not reveal what charges had been brought against the group or Dayna and Heather in particular. As their interrogation stretched on for weeks, they were moved from one squalid, parasite-infested prison to another, always sharing a single cell with the other female SNI workers. The toilet was makeshift, and there was no shower. They had nothing to do but wait.

"We have been treated well," Dayna wrote later to her family and friends,[7] "but it has been heartbreaking to see and hear others being severely beaten around us. The female guards that come each day to look after us have not been paid in two months. They are hungry. We give them any food we have left over to take to their families. . . .

"We meet in the mornings and evenings every day for one or two hours. We sing a lot! Heather and I even wrote a song. Some of the others have written songs too. . . . Pray that we can grow in our love for one another. Six ladies in a small place 24-7 can be a challenge, so we are learning to be patient and kind to one another. Most of the time things are fine, but when one gets down, it affects all of us."[8]

The last comment may have been in reference to the differing responses to imprisonment that Dayna and Heather were experiencing, stemming from their dissimilar views about their potential fate. Dayna believed the worst they might experience was five years in prison. She was getting a taste of that already and felt she could survive. Heather saw the situation more gravely, believing they could be hanged. As imprisonment stretched into weeks, she shook uncontrollably from fear and frequently isolated herself from her fellow inmates.

"For a month and a half, the fear escalated," Heather shared later. "I feared that the religious police were going to execute us; I feared that we'd spend our whole lives in prison; I feared that a terrorist group would know where we were and kill us; eventually I feared that we would lose our lives from a bomb. I was immobilized at times."[9]

On September 1, Dayna, Heather, and the other SNI workers were transported to another location where a chief justice asked if they had a lawyer. The SNI workers were stunned. "They didn't even tell us there was going to be a trial, and now they want to know if we have a lawyer?" Dayna protested.

"Now you are informed," the chief justice replied.[10]

As the trial slowly proceeded, it appeared sentencing would be light. Then came 9/11. The trial stopped, and the women were left to ponder their fate. In late September Heather came to a turning point in her battle with fear when she realized she could continue to worry or she could place her trust in the hands of the God she had come to Afghanistan to serve. Remembering the Scripture that said, "If you lose your life for my sake, you will find it" (Matt. 10:39), she began through prayer to place her fears into the hands of Jesus.

On October 6, the Taliban supreme leader, Mullah Mohammed Omar, turned the arrested prisoners into hostages by offering to release them if the United States "stops its mass propaganda of military action against the Afghan people."[11] The Bush administration rejected the offer and launched its military campaign against Afghanistan the following day. Even for prisoners like Dayna who felt confident they would not be killed, the next five weeks proved to be a harrowing test of faith and fortitude as bombs began falling everywhere.

On November 13, one of the SNI workers who had a small transistor radio learned that Kabul was on the verge of falling to the Northern Alliance. Taliban soldiers rushed the prisoners into a van filled with rocket launchers. Three hours later they were herded into a large metal container sitting in the middle of a field. Terrified that they would be locked in and left to die, Heather stood in the doorway and would not budge. In the morning they were taken to a prison in Ghazni, about eighty miles from their previous location in Kabul. Heavy gunfire erupted. The Taliban guards deserted the prison and ran. Following thirty minutes of eerie silence, an Alliance soldier burst in with rounds of ammunition around his neck. "You're free, you're free! The Taliban have left!"

Freedom was one thing; safety was another. The Northern Alliance contacted the United States military to arrange a time and place for the Americans to be picked up. In the early hours of November 15, Dayna and Heather stood with several Alliance soldiers in a deserted field waiting to be rescued. As hours ticked by, they could hear helicopters in the vicinity, but the pilots could not find them in the utter darkness of their rural surroundings. Although the women did not want to attract enemy attention, they knew they had to do something to let the Americans know where they were. Heather suggested they set their head scarves on fire. Within minutes, helicopters appeared and whisked the women to Pakistan, where they met their families.

In 2002 Dayna and Heather published a book about their experience.[12] They also produced a CD containing the songs they had written while in prison. Proceeds from the sale of both items go directly to the nonprofit organization they founded called the Hope Afghanistan Foundation,[13] dedicated to bringing relief and hope to the people of Afghanistan. Someday they hope to return to Afghanistan.

Questions/Thoughts for Reflection: Hope is crucial to the survival of any difficulty, no matter how light or severe. For a time during her captivity, Heather Mercer lost sight of the foundation of her hope—Jesus Christ. She suffered tremendously until she realized that as long as she continued to hope in her own capacity to survive or in the American military to rescue her, she was losing her ability to cope with her situation. When she began to trust in Jesus Christ, she found she could face her circumstances, even the possibility of death, with courage and strength. Where is your hope today?

Prayer Focus: Dear Holy Spirit, in the midst of trouble, help me to sing with the hymnist:

> My hope is built on nothing less
> Than Jesus' blood and righteousness.
> I dare not trust the sweetest frame,
> But wholly trust in Jesus' name.
>
> On Christ the solid Rock I stand,
> All other ground is sinking sand;
> All other ground is sinking sand.[14]

Fern Nichols

(b. 1945 – d.—)

*"We are in an unseen, spiritual battle for our souls. This is what's
so hard to get across to Christians today. We wouldn't dream of
leaving our houses without putting our clothes on, yet we don't
think twice about not putting our spiritual armor on . . . not
praying before beginning each day."*
—Fern Nichols

Fern Landsem's feet didn't even reach the floor as she swung her legs
back and forth during the prayer meeting at the little Baptist church
in Portland, Oregon. Week after week she sat with her mother and three
siblings, surrounded by quiet voices that rose and fell in the peaceful setting. It mattered little that she had no idea what was being said or why.
She simply loved being there. At home a day never passed when grace was
not said before meals or prayer was not offered up in the car before a trip
or at bedtime. It was as natural as breathing and just as indispensable.

As she grew up, prayer continued to permeate Fern's life, as she lead
Sunday school, played the organ during worship services, and presided
over the Youth for Christ meetings at the local high school. Later, at the

Oregon College of Education, she became involved with numerous Christian organizations on campus, including Campus Crusade for Christ, where she met Rle Nichols. Two years after graduating with a degree in education, Fern and Rle married. As a coach with Athletes in Action, Rle's work led the couple to Indiana, then Abbotsford, British Columbia, where Tyrone, the eldest of their four children (three sons and a daughter), received a scholarship to play basketball at a nearby Christian junior high school. Having had no experience with a Christian school before, Fern assumed there would be a parents prayer group. She attended the first women's auxiliary meeting of the year and asked, "When do you get together to pray?"

The president of the group responded, "We don't. But it sounds like a good idea. Why don't you share what you have in mind at the next meeting and see what happens?"

The following month Fern outlined her idea to the group. They would gather together for a full hour of prayer once a week, saving refreshments and socializing for after the prayer time. The hour would be divided into four segments—adoration, confession, thanksgiving, and supplication. During the time of supplication, they would pray specifically for the needs of the school, the teachers, and the students. Twenty women attended the first meeting. A few expressed reticence about praying out loud, while others could not imagine praying for such an extended period of time. All were willing to give it a try. It was a period of growth for everyone. By the time the school year ended, many of the women said their time together in prayer had revolutionized their lives.

"Throughout the Gospels," Fern explains, "Jesus talked about the importance of corporate prayer, praying together with one heart and mind. Prayer is always critical, but something special happens when we pray *together.*"

The following year the Nichols' second son, Troy, was also ready to start junior high school. Fern and Rle decided they wanted the boys together, so they pulled Tyrone out of the Christian school and registered both boys in the local public school. For Fern, after such a positive experience the year before, sending her boys to a school with no prayer support was like hurling them into a dark cave with no torch. Surely there was at least one other mother at the new school who would be interested in praying with her. Asking the Lord for guidance, a woman's name came to Fern's mind. The woman responded eagerly, and together they came up with a list of a few more mothers who might be interested in joining them. The following week five women met in Fern's home to pray. As the months passed, other women joined the group.

Looking back, Fern now claims that year, 1984, as the beginning of the organization she later founded, Moms In Touch International (MITI).[1] "I had no idea I was starting anything. I just knew prayer was the answer to what my children needed as they went out into the world."[2]

The following year Athletes in Action moved its headquarters to San Diego, California. The Nichols family followed, settling in nearby Poway. As Fern began to meet other mothers from her children's schools, she formed new prayer groups, following the tried-and-true pattern she had used previously. More groups cropped up in outlying communities as news of the concept spread. Slowly churches and school districts outside the San Diego area began calling on Fern to speak about her new organization.

In January 1987, a group of thirty-five women gathered for a retreat to pray and thank God for what he had been doing. They prayed for all the schools throughout Southern California represented in their gathering. Suddenly one of the women blurted out, "Why not pray for the west coast—California, Oregon, Washington?" Another chimed in, "How about the entire United States?" Followed by, "Why not pray for schools around the world?" After more prayer a final woman voiced the concern they were all thinking, "How are we going to tell all the mothers of the world about Moms In Touch?" Someone suggested Dr. James Dobson's organization, Focus on the Family, whose ministry already had a worldwide audience. Before the end of the weekend, the group prayed in earnest that God would somehow open this door. Then they waited.

In the spring of 1988, Fern was stirring spaghetti sauce on the kitchen stove when her phone rang. It was a representative from Focus on the Family. They had been receiving scores of letters and telephone calls from individuals and churches asking for information about MITI. Would Fern come to Los Angeles to share with Dr. Dobson about what she was doing? Three months later she and eleven other women sat down in Dr. Dobson's office. One by one they shared what MITI meant to them, their children, and their children's schools. Dr. Dobson immediately arranged to air a broadcast featuring all twelve of the women, spanning three days. No one could have anticipated the response, as twenty-three thousand letters flooded Focus on the Family,[3] and thousands more arrived at MITI's headquarters in Poway. To help MITI respond to the deluge of correspondence, Focus on the Family helped to prepare a booklet outlining Fern's four steps to prayer and how to start a MITI prayer group. Fern believes that what happened after the Focus on the Family broadcast was a direct result of their prayers at the 1987 retreat, as suddenly MITI prayer groups began to sprout up all over the globe.[4]

The organization grew steadily through 2002. Then, inspired in private prayer, Fern launched Vision 2003, praying that by the end of that year, God would provide a prayer group to every school in every city throughout the United States, both public and private. When asked by a journalist in mid 2003 what would happen if MITI did not reach its goal, she replied, "The Lord didn't promise me that this goal would be reached. He said, 'Set the goal out there and get going.' If you don't have a goal, you aim at nothing."[5] Indeed, 2003 saw another explosion of growth with the release of two books, both written by Fern: *Prayers from a Mom's Heart* and *Every Child Needs a Praying Mom.*[6] MITI's current objective, called Vision 2004 and Beyond, is a continuation of its 2003 goal. "We've made a huge dent, but there are still thousands of schools to be reached in America through prayer." In addition to the traditional prayer groups representing individual schools, groups are also forming for mothers of special needs children, for grandmothers, and regionally based groups focusing on college-age children.

While MITI's primary purpose is to ask God to raise up women who will take time out of their busy lives to pray and equip them to form and lead prayer groups, Fern has her own personal goals, as well.

> We are in an unseen, spiritual battle for our souls. This is what's so hard to get across to Christians today. We wouldn't dream of leaving our houses without putting our clothes on, yet we don't think twice about not putting our spiritual armor on . . . not praying before beginning each day. I meet Christians every day who wonder if their prayers are being heard, if they are making a difference. They feel like giving up.

I want to tell them that just because they aren't seeing immediate results does not mean their prayers are ineffective. Sometimes the tangible results of prayer are delayed in coming, but they always come. We must persevere, trusting that our prayers are touching heaven.

Questions/Thoughts for Reflection: Do you remember the story of Balaam's ass, as told in Numbers 22, who saw the Lord's angel when her master did not? Three times Balaam kicked and whipped the ass to drive her forward. Out of fear for the angel standing before her—whose sword was drawn to kill Balaam—the ass would not budge. O, that we had the eyes of Balaam's ass, to see the spiritual dimension of our world, which is more real than what we with our limited vision call reality!

Prayer Focus: Heavenly Father, through prayer, "open my eyes that I may truly see . . . incline my heart that I may desire, order my steps that I may walk in the ways of your commandments."[7]

Anna Nitschmann

(b. 1715 – d. 1760)

"When she spoke or prayed or sang, all hearts stood open to her."
—**Moravian church saying regarding Anna Nitschmann, www.gospelnet.com**

M any women throughout Christian church history have served in leadership capacities. But few have had the impact of Anna Nitschmann, the youngest female leader in the history of the Moravian church.

Over three hundred years before Anna was born,[1] the Moravian movement began in Moravia[2] in Eastern Europe. Jan Hus, a young professor of philosophy and rector of the University in Prague, led a protest against the doctrinal positions and excesses of the Roman Catholic Church, its clergy and hierarchy. He was burned at the stake for heresy on July 6, 1415. But persecution did not stop the reformation spirit of Hus's followers. Gathering on a large estate one hundred miles east of Prague, they organized the Moravian church, taking the official name of *Unitas Fratrum*[3] in 1457, nearly sixty years before Martin Luther and the Protestant Reformation.

Heavy persecution persisted for the Moravian community, which continued to print Bibles and hymnals in its members' indigenous language in direct opposition to the Catholic Church's position. Over the next 250 years, the Moravian church spread outside its native land to other parts of Europe. In 1722, several Moravian families found refuge on the estate of Count Nicholas Louis von Zinzendorf, a pietist nobleman in the Saxony region of Germany. A student of the Bible himself, he was sympathetic to the Moravian's desire to read the holy Scriptures in their own tongue. The families built a small community on the Count's estate, calling it Herrnhut.

Soon more Moravian refugees arrived, including Anna Nitschmann, whose father and eldest brother had recently escaped from prison in Moravia where they had been arrested for heresy. Just entering adolescence at the time, Anna was a rebellious child. A witness to what she considered petty bickering and disharmony in the growing Moravian church community, she wanted no part of it. When pressed about her lack of conversion, she would snap back, "First get converted yourself, then talk to me."

Over the next few years, Count Zinzendorf, now Herrnhut's religious leader, strengthened the structure of the church, with men and women of various ages and marital status divided into "choirs" for the purposes of mentoring and worshipping according to shared life experiences. This structure was common to eighteenth-century society of the time. What was not common was the growing prominence women were gaining within the community, beginning with Anna.

On August 13, 1727, the Herrnhut community held a worship service. Following Communion an unusual spiritual revival swept over the people. Their eyes opened to their damaging feuds and quarrels; they vowed to make deliberate changes to overturn their disunity. Relationships that had been broken for years were restored. Among those deeply affected was young Anna, who dedicated her life to the Lord's service, choosing a life of ministry over marriage. She immediately organized other girls in the community into a special "Single Sisters" club, where even marriage would take second place to being a devoted disciple of Christ in worship and ministry. In her desire to demonstrate her devotion, Anna began writing hymns, an honored task that until then belonged predominantly to European men.

Anna's leadership skills did not go unnoticed. In 1730, an important election was held to choose new officers. One role needing to be filled was that of chief eldress over the women in the burgeoning Herrnhut community. Four names were selected and written on pieces of paper, women of various ages who had shown exceptional leadership qualities. One name was that of now fourteen-year-old Anna. When the lot fell to her, she stepped forward.

"Anna, no." Count Zinzendorf had held his tongue when young Anna was selected as a potential leader. Now he pulled the girl aside. "Refuse the appointment. You are too young for this kind of responsibility."

"May I remind you, sir, that I accept this appointment as from the Lord? If my lot was drawn, it is God's will,"[4] the young peasant girl said, thus becoming the youngest female leader in the history of the Moravian church.

As chief eldress, Anna took an active role in discussions and decisions affecting the Moravian community. She was even invited to sit in the place of leadership at the session meetings of the Moravian synod.[5] The women of the community thrived under her leadership, while the community itself continued to grow by the thousands.

Keeping Christ's Great Commission in mind, Count Zinzendorf encouraged the leaders to take the gospel message to the far reaches of the earth. Anna was one of the first to adopt the new missionary vision. She joined a special group, called the Pilgrim Congregation, whose undertaking would be the worldwide spread of the gospel and the Moravian church. As part of this group, she was responsible for sending the first Moravian missionaries to the West Indies. She herself came to America in 1741 and helped found Moravian congregations in Bethlehem and Nazareth, Pennsylvania.

To the early Moravians of the Herrnhut community, Anna became known as the *Selige Juengerin,* the Blessed Woman Disciple. In 1746, she was named Mother of the entire Moravian church. Over her lifetime she refused two offers of marriage. Finally, after the death of Count Zinzendorf's wife, she married the Count in 1757. By the time of her death in 1760, Anna had written more than thirty hymns, which are still published in the Moravian German hymnal, and had commissioned more than two hundred missionaries.

Questions/Thoughts for Reflection: In an age when disputes persist between and within denominations about a woman's role in church, women continue to minister faithfully and effectively in a myriad of leadership roles within the church at large. Take a moment to consider your own church or denomination's stance on this issue. Do you think the Moravian Church motto—"In essentials, unity; in nonessentials, liberty; and in all things, love"—which Anna Nitschmann lived by, would in any way help your congregation or denomination?

Prayer Focus: Jesus, while on earth, you taught your disciples that the world would recognize them as Christians by their love for one another. Teach us this day what it means to love one another in the midst of the disagreements that divide us.

Kathleen Norris

(b. 1947 – d.—)

> *"I am not a monk, although I have a formal relationship with the Benedictines as an oblate, or associate, of a community of some sixty-five monks. As a married woman, thoroughly Protestant, who often has more doubt than anything resembling faith, this surprises me almost as much as finding that the Great Plains themselves have become my monastery, my place set apart, where I thrive and grow."*
> —Kathleen Norris, *Dakota: A Spiritual Geography*

Perhaps more than any other contemporary voice in America, Kathleen Norris has helped bridge the gap of understanding between Protestants and Catholics and has given the nation a fresh perspective of historical Christianity's ancient contemplative roots. Unsuspecting of how her readers would respond, she openly shared her personal search for her Christian roots at a time when sex and drugs were more popular than religion. If *The New York Times* bestseller list is any indication, the nation has been hungry to hear her words.

As a child growing up in the 1950s, Kathleen's family, including two sisters and a brother, was steeped in the traditional rituals common to

Protestant America. Her paternal great-grandfather being a Methodist circuit rider and a chaplain in the Conferderate army, her grandfather being a Methodist minister and her father a church choir director, Kathleen was expected to attend Sunday school every week and sing in the cherub choir. But "church was music" to her in those days, when a pale blue choir robe with voluminous sleeves and a floppy bow tie made her feel like an angel.

Kathleen thrived in this environment for many years, her radiant, simple faith sustaining her through moves from her birthplace in Washington D.C. to Virginia and then Illinois, where she attended confirmation classes. Then adolescence set in, a time of natural cynicism. While school was introducing her to various world philosophies and religions, the kindly minister and other adults "who taught Sunday school and confirmation classes seemed intent on putting the vastness of God into small boxes of their own devising,"[1] raising more questions for the inquisitive younger teenager than they had answers. Most troubling was the vocabulary she was learning—words like *dogma, sin, washed in the blood, hell*. Was she to accept these concepts in a literal sense? Kathleen's paternal grandmother, Beatrice Norris, said unequivocally yes. But her grandmother's religious fervor backfired. Rather than drawing Kathleen closer to God, her zeal "told me that as a thinking and questioning person, I had no business being in church."[2]

Another move, this time to Hawaii, found Kathleen in high school, attending Sunday school classes at a politically active United Church of Christ where she was taught to interpret the New Testament according to the concepts of existentialist philosophy. Juxtaposed against her Grandmother Norris's strict beliefs, religion became a confusing issue. During this time Kathleen started writing, mostly poetry, which was easier to accept as a substitute for faith than reconciling her questions and doubts.

In the midst of her years of searching, Kathleen and her family spent every summer in Lemmon on the western Plains of South Dakota, where Kathleen's maternal grandparents, Frank and Charlotte Totten, lived. Then as now, to most people, Dakota was a harsh, solitary place. But to a child brimming with imagination, it was paradise. In contrast to her Grandmother Norris, Grandmother Totten had a "livable faith" and a broad-mindedness that allowed her to remain open to the world.

In the late 1960s, Kathleen left her relatively sheltered life to attend Bennington College in Vermont, saying goodbye to all thoughts religious as well. Besides offering an excellent writing program, Bennington was a hotbed of political activism, sexual experimentation and drug use. Immediately after graduation, she moved to New York City and worked for six years as arts administrator at the Academy of American Poets. As a struggling poet herself, she was drawn to Greenwich Village, where she published her first book of poetry[3] and met her husband, fellow poet David Dwyer.

While basking in her first publishing success, it began to dawn on Kathleen that the drug culture and continual nightlife of the Village were not conducive to what she hoped would be a long writing career. She began yearning for the simpler days she had experienced in South Dakota. Looking back, she realized those hours of watching her Grandmother Totten bake using a tattered wooden spoon and breadboard, listening as the wise old woman expressed her quiet faith, had fed her soul deeply. Like a gnawing hunger, a voice within told her she needed to reconnect to the less complicated life she had left behind.

In 1974 that opportunity came. When Charlotte Totten died (Frank Totten had passed away years before), Kathleen's family in Hawaii was reluctant to make the trip to South Dakota to settle the estate. Kathleen offered to move into the Totten house and manage the land and cattle interests that had passed to the family. Her husband David agreed, expecting to stay for only a few years. Kathleen's friends thought she was crazy. "You'll starve for mental stimulation," they said. "Your inspiration will dry up." But the desire for change was powerful. Ignoring her friends' advice, Kathleen packed up their household and moved west.

Once in Lemmon, grant funds for writing soon evaporated. Kathleen and David had to find creative ways to earn a living (bookkeeping, computer programming, library work, a cable business, etc.). Meanwhile Kathleen made numerous visits to Spencer Presbyterian Church in Lemmon, the church where her Grandmother Totten had been an active member for more than sixty years. But she eventually gave up; too much emotional baggage still existed from the past. For nearly ten years she stayed away, yet memories of those first few visits—the spine-broken Bibles carried under the arms of the old women in the congregation carried a message: "There is more here than you know"[4] combined with her own childhood memories of the place, continued to intrigue her.

Finally Kathleen began to feel at home on the plains. She had made numerous friends, including a clergy couple who had become the pastors at Spencer. However, despite having a few more published poems under her belt, her true literary voice still eluded her. She struggled with depression. Sensing a need for renewal, she again turned to Spencer, where her clergy friends welcomed her. They also invited her to a Benedictine monastery in western North Dakota for a personal retreat. While there, a man appeared in a nearly new Jeep, handed over the title and keys, and walked away. Learning that the gesture was part of some healing process in his life, the sisters promised to pray for him.

Awed by the incident, Kathleen realized that she, too, was on a journey, a road to discover her own "spiritual geography."[5] This became the starting point of her conversion, which she says begins for each individual with knowing who we are and where we come from. "Religious conversion . . . doesn't come out of a vacuum, but it might come out of a very messy life. Out of someone who really isn't even aware that God is working in the world."[6]

Over the next few years, she went on several retreats to Benedictine monasteries in the area. She came to cherish the Liturgy of the Hours,[7] *lectio divina*,[8] the Benedictine motto,[9] and St. Benedict's Rule.[10] Stories of the monks' communal experience—so similar to ordinary family life—as well as the stories of the Desert Fathers[11] and the saints of the Catholic Church, appealed to the writer within her. Even the long periods of silence she encountered as part of the retreats were a comfortable fit. To her surprise each of these processes nurtured her soul and helped her reclaim her own Protestant roots. For the first time in decades, she could relax and allow God to transform her through a growing relationship with him, a relationship that continues to teach her how to love God, her neighbor, and herself.

Step-by-step she also began to make sense out of Sunday morning worship services. In 1985, she became a member of the Spencer church. Still, the draw to the Catholic tradition and the contemplative aspect of monastic life was strong. In 1986 she joined Assumption Abbey in Richardton, North Dakota as an oblate.[12] "I can't imagine why God would want me, of all people," she told the monk who was her oblate director. "But if God is foolish enough to take me as I am, I guess I'd better do it."[13]

Kathleen has spent the last two decades moving ever more comfortably between visits to several Benedictine monasteries (including two nine-month stints at St. John's Abbey in Collegeville, Minnesota) and two local Presbyterian churches—Spencer in Lemmon where she is a member, and Hope in nearby Keldron, where she is frequently asked to speak. She found her literary voice, which exploded with three back-to-back best sellers about her spiritual pilgrimage.[14] Currently she is facing a new challenge, caring for her husband David who is suffering from cancer. Knowing that God does his best work in the midst of chaos, she finds peace even in this day-to-day uncertainty.

Questions/Thoughts for Reflection: For centuries the Catholic and Protestant faiths have been at odds, ranging from verbal disputes to bloody wars. In her books Kathleen Norris has succeeded in exalting the many elements common to both faiths, the Protestant church's deep roots in the Catholic tradition, and what each can learn from the other. Through her personal struggle, she has also given us new handles by which to hold on to our Christian beliefs.

In the midst of growing religious pluralism in our society, how can you create inroads to peace? While Jesus Christ calls us to be faithful to him as the way of salvation, we are also called to be gentle toward those who do not believe as we do. Think about the religious mix found among your family and friends. In what ways can you be a peacemaker while remaining true to who you are in Christ?

Prayer Focus: Jesus, you said, "Blessed are the peacemakers, for they will be called sons and daughters of God." Help me to be a gracious example of your truth and love to those around me.

Janette Oke

(b. 1935 – d.—)

"I see my writing as an opportunity to share my faith. We live in a hurting, confused world that is searching for answers and purpose. . . . My hope is that my books, which I do not regard as 'romance novels' but as slices of life, will show readers that a personal faith in God and the fellowship of family and selected friends will bring harmony and inner peace to their lives. If my books touch lives, answer individual's questions, or lift readers to a higher plane, then I will feel that they have accomplished what God has asked me to do."
—Janette Oke, www.janetteoke.com

The Great Depression was in full swing when Janette Steeves was born in 1935. As the sixth of nine children growing up on a farm on the Canadian prairie, she had little more than a houseful of love and laughter, as well as a family heritage that dated back hundreds of years—her mother being the progeny of Puritan immigrants and her father a German descendant whose family came to Canada in the 1700s. Prairie life surrounded Janette, both in fact and in her dreams. She loved the rugged beauty of her environment and the rustic, simple life she and her family led. When she wasn't going to school and working the farm alongside her siblings, she was reading about the opening of the Canadian West, the pioneers who occupied the virgin territory, and their anvil-tested faith, which resembled her own family's in so many ways. Absorbing their stories, she found her own difficulties easier to bear.

Entering Mountain View Bible College in Didsbury, Alberta, Janette had two hopes in life: to become a wife and mother and a published novelist. She met a nice young man at Mountain View named Edward Oke and wondered if he would someday be her husband. But first things first. Both her dreams would have to wait until her education was complete. Soon after graduation in 1957, she and Edward married. After pastorates in Calgary and Edmonton in Canada, and Indiana in the United States, the couple returned to Mountain View, where Edward became president of the college.

As a parent raising four young children, including a set of twins, Janette still yearned to write. Her life was different now from her hardworking farm days, but memories of the prairie were still as vivid as the sun that rose each morning, illuminating the nearby Canadian Rockies. Colorful plots and characters frequently danced in her head while she changed diapers and washed dirty faces. But if her childhood taught her anything, it was that life needs to be prioritized, and dreams outside of her God-given responsibilities must be put in their proper place. "My family has always been first," Janette says, looking back over the years. "That's why I put off writing for so many years. If I had to give up anything even now, the writing would be first. It wouldn't be a big decision. I don't see myself as a professional writer. I see myself as a wife and mother and grandmother who writes. It's a busy corner of my life, but it's just a corner."[1]

Once her children had entered the active teenage years, Janette turned her attention to the stories that had filled her mind for almost two decades. But how to begin? Her college education had not included writing classes. Writing conferences were scarce. And she wanted to write *Christian* fiction, a genre that had hardly been broached by the early 1970s. "As a fiction reader myself, I found that I was needing to go to the secular shelves to find books and often, I was not liking what I was finding."[2] With no guideposts to light her way, she turned to prayer. After many nights on her knees, she felt the nudging of God to begin to write and leave the rest up to him. She sat down with pen in hand and began: "The morning sun shone brightly on the canvas of the covered wagon, promising an unseasonably warm day for mid-October."[3] The resulting book, *Love Comes Softly*, was published in 1979. It remains her single best-selling title, with more than one million copies sold.

In the decades since, Janette has written nearly seventy-five books. Although most are fiction, they are founded in the tragedies and joys of real life. Coming from a large family, she has experienced a great deal of suffering over the years. She watched as two of her sisters raised handicapped children; her own firstborn son died at an early age, and she lost a grandchild to sudden infant death syndrome. "It isn't that God protects us from all of these tough things in life—What I want to emphasize is the fact that He's there to help us through these things. . . . He's holding you steady. He's going to see you through this. Someday you will come out on the other side. God hasn't deserted you."[4] An esteemed speaker at Christian writing conferences, Janette now gives tips to audiences from around the world. A repeated question at these gatherings is where her book ideas come from. "I don't know if a writer can tell you how he or she gets ideas," Janette responds. "Ideas come. A writer never knows what might spark an idea for a story. All of life serves to present ideas. Perhaps the only difference is that writers are 'tuned in,' looking and watching for ideas that others might miss."[5]

As the years have passed, her children have had children, and she looks forward to great-grandchildren. One thing is of utmost importance to Janette—consistency. Her life must remain true to who she is. "I want my Christian life to be consistent for the sake of my family, for my grandchildren, also for my church community. I feel it is important to be consistent in your Christian walk, to live the life you claim."[6] As in her own life, she tries to create stories and situations that allow her fictional characters to remain true to their beliefs, as well. "I want to show [readers] that faith in God is much, much more than going to church on Sunday. It has to embrace every part of your living, every part of your life. It's not a bunch of rules: it's a relationship."[7] Indeed, it is difficult to pick up one of Janette's books without the message of Christian faith quickly becoming apparent. For her Christian integrity and high-quality writing, she has been awarded numerous honors, including the Gold Medallion Award, the Christy Award of Excellence, the President's

Award from the Evangelical Christian Publishers Association, and the Life Impact Award from the Christian Booksellers Association International. Her books have been translated into fourteen languages and hold a combined sales record of over twenty million copies.

Juxtaposed against her gigantic writing success, Janette leads a quiet life with her husband on the Canadian prairie. When the urge to write strikes, she heads for the solitude of the family's condominium high up in the Rocky Mountains. Recently she and her siblings restored their parents' prairie farmhouse, which now serves as the Oke Writing Museum and Steeves' Historical House, a living legacy to a vanishing way of life.

Questions/Thoughts for Reflection: Everyone needs dreams; they are a crucial part of the human experience. Just as important is the ability to prioritize our dreams along with everyday realities. There is no more tragic existence than the one that pursues a dream, only to find at the end of life that the truly significant things somehow were missed. Janette Oke's life displays a remarkable balance and sense of timing, most likely because of her deliberate efforts to prioritize her daily activities.

When setting your own priorities, the following simple guidelines can make the difference between a satisfying life and one that is fruitless and unfulfilling: (1) Prayerfully decide what is truly important. (2) Discover where your time, energy, and money are currently being spent. A brief evaluation will bring to light any discrepancies between what you hope to accomplish in life and where your current resources are taking you. (3) Make a plan to align your time, energy, and money with your ultimate goals. (4) Follow through on the changes you deem necessary. Take time occasionally to reevaluate, making sure your objectives and means to achieve them are still on track.

Prayer Focus: Dear Jesus, without your leadership and direction I am hopelessly lost. Help me to prioritize my days so that when I am at life's end, I can close my eyes at peace with myself and you.

Janet Parshall

(b. 1950 – d.—)

"I often refer to the fact that God has called me to Babylon. When I got saved when I was six, I was absolutely certain the Lord would call me to a foreign mission field. In some respects, it is a foreign mission field. It's a different world here in Washington, D.C., and I view myself as a war correspondent. I believe that through the power of this microphone, my challenge is to take everything that's happening to Washington and send it back to parents, so that they in turn would be equipped as Scripture says we're supposed to be, and so they will turn and look well to the ways of their own household."

—Janet Parshall, www.awana.com

Not many people can boldly state, "We live in a world of terror color codes not by accident but by divine appointment,"[1] and get away with it. To think that God has *anything* to do with the terrorism that threatens our nation is an unsettling thought. But when Janet Parshall speaks, millions of Americans listen.

Janet did not aspire to be a news commentator and popular radio talk show host. Following graduation from Carroll College in Waukesha,

Wisconsin with a degree in music, she went to work as a teacher. After marrying her husband Craig and moving to Virginia, she followed her heart's desire to stay at home with her four children. At a time when all of her colleagues were swept up in the tornado of the feminist movement, she quit work so she could pursue what some at the time called an "illegitimate profession" (motherhood). "I'd step out my front door during that time and look up and down the street. I thought it was Death Valley because nobody was at home."[2] But Janet was never idle. She actively supported the children's schools, getting involved in volunteer functions and serving as president of the PTA.

Always an avid news follower, she has made it a lifelong point to stay informed on issues pertaining to culture, government, and family. So when she began to see the dark side of the dominant culture encroach on the social environment in which her children were growing up, "fingerprinting their lives with something other than absolute truth," she became alarmed. "I would sit around the dinner table with my precious treasures, knowing what was on the evening news. I wanted to hide them."[3] But running away or burying our heads in the sand is not what Christians are called to do. Neither is complaining about the problem while at the same time being unwilling to vote the issues or get involved as part of the solution, Janet says.

Once her children were out of elementary school, Janet turned her attention back to the workforce. While she saw teaching as an important profession, she wanted to get involved in something that would be informative to parents and have a direct impact on society, no matter how small. Through a unique set of circumstances, she landed a job at a mom-and-pop radio station just outside of Washington, D.C., where she investigated local news stories, provided commentary, and spoke with listeners on the air. Her audience instantly responded to her concise, conversational style, finding her to be a good listener as well. As the show's ratings and audience grew along with Janet's popularity, it became an innovative platform for her to invite a wide variety of guests to come and discuss issues that pulled at the heartstrings of parents across America. No topic was taboo, from homosexuality and pornography to TV sex and violence to euthanasia and the sanctity of life. Civil rights, civil disobedience, civil responsibility—all became part and parcel of her radio existence. Talking about so many politically incorrect subjects, Janet's own fame has come as a complete surprise. But like everything else, she has theories about that, too. "I am a bit of an anomaly, a female non-liberal doing talk radio in America's backyard [the nation's capitol]. I happen to be a wife and a mother, . . . and there's not an issue we address that doesn't deal with the family."[4] All things considered, she would like to think that home and family are the *true* dominant culture in America, not what is seen in the news or on television.

Syndication of Janet's show, called *Janet Parshall's America*,[5] put her name on the map from coast to coast. According to recent NBC *Today Show* statistics, Christian talk radio is the fourth largest media format in America, due in large part to Janet's upbeat programming and what *The Washington Times* calls her "kitchen table culture commentary."[6] So it came as no surprise when, after 9/11, millions of Americans turned to *Janet Parshall's America* for explanation and hope.

"We live in a world of terror color codes not by accident but by divine appointment," Janet said in a broadcast that captivated audiences across the country. "God has purposely placed us in the midst of these threats to live out the Great Commission."[7] In a nutshell that summarizes Janet's entire worldview. Christians are intended to be salt and light to a stagnant, dim world. Knowing that few people will intentionally look for opportunities to share the light of Christ, God has made it easy by bringing the challenge right into our homes.

As listeners can attest, numerous topics hit Janet's hot button. High on the list is the average American Christian's growing tendency toward biblical illiteracy. "If we don't study God's Word and hide it in our hearts so that we don't sin against God, how will we endure when tempestuous times come?"[8] Only when Scripture exists as a vital, dynamic influence in one's life, Janet explains, can the believer go out into the world and fulfill the Great Commission. Another concern is most American Christians' preoccupation with creature comforts. "Oswald Chambers once said, 'God is not concerned with our comfort; he's concerned about our character.' That is still true today."[9] Finally, as Janet often repeats on her shows, no matter who you are, what your schooling or occupation, *get involved*. "Sometimes I still stand in front of a mirror and shake my head, thinking, *I'm a mom. How in the world did I end up in politics?* Well, I ended up there because that's where God called me to serve. God will use anyone who says, 'Lord, Here am I. Send me.'"

Janet Parshall's America has been nominated for the National Religious Broadcasters Talk Show of the Year as well as Best Produced Radio Program of the Year numerous times. Janet herself has received many awards and is a frequent guest on dozens of print and broadcast newsmagazines, radio shows, and television programs. Her name appears on several Who's Who lists. In a 1998 issue of *TALKERS Magazine*, the National Association of Radio Talk Show Hosts rated Janet in the top one hundred out of five thousand hosts spanning fourteen hundred shows nationwide. With her children grown and more time on her hands, Janet has been making regular public appearances across the country, and has coauthored three books with her husband.

Questions/Thoughts for Reflection: Janet Parshall believes that the answer to many of America's woes is a biblically-literate body of Christian believers who will boldly and graciously live out their faith. How well do you know your Bible? If a Jew or a Muslim or even another Christian asked you what you believe and why, would you be able to back up your answer with Scripture? What about sin? The next time you are tempted by evil, will you—like Jesus in the desert of temptation— be able to answer back with, "It is written . . ." or will you be tossed about like a sailboat adrift in a tempestuous sea?

Prayer Focus: Holy God, help me to hide your word in my heart, so that I might not sin against you!

Perpetua and Felicitas

(b. "unavailable" – d. "unavailable")

"Father, do you see . . . this vessel lying here to be a little pitcher or
something else? Can it be called by any other name than what it is?
Neither can I call myself anything else than what I am, a Christian."
—Perpetua, from her journal

Times were dark for the Roman Empire in the year AD 203. The
Emperor Pertinax had been killed by mutinous soldiers in Rome a
few years before, and Septimius Severus, spurred on by a conviction in
his destiny to gather the splintered empire back together, had begun his
reign as new emperor with an iron fist. Believing Judaism and
Christianity to be obstructions to bringing the civilized world under his
control, Severus forbad conversion to both faiths. The persecution of
Christians was especially cruel along the northern coast of Africa, where
the city of Carthage sat as a gleaming metropolitan jewel among the
other coastal towns.

But as happens even in the midst of the most troubling times, life
went on for the inhabitants of that city. One woman in particular,
twenty-two-year-old Perpetua, led a busy life. As a wife and mother of an

infant son, she embraced the message of Jesus Christ's sacrifice on the cross and began a regimen of training in the Christian faith. The daughter of a nobleman, Perpetua was well educated and held considerable influence for a woman of her time.

Early in AD 203 Perpetua was placed under twenty-four-hour surveillance because of her new-found beliefs, along with several other catechumens—three men by the name of Saturninus, Secundulus, and Revocatus, along with his young servant girl, Felicity. That night Perpetua's father visited her, his face wet with tears.

"My daughter, why are you bringing this reproach on me? Renounce this nonsense and come home."

"Father, do you see this vessel lying here to be a little pitcher or something else?"

"I see it to be a pitcher."

"Can it be called by any other name than what it is?"

"No, of course not."

"Neither can I call myself anything else than what I am, a Christian."

Incensed, Perpetua's father lunged at her as though he were going to tear out her eyes. But he caught himself and left her, swallowed up in his grief and rage.

A few days later, facing arrest and possible death, Perpetua and her friends knew they must make their faith publicly known as a source of encouragement to one another as well as other Christians in the city. They were baptized before a small crowd of believers. In prayer amidst the waters of baptism, Perpetua sensed the Holy Spirit speak to her heart. From that time forward she must pray for nothing else save endurance to withstand what was to come. Within a few days soldiers dragged the converts away to the lower depths of the Carthage prison. In her journal[1] that night, Perpetua wrote, "O terrible day! O the fierce heat of the shock of the soldiery, and because of the crowds! I was especially distressed by my anxiety over the care of my infant."

Knowing how Perpetua would be pining for her son, two deacons of the local church, Tertius and Pomponius, bribed her guards to allow the young mother to leave the dungeon for a few hours and nurse her child in more pleasant surroundings. After several more days, remembering how the prisoner blossomed in the presence of her son, the guards finally relented to Perpetua's pleading and allowed the baby to stay with his mother during her imprisonment. Soon Perpetua's journal included this entry: "After I obtained my infant to remain in the dungeon with me, I grew strong and was relieved from distress and anxiety about him. The dungeon became to me as it were a palace, so that I preferred being there to being anywhere else."

One afternoon Perpetua's brother, who shared her Christian faith, came to her. "Lady, my sister, you are now in high honor such that you may ask for a vision and it will be granted to you. Ask of God, therefore, whether this be a passion or else deliverance."[2] Perpetua, who felt confident in her relationship with her Lord and did not doubt that he would grant her request, replied to her brother that she would give an answer the following day.

That night Perpetua saw a vision in which a ladder made of bronze rose up to the heavens. At the ladder's base a giant serpent lay in wait for anyone daring enough to climb the ladder. Saturus, Perpetua's spiritual instructor, who was not with his students at the time of their arrest but who afterwards gave himself up to the authorities, scaled the ladder first, then called down to his friend: "I am waiting for you, but be careful that the dragon does not bite you."

"In the name of the Lord Jesus Christ, he shall not hurt me," Perpetua replied.

As she raised her foot to the first rung, the serpent raised his head. Perpetua stepped on the snake's head and pushed herself up to the next rung. When she had gained the top, she saw a lovely garden covered with a fine mist and a white-headed man sitting in shepherd's apparel. "Welcome, my child," the man said and held out some sweet curd for her to eat. At that moment the prisoner awoke from her vision with the lingering taste of sweetness on her lips. At once she called her brother. "It is a passion; I know it now." From that time forward Perpetua and her friends set their minds on heaven.

Days later the city stood paralyzed by the breaking news: Perpetua and her friends would stand trial for their crime. Perpetua's father, who had stayed away from the prison, now threw himself at his daughter's feet once more.

"Have pity, daughter, on my gray hairs. Have pity, my lady, on your father, if I am worthy to be called father by you! If with these hands

I have brought you up to this flower of womanhood—for I have preferred you before all your brothers—do not, I beg you, make me a reproach to men. For the sake of your brothers, your mother, and your aunt; for the sake of your son, who will not survive your death; give up your resolve to do this thing. You will destroy us all!" At this, Perpetua's father burst into tears and kissed his daughter's hands.

Perpetua's heart ached. She loved and respected her father, yet she could not relinquish her faith. Saddened that he could not understand her resolve to die for Christ, she tried her best to comfort him. Squeezing his hands within hers, she said, "Dear father, whatever shall be done at this tribunal will be God's good purpose and pleasure, not my own. I'm sorry."

At this, Perpetua's father slid his hands out of his daughter's and left.

During the time of their imprisonment, Perpetua and Felicitas became fast friends, and Perpetua learned of Felicitas's deepest dread. Because the servant girl was pregnant and Roman law forbade the execution of a woman with child, she feared her execution would be stayed until after the baby was born, by which time her friends would already be martyred. For days the women prayed that they should be allowed to face death together.

One night, as the captives were eating the evening meal together,[3] the coliseum guards burst in and took them to be tried before Hilarianus. The procurator had just received the authority to execute matters of life and death in the place of the proconsul Minucius Timinianus, who had recently died. Testing his new power, Hilarianus interrogated Perpetua's friends, who all confessed to the crime of conversion to Christianity. He then turned to Perpetua.

"Do you see your father, standing here? Spare his gray hairs! Spare your infant son! Offer sacrifices for the emperor's prosperity."

"I cannot, for I am a Christian."

Hearing his daughter's fateful words, Perpetua's father flung himself at her but was caught by the guards and beaten. The prisoner cried in horror as her father succumbed to each blow, then was released to his home.

"Take them away!" Hilarianus growled. "We'll see how strong their faith is when they are face-to-face with death."

That night Perpetua sent word to her father to return her son to nurse at her breast, but in his anger and grief he refused. Tradition has it that by an act of God, the child was immediately weaned, and Perpetua's milk dried up, alleviating her pain.

As the day of execution drew near, Pudens, the assistant overseer of the prison, moved by the prisoners' faith and courage, began permitting a great many visitors to see them. Among these was Perpetua's father, to make one final plea. Throwing himself to the ground, he plucked out his beard and cursed the day he was born. Perpetua grieved over his unhappiness, but her resolve remained strong.

Three days before their execution, the captives—except for Secundulus, who had fallen ill and died in prison—prayed in one accord for Felicitas to be delivered of the child in her womb. She wanted to die in the comfort of her friends, especially Perpetua. Immediately after the prisoners' prayers, Felicitas went into labor. The birth pains were hard, and she cried out in pain. One of the prison servants who accompanied her in her labor taunted her. "You cry now; what will you do when you are thrown to the wild beasts?"

To the servant's amazement Felicitas answered, "Now it is I who suffer; then there will be One within me who will suffer in my stead." After many hours of labor, she gave birth to a daughter and handed her to a couple to raise as their own child.

With their execution one day away, Perpetua saw one more vision in which she was transformed into a man and the wild beasts promised by the procurator turned into an Egyptian warrior. She fought with him and prevailed and was given a green branch laden heavy with apples of gold. When she awoke, she wrote her last journal entry: "I perceived that I was not to fight with beasts but against the devil himself. Still I knew that victory awaited me." Setting down her pen, she joined her friends for a final agape feast[4] featuring their favorite foods, according to Roman custom for the condemned.

March 7 dawned sunny and warm. In celebration of the Emperor Geta's[5] birthday, an exhibition of gladiators was to be held in the city's coliseum, including the execution of Perpetua and her friends.[6]

Revocatus, Saturninus, and Saturus were handed the garb of the priests of Saturn[7] and forced to put them on. Entering the forum before the women, their eyes fell on Hilarianus. "You judge us," they yelled, "and God you!" Revocatus and Saturninus were thrown immediately to a leopard and then a bear, but the men survived both, sustaining severe wounds.

Meanwhile, Perpetua and Felicitas were given the ceremonial dress of the priestesses of Ceres[8] to wear. But the women refused. "We are the true brides of Christ," they declared. "We will not wear outfits befitting heathen priestesses."

To mock the captives' dignity, the guards wrapped them naked in netting. But the crowd shuddered to see Perpetua, her tender youth bared before them all, and Felicitas, her breasts dripping with milk after her recent childbirth. The audience had come for the sport, yes, but this scene was too much for even them to bear. The women were brought back into the den and given their own clothes to put on, then sent out again. Entering the amphitheater hand in hand, the two burst into song. The crowd awed in amazement at the sight of the women, their heads held high, gladness on their faces. The pair looked more like two saints entering the gates of heaven than two criminals who were about to be mauled to death.

A bull was released upon the two women. It charged Perpetua first, throwing her to the ground, then turned on Felicitas. Dazed, her robe torn and her hair disheveled, Perpetua fumbled around the ground for her hairpin and neatly fastened her long hair once again. Seeing Felicitas on the ground, she held the fabric of her robe together to protect her modesty and went to her friend's side. The pair was allowed to rest at one of the coliseum gates while Saturus took his turn with the beasts.

Saturus, who detested bears, hoped to die from a single bite of the leopard. But a boar was loosed upon him first. As soon as the gladiator released the animal, it turned and tore into its handler, who died. Next a bear's cave was opened to the forum, but the beast refused to leave the comfort of its quarters. Finally, a leopard was sent into the amphitheater. The great cat leapt at Saturus's throat, killing him almost instantly. Perpetua saw her instructor dead on the ground. True to her vision, he had gone before her into heaven and would be awaiting her there.

Rousing herself, she exclaimed, "When will we be thrown to the beasts?"

Felicitas replied, "Look at the gashes on our bodies and the blood covering our clothes. We have already confronted them!"

The roaring audience, its thirst for blood not yet quenched, turned its attention again to the women. "Bring them forward. We want to see their slaughter with our own eyes!" the crowd jeered.

Perpetua and Felicitas moved to the center of the coliseum, near where Revocatus and Saturninus stood. Friends in death as in life, the two women held each other close. Several gladiators approached the group from different directions, their weapons raised. The men stood valiantly as the swords pierced them through and fell to the ground. Then, with a final blow, they were beheaded.

Perpetua and Felicitas exchanged a kiss of peace, then waited with eyes fixed on each other for their fate. Felicitas's death was swift, but the young, inexperienced gladiator assigned to Perpetua fumbled his sword, piercing her between the ribs but missing her heart. Perpetua cried out in agony as the youth withdrew the blade. Gathering her strength and her wits, she cautiously raised the blade to her throat.

As Perpetua's body sank to the ground, a whisper rushed through the crowd, "Perhaps so great a woman could not else have been slain except she willed it."[9]

Questions/Thoughts for Reflection: Today's culture rewards individualism over our need for community with others. Yet Christianity is inescapably communal. As this historical account has survived through the ages, Perpetua, Felicitas, and their "death row" companions have been praised above all else for their mutual support in death as well as their faithfulness to one another in life. Can you imagine how different these two young women's last moments on earth might have been had their friendship not been as deep as it was?

Prayer Focus: Dear Jesus, as you have promised never to leave or forsake me, help me to be there for my family and friends and even for those around me whom I do not know. Help me to show kindness and gentleness to other people, never knowing how my words or actions might affect them but trusting that you want to use me to be a blessing.

Patti Pierce

(b. 1943 – d.—)

*"When I think of what God has done through Women at the Well,
I'm in awe. I just smile and giggle; it's all I can do. I know
who I am and who I'm not. I know what I'm capable of
and where my weaknesses are. In my wildest dreams I would
never have imagined God using me in this way."*
—Patti Pierce, personal interview

For Patti Pierce life in the mid-1980s was hectic but rewarding. As head of a dynamic singles ministry at Menlo Park Presbyterian Church in Menlo Park, California, she had her hands full planning activities and leading Bible studies for a group of 650 singles, most under the age of thirty-five. Some of the men and women in the group were struggling with relationships, some were looking for direction, and some simply wanted to know more about God. To help them resolve their issues, Patti found herself doing a lot of one-on-one counseling. Her work also entailed developing a leadership team and serving as the director of women's ministries. As if all these activities were not enough, she was wife to a busy general contractor named Bill and mother of two girls, Carrie and Lindsay.

Then one day in 1987, she experienced a paradigm shift. Her teenage daughter Carrie had been wrestling for some time with her self-esteem. Finally, Patti and Bill decided she might benefit from professional counseling and made an appointment for her to see their therapist friend, Susan. Carrie and Susan had met twice when Patti had a strong sense that she should speak privately with Susan about her own personal history in case it was important to Susan's work with Carrie. "You see, when I was a child, my father, who was a minister, molested me repeatedly," Patti shared quietly. "He only recently acknowledged what happened in the past, and we've had several discussions about it, in private of course. The girls don't know. It's been causing some tension."

Susan was thoughtful for a moment. "I'm glad you told me this, Patti. It's an important piece to this puzzle. For some time Carrie has been feeling like something is amiss in your larger family, and she feels she's the cause of it. It has affected how she thinks about herself. Knowing what you've just told me, I would say there is nothing wrong with Carrie at all. She's simply been picking up on the tension within your family. She doesn't need therapy, but *you* do."

Patti had long known her childhood experiences had left her emotionally wounded. Yet she had never dealt with the memories except to shove them deep into the graveyard of her mind. Now those old bones were returning to haunt her entire family. For the next five years she attended regular therapy sessions. Meanwhile, economic recession hit the Bay area, and Bill's business began to suffer. Patti continued working at the church, but it was becoming more and more difficult for them to make ends meet.

During this period Patti was counseling a woman from the church who had recently been raped. The woman was devastated by the event, along with the distress of a pending civil suit. The two women prayed together frequently, with Patti lending moral and spiritual support. One spring day in 1992, the woman arrived at Patti's office full of smiles. The case had settled out of court for a large sum of money. Although Patti was genuinely happy for the woman, deep down she felt as though her heart had been pierced through with a knife. She couldn't help feeling that God had forgotten about her own situation. Hadn't she been traumatized by her father's incest so many years before? Wasn't she still learning to cope with the long-term effects of her past? Yet this woman had been blessed with financial compensation for the wrong done to her while she and Bill were struggling to the point of possibly selling their house just to keep their now-college-age daughters in school.

When Patti got home that evening, she wrapped a scarf around her neck and went outside. Her daily walks often took her down secluded paths around a nearby reservoir where tall pines sheltered her thoughts from the outside world and she could pray uninterrupted. This time her thoughts took her places she did not want to go. Unwelcome interludes with her father. Concerns about financial instability. Uncertainty about where God was in the midst of her predicament. All her life she'd been taught that she could trust God; all of a sudden she realized that trust had been hard to come by. She stopped in her tracks.

"God, where are you?" Patti shouted toward the towering treetops. "Why are you allowing all this to happen? Don't you care what happens to me and my family?" For the next hour she bared her soul to God, articulating thoughts and feelings she had never dared express before. Above all there was a growing realization of how deeply her past had scarred her life, distorting her view of God. The intensity of those minutes, speaking candidly with God from the depths of her being, was unlike anything she had ever experienced.

When she arrived back at home, Patti felt a wonderful sense of release, like a heavy burden she had been carrying around completely unawares had vanished. She fell into a deep, refreshing sleep. When she awoke, a single thought was foremost on her mind: *Everyone needs a place where they can bare their souls to God.*

She had been working with hundreds of single adults and other women for years, yet only now did it occur to her that while she had been feeding their minds and keeping them busy with wholesome activities, their spirits might well be starving for an intimate relationship with God. It was as if the activities were inoculations, helping them get from one week to the next without teaching them how to sustain a relation with God that is deep, honest, and satisfying. *What does that kind of relationship look like?* she asked herself. *How does one achieve it? Is intimacy with God something only the lucky experience, or is there a process by which anyone can know the presence of God in a personal way?*

She did not have all the answers to the questions that flooded her mind, but she was determined to find them. She called together a group of close friends and learned that they, too, experienced the same longing to know God more deeply. For the next several months, the group prayed together about how to meet the deep spiritual hunger for God that many people face. From her own experience Patti believed that meeting God in silence and solitude was important to the process of receiving healing and freedom. If, due to our frantic lifestyles, we cannot hear his voice, how can we expect to receive what he wishes to impart? Believing the Bible to be God's Word, she knew the truths found therein would be relevant to people's needs and should also be part of the process.

In June 1994, Patti and the group[1] determined that what people need is a safe place where they can get away from their normal routines and meet with God, a place to build a relational bond with him in addition to the cognitive one that most Christians have already formed—to really get to know God and be known by him. They also need a process for learning to develop and sustain intimacy with God, as well as resources to help them practice the process in their own private moments no matter what their spiritual level was.

The group decided to invite thirty-two key Christian women church and community leaders from the local area to a retreat, to share their vision and test the material Patti had been developing. The retreat was a success. Over the next six months, these women hosted coffee clutches around the Bay area to pass on the vision to others and raise seed money to start Women at the Well,[2] a nonprofit organization that could turn the growing dream into a reality. By December, thirty thousand dollars had been raised, and Women at the Well was launched. Patti knew that if she was to be the executive director of this new venture, she would have to quit her job at the church. Believing this to be God's calling, she turned in her resignation. She and Bill sold their house, using the proceeds to help supplement Bill's income (his business was flourishing again, and they were no longer struggling financially).

Her time now free to devote to Women at the Well, Patti began leading day and weekend retreats, using the facilities at a nearby Catholic seminary. In 1998, the organization rented a small house in Menlo Park. An older home on a main thoroughfare, inviting décor and gardens soon transformed it into a center where people could come and spend an hour, a day, or even a weekend meeting with God. Various resource materials were made available for visitors' use, including guides for personal retreats written by Patti.

By 1999, Patti realized that she personally could no longer keep up with the spreading work of Women at the Well, which had now extended into Southern California. Several women began to help with retreat leadership, but that still did not address the greater problem of being a small organization trying to meet the needs of so many people. Through prayer Patti felt God nudging her toward another area of work: spiritual mentoring. She had been training mentors through Women at the Well since 1996, while she herself was being mentored by people like Eugene Peterson, author of *The Message,* and poet Luci Shaw. In 2001 she developed a program to equip leaders from any locale to train their constituents to be mentors, who could then help others with their own spiritual formation.[3]

The ministry of Women at the Well is still evolving. In 2003, with the mentoring program going strong and requests coming in from churches desiring training in order to give their congregations a more structured spiritual formation program, Patti is once again stretching the organization to incorporate a church training program. However, one thing will always remain the same: Women at the Well will continue to offer a place for people to experience an authentic connection with God through Jesus Christ and a practical process to learn how to listen and notice the ways in which God speaks to their everyday lives.

Questions/Thoughts for Reflection: In C. S. Lewis's book, *The Problem of Pain,* he states that "God whispers to us in our pleasures, speaks in our conscience, but shouts in our pain. It is God's megaphone to rouse a deaf world."[4] While pain and suffering are not focal points of Women at the Well's ministry, they are oftentimes trigger points that bring people to the ministry in search of a deeper understanding of and relationship with God, just as Patti herself experienced.

Has some painful life experience caused you to wonder where God is in the midst of it all? On a scale of 1 to 10, how would you rate your own intimacy level with God? Take a moment to write a letter to God, expressing what you would like your relationship with him to be and any feelings you have that might interfere with that kind of relationship. Then spend some time in prayer, using the following as a springboard.

Prayer Focus: Dear God, I want to believe you care deeply for me. But when I think of. . . .

Puah and Shiphrah

(b. "unavailalbe" – d. "unavailable")

"But the midwives feared God, and did not do as the king of Egypt commanded them, but saved the male children alive."
—Exodus 1:17

Israel's son Joseph was long since dead, as was the Pharaoh under whom he had served. The children of Israel, who had come as friends to the land of Egypt, were now slaves under the ruling pharaoh's heavy hand. Nevertheless, they multiplied and grew to be a powerful nation, and "the land was full of them" (Exod. 1:7). In fact, the descendants of Israel had grown so great in number that the new pharaoh, most likely Rameses II, of Egypt, became concerned. Might these slaves someday join with his enemies, overrun his land, even overthrow his throne? Something must be done.

So Pharaoh increased the workload of the Hebrew people. For every quota of mortar and brick they had to make, now they must make two. For those working in the fields, hours of labor were added per day and enforced by the crack of a whip. The city walls of Pithom and Raamses,

Pharaoh's newest storehouse cities, must now go up higher and faster, or there would be hell to pay. Besides, busy hands are happy hands, the king mused cruelly. No time for idle thoughts of escape or revenge. And certainly no energy for lovemaking at the end of a long, hard day.

But Pharaoh's plan failed. The more miserable he made the Israelites, the greater their numbers grew. His own people dreaded their presence in the wilderness camps outside their homes.

One sleepless night an idea came to Pharaoh, a foolproof plan to demoralize the Israelites and decrease their numbers. Why hadn't he thought of it before? In the morning he called the Hebrew midwives before him.

"Which of you supervises the rest?" Pharaoh demanded.

The women looked around at one another. Had they done something wrong? Finally, two stepped forward.

"Names."

The women bowed. "Shiphrah and Puah, your excellency."

"Shiphrah and Puah, hear the charge of Pharaoh, king of Egypt," the ruler bellowed in the presence of the others. "You are all to continue on with your duties as midwives to the Hebrews, as before. When the women are about to deliver and they sit on the birth stools, if you see that the child is a daughter, you shall allow it to live. However, if it is a son—" Pharaoh paused, measuring out the next few words. "If it is a son, you shall kill him."

The midwives gasped. Many began to sob, choking down the whys that filled their hearts but could never be asked or answered. No one could call into question Pharaoh's wisdom.

"If you do not obey my command," Pharaoh continued, "I assure you, the cost of your disobedience will be your own lives."

The women left Pharaoh's presence in silence, but as soon as they were outside the palace, their chatter filled the streets leading to the Hebrew camps outside the city walls.

"How can we do such a thing?" they asked one another.

After a great deal of talk, they came to a unison conclusion. Even at the threat of death, they could not, would not, take the innocent lives of the newborn boys, as Pharaoh had instructed.

"But what will we tell him when he learns we have disobeyed him?" one of the women asked. "Surely his soldiers will be watching."

Shiphrah and Puah nodded at each other in agreement. "We've been discussing that. . . ."

Days turned into weeks and weeks into months. Pharaoh's guards lurked around the Hebrew camps watching for signs of swelling bellies, signaling a birth in the near future. Try as the new mothers might to hide their newborn sons, the truth was obvious. There was no mourning in the camps, and no burials were taking place for infant children. The Hebrew population continued to grow.

One day the inevitable happened. Shiphrah and Puah were again called into Pharaoh's presence, his clenched fists revealing the fury they feared would be released upon them.

"Why did you deliberately disobey me?" The king paced in rage. "Answer me!"

"Your excellency," Shiphrah began, her forehead pressed against the floor in a low bow. "The Hebrew women are not like the Egyptian women, who are not used to hard work and are weak in the final hours of their delivery."

"That's right," Puah agreed, gathering her courage. "The Egyptian women need assistance even to crouch onto the birth stools."

"But the Hebrew women work all day and are lively and strong," Shiphrah continued. "They give birth before we even have a chance to be called."

Both women trembled as they remained in subservient positions on the floor, awaiting Pharaoh's verdict. Would he believe their tale?

To the women's relief, Pharaoh dismissed them from his presence. As the months passed, more sons were born to the Hebrew people, and the nation of Israel thrived. Because the midwives honored God, desiring to obey his command over Pharaoh's, God blessed them and gave them families of their own (see Exod. 1:21).

Questions/Thoughts for Reflection: What does it mean to fear (or honor) God more than man? Aren't we told in Scripture to obey those in authority over us? For those who are faced with these questions, the choice at hand might mean obeying one of God's laws while seemingly breaking another. Is it possible to do both at the same time? This was the dilemma Puah and Shiphrah faced. While the Ten Commandments had not yet been issued, the midwives knew that Jehovah would not want them to lie or behave dishonestly. Yet a deep conviction gripped their hearts that they must not carry out Pharaoh's command to murder innocent children. What were they to do? *What would you do?*

Prayer Focus: Most holy, just, and merciful God, it is not easy to know what to do in all circumstances. I want to do what is right in your eyes, but that choice is not always clear or easy to follow. Please help me to love who and what you love and to feel compassion toward whomever and whatever touches your heart so that when I am faced with a moral dilemma I will choose wisely and *your will* will be done.

Condoleezza Rice

(b. 1954 – d.—)

"When I'm concerned about something, I figure out a plan of action,
and then I give it to God. I just ask to be carried through it.
God has never failed me yet."
—Condoleezza Rice, *Essence* magazine

"Condi, honey, come take a look at this dress. Do you want to try it on?"

Seven-year-old Condoleezza Rice nodded eagerly. It wasn't often that her mother took her shopping in the downtown Birmingham, Alabama department stores. Angelena Rice took the dress off the rack and handed it to her daughter. The pair strolled toward the fitting room, then stopped as a store clerk barred their entrance.

"I'm sorry, ma'am, but you'll have to use the storage room in the back of the store. These rooms are for whites only."

Angelena stared coolly at the clerk. "My daughter will change in one of your dressing rooms, or I will take my business, and your commission, elsewhere."

The clerk's cheeks blushed. "Well, let me see, maybe your little girl can use this room, here at the end of the hallway. I'll just stand here and make sure you have everything you need."

Upon entering the remote dressing room, Angelena chattered idly to her daughter while buttoning up the back of the dress. All the while, Condoleezza wondered why the lady was standing outside their dressing room door. *Is she afraid we'll steal the dress or that someone will see us?*[1]

It was a frozen moment in time in 1961 that Condoleezza would never forget. She realized that being black meant being mistrusted or receiving second-rate treatment. From her mother's response to the store clerk and her patient determination, Condoleezza also learned she could stand her ground.

Condoleezza Rice has spent the rest of her life doing just that.

Born on November 14, 1954, Condoleezza (which means to play "with sweetness" in Italian musical notation) grew up in a Birmingham still crippled from decades of black oppression under the Jim Crow laws.[2] Beginning with her grandfather, John Rice Sr., who was the son of house slaves, education became a crucial component of the heritage that would be passed down through the Rice family. Recognizing that "book learning" was the key to a brighter future, Granddaddy Rice, as Condoleezza affectionately calls the man who died two years before her birth, attended Stillman College in Tuscaloosa in 1918, eventually becoming a Presbyterian minister. John Rice Jr., Condoleezza's father, also a Presbyterian minister, went on to serve as dean of Stillman College as well as vice chancellor of the University of Denver. Condoleezza's mother, Angelena Rice, was also well educated, and taught science and music in an all-black high school.

While John and Angelena felt strongly about the emerging civil rights movement, they were not activists. They believed in fighting racial prejudice of the mind. Within the church and public school settings, they inspired many young blacks to see themselves as equals, and they left nothing to chance with their only child. Condoleezza could read at an age when most children were just beginning to walk. By the time she was three, she was learning to figure skate, dance ballet, speak French, and play what became the love of her life—the piano. Condoleezza's parents initiated these pastimes into their daughter's life to overcome the racism that would surely confront her as she grew up. Perhaps, if she excelled at the activities prized by white society, she would be accepted on her own terms and not judged simply because of the color of her skin.

But with all her parents' efforts, nothing could completely shield Condoleezza from the racial hatred that at times permeated Birmingham. In September 1963, two years after her department store "awakening," a dynamite blast at the Sixteenth Street Baptist Church killed four little black girls, including Condoleezza's childhood friend, Denise McNair.

After that Condoleezza's personal drive began to take her where her parents' efforts could not. Due to a tireless work ethic and staunch self-discipline, at fifteen she entered the University of Denver as a music student, intent on becoming a concert pianist. Surrounded by what she considered more capable musicians, she decided her skills would likely land her a position as an accompanist at best, or perhaps a piano instructor, "teaching thirteen-year-olds to murder Beethoven."[3] A political science professor who specialized in Soviet studies wooed Condoleezza away from music to her graduate major, international politics. At age nineteen, she graduated cum laude. A year later, in 1975, she graduated from the University of Notre Dame with her master's degree. By age twenty-six she had a doctorate from the School of International Studies at the University of Denver and had begun to serve as an assistant professor at Stanford University.

But education and hard work are only half the story of Condoleezza's upbringing. Being the child of a minister, she grew up holding hands with prayer and Scripture, resulting in a deep faith in God. However, there comes a time in each person's life when she must either reject or claim for herself what she was taught as a child. Condoleezza's defining moment came when, as a twelve-year-old, she was visiting her grandmother along with several other family members. During the visit her Uncle Alto became sick and needed immediate medical attention. While the rest of the family ran anxiously about the house, Condoleezza's grandmother sat calmly praying on the edge of the bed beside her son.

"Grandmother, aren't you worried about Uncle Alto?" Condoleezza asked.

"God's will be done."[4]

Seeing her grandmother's trusting spirit, Condoleezza realized that God really *could* be trusted with any crisis, no matter how great. Little did she know then that this lesson in faith would carry her through many turbulent times in the future.

Beginning in 1981 and through the early '90s, Condoleezza served on the Stanford University faculty, where she earned numerous teaching awards. From the fall of 1989 through the spring of 1991, she left Stanford temporarily to serve as the director of Soviet and East European Affairs on the National Security Council. In this capacity she advised President George H. W. Bush about the reunification of Germany and the conversion of the former USSR to individual democratic states. In 1993, amid tremendous controversy, she became Stanford's youngest, first black, first female provost, a post she held for six years. During this time, besides instigating huge budget cuts to improve the school's financial stability and a conscious effort to racially diversify the faculty, she helped found the Center for a New Generation, an after-school program in the Palo Alto community, to help impoverished children.

In 1999, Condoleezza left Stanford permanently to join George W. Bush's presidential campaign, counseling him about foreign affairs much as she had done with the senior Bush earlier in the decade. When the president-elect took office in January 2001, he immediately named Condoleezza as his National Security Advisor. "America will find that she is a wise person," Bush said during his media ammouncement. "I trust her judgment."

When Secretary of State Colin Powell resigned from his duties just days after Bush was elected to a second term in office, the president nominated Condoleezza to the post. "In Dr. Rice, the world will see the strength, the grace, and the decency of our country," Bush said. "Dr. Rice has a deep, abiding belief in the value and power of liberty, because she has seen freedom denied and freedom reborn."

Condoleezza accepted the senate-confirmed appointment with the dignity Americans have come to expect from her. Immediately she set forth goals for her new post: "One of my highest priorities as secretary [of state] will be to ensure that [the Foreign Service and the Civil Service] have all the tools necessary to carry American diplomacy forward in the twenty-first century."[5]

The job is sure to be her toughest yet. Condoleezza has conceded in the past to being overwhelmed at times. Amid renewed peacekeeping efforts between Israel and Palestine with a new PLO leader, ongoing conflicts in both Afghanistan and Iraq, and growing nuclear threats from several fronts, her new job may well summon more of the same. When this happens, she momentarily sets everything aside and focuses once again on prayer and Scripture, especially Romans 5,[6] where she finds the assurance of peace with God and the promise of hope even in the most difficult circumstances. "When I'm concerned about something, I figure out a plan of action, and then I give it to God. I just ask to be carried through it. God's never failed me yet."

Questions/Thoughts for Reflection: Undoubtedly nothing seemed so impossible at times as a just society in which Condoleezza Rice could grow up. Nothing seemed more impossible to the world than the fall of the Berlin Wall or the end to the Cold War. Yet God saw Condoleezza through these arduous times. Due to her efforts many people around the world have experienced a better life. Imagine for a moment what might happen if you faced your own challenges head-on, coupling discipline and a strong work ethic with prayer and Scripture as Condoleezza has done. Can you envision a better tomorrow for yourself and for those around you?

Prayer Focus: Dear Lord Jesus, you faced the most difficult challenge of all—death on the cross to redeem mankind. Surely you can help me to face the challenges of my life. Teach me to set aside daily time for prayer and reading the Scriptures so that from them I might gain strength.

Rikka

(b. "unavailable" – d.—)

"Jesus was willing to die for me and shed his blood on the cross.
Jesus did this for all of us, so it doesn't matter what happens to me.
I am willing to suffer for Him."
—**Rikka, personal interview**

When Rikka[1] became a Christian, she never imagined that someday, because of her faith, her life might be required of her.

Petite, with expressive eyes and silky black hair that catches the breeze, Rikka is a typical teenager. She is outgoing and enjoys attending classes at a nearby Christian high school. But Rikka lives in Indonesia, where being a Christian can be dangerous. A day never passes that she does not renew her commitment to Jesus Christ or think about what the consequences of her faith might be that day.

A collection of 13,500 islands, Indonesia boasts one of the largest Muslim populations in the world. Although the government promotes a philosophy called *Pancasila,* meaning that all its citizens are free to follow any of the major world religions, every citizen must carry an identification card that includes religious preference. As in many Islamic countries, powerful Muslim extremists in Indonesia have vowed to annihilate the Christians in their midst (who make up approximately 15 percent of the country's population). However, the daily occurrences of rape, beatings, and beheadings, as well as church burnings, have only served to unify the Christians living in Indonesia, including those in Rikka's hometown.

Recently Rikka spent several months helping to plan a school-sponsored Bible camp for the youth in her community, the first of its kind. She could hardly wait for the first evening meeting, which went by without incident. On the second evening the students were having fun and singing boisterously when the leaders told them to quiet down. Not long ago Muslim extremists had burned a pastor alive inside his church because he would not renounce his beliefs, they said. What would the students do if their faith were similarly tested? The students became silent. They had heard stories of religious persecution in their country, but none had experienced it firsthand.

At that moment broken glass showered the room as a large stone crashed through the window and rolled to a stop at the students' feet. A barrage of stones followed. The lights went out. Hunkered down on the floor, Rikka felt a sharp blow to her head. She reached up to find blood streaming from the wound. Disoriented, she could not tell what was happening around her. "We must pray. Don't panic, pray," she cried out. "Ask God to help us."

A mob broke into the room, the sound of angry shouts outdoors now mingling with the screaming and crying inside. In pairs men grabbed the students one by one and dragged them outside. Rikka could hear sticks beating across her friends' backs, their cries rising above the sound of scuffling feet as more men ran from building to building. Rikka's heart raced. She felt vulnerable hunched down in the middle of the room, but terror had glued her to the floor. She could not move.

Suddenly a tall form with long hair grabbed Rikka's arms and forced them behind her back. With her arms pinned behind her, another man challenged her in the darkness.

"Are you a Christian?" the second man shouted.

"We are all Christians," Rikka whispered.

The man picked up a piece of broken glass from the floor and held it against Rikka's stomach. "Repeat after me," he demanded. "I renounce Christ and bow down only to Allah. Repeat it!"

Rikka cried. In her heart she prayed, *Save me! Help me not to deny You.*

When she did not respond, her attacker pressed the glass closer to her body, the sharp point piercing her cotton shirt. With each sob the shard of glass punctured Rikka's skin. "Do you believe your God can help you now?"

"Yes. I belong to God, and I believe he will save me."

Furious, the man tossed the glass away and grabbed a nearby stick. "You think I am not strong? You think I cannot break you?" he shouted, cracking the stick across her back and shoulders.

Rikka tried to brace herself for the blows, but each one knocked the wind out of her and seemed worse than the one before. Soon she had no energy left to cry, but inwardly she continued to pray, *Keep me strong; help me not to deny You.*

In exasperation Rikka's assailant threw the stick on the floor. "You are strong too. You are stronger than I am." He motioned to his accomplice to release their captive, then left her bruised and bleeding.

Neither Rikka nor her friends were seriously injured that night. Many others in Indonesia and throughout the world are not so fortunate. For them, choosing to be a Christian means choosing a life of hardship, harassment, imprisonment, even death. In such an environment, one's faith is quickly tested. Often that faith is valued more highly than life itself.

The tenacity of Rikka's faith may seem foolish to some living in the free world. After all, what are a few words if they would spare her from harm? Yet Rikka and thousands like her in religiously repressed countries thank God daily that they are counted worthy to be persecuted for their faith. They pray not to be relieved of their suffering but that through it they will remain faithful to the One who initially suffered on their behalf. Like Jesus they pray for God to forgive their persecutors.

Rikka stands as a symbol to the Christian world of the possible consequences of following Jesus as well as the devotion to Christ we are all capable of with God's help. Because Rikka willingly endured personal suffering for the sake of her faith, we can now draw courage, strength, and healing from her experience. We learn the ultimate meaning of commitment from her example and have a tangible image of what devotion to God looks like. Through her affliction, a portrait of the kingdom of heaven emerges (see Matt. 5:10).

Questions/Thoughts for Reflection: Rikka's story is hard to hear. It's easier to put it out of our minds than think it happens around the world every day, much less that it could happen to us. But think about Rikka's experience for a moment longer. Do you think she was foolish to keep proclaiming faith in Jesus Christ, knowing that doing so would mean more agonizing pain? What was the outcome of her refusal to deny Christ? How might things have been different, for her and her attacker, had she renounced Christ?

Prayer Focus: Dear Holy Spirit, I cannot imagine a time when I would need you more than if I were to face persecution like Rikka faced. Help me to trust that when Jesus said he would never leave or forsake us, he meant also in sickness, persecution, pain, even death.

Edith Schaeffer

(b. 1914 – d.—)

"I dream of a room with a fireplace, a round table with comfortable chairs for six, a lovely teapot with a collection of cups, and a tiny kitchen to make lemon-cream scones. All for the purpose of talking to people: actors, musicians, philosophers, artists and seekers, because Jesus said we're supposed to be a light in a dark place."
—Edith Schaeffer, personal interview

Rebuilding war-torn Europe after Hitler's regime of terror was a slow process. Slower still was the healing of broken hearts and spirits. While people once again began filling churches in search of answers, pastors themselves struggled to make sense of the reality that emerged from the surrounding rubble. If God existed at all, what kind of God was he to allow such death and devastation?

Edith Schaeffer recounts this point in history with solemn wonder. Is it possible that God used a simple American pastor's wife to help encourage a battered Europe and rekindle a faith near dead? This dawning of a new era in her life began in 1947, when the Independent Board of Presbyterian Foreign Missions commissioned her husband, Francis

Schaeffer, to take a leave of absence from the church in St. Louis where he was pastor and travel abroad to study the spiritual health of Europe. In her husband's absence Edith read his letters aloud to their three small children—Priscilla, Susan, and Debbie. Daddy would return soon, she assured them, and things would get back to normal.

But when we follow God's call, life can be anything but normal! After three months of grueling travel through thirteen countries, Francis's findings were alarming: Christian churches in Europe were faltering, and too many children were being raised with no knowledge of the biblical Christ. Soon after filing his report with the Board, a letter arrived from them with an unexpected request: Would Francis and Edith consider moving to Europe "to help strengthen the things that remain"?

Faced with this life-changing decision, Edith exhibited a pattern of prayer that would become the hallmark of her personal faith and ministry. Sensing God's call to move in early 1948, the Schaeffers rented Chalet *Bijou* in the village of Champéry, Switzerland. In addition to representing the Independent Board and helping to organize the International Council of Christian Churches, Francis began to lead Bible studies for children and young people from the local community. Before long a steady flow of people of all ages and walks of life beat a path to the chalet for conversation and morning coffee or afternoon high tea. While Francis led daily discussions around the fireplace in their living room, the task of feeding the continual stream of people fell to Edith. She enjoyed reliving what she had experienced as a child, when, growing up in a missionary family, dinner guests were a regular part of life. Rather than being a burden, the guests provided a welcome outlet for gracious hospitality.

May 1954 found the Schaeffers—including Franky, the newest addition to their family—back in the United States on furlough. Amidst visiting with family, Francis spoke to scores of audiences on topics he had been studying while in Switzerland, such as the validity of absolute truth and a literal interpretation of the Bible. But his views were not well received. It soon became apparent that if they were to return home to Chalet *Bijou,* it would be under a cloud of disapproval from the Board that had sent them to Switzerland in the first place.

Again Edith spent weeks prayerfully waiting to see how the future would unfold. While her husband was earning a name for himself as a well-known albeit controversial intellectual theologian, she began to formulate opinions of her own about what their family was going through in terms that thousands of people around the world would later relate:

Timing is what impresses me most about when the Lord is pushing, pulling, clearing the path, putting up a signpost— whatever way you want to look at His guiding your steps to the next stepping stone. . . . Patience involves a period of time of not having an answer or solution to some critical problem or difficulty in your life. Patience is real, over and over again in a diversity of situations, if it is to be a growing quality. Perfect? Never. But gradually we are meant to look back on shorter or longer periods of patience in the midst of "impossibility."[1]

In September the Schaeffers returned to Europe on board the ocean liner *Île de France*. The future was still unclear yet full of promise. Hadn't the Lord touched the lives of the hundreds of visitors who had experienced their Swiss hospitality? Hadn't he cared for their needs as well? But the cloud of uncertainty that had followed them into the Atlantic darkened when three-year-old Franky became ill. Edith spent the rest of the voyage trying to keep him quiet and comfortable. Once in Switzerland, she would take him to see a doctor. But she didn't have to wait until then for a diagnosis. In Paris, where they waited for a train that would whisk them home, the family went sightseeing for the day while Edith watched little Franky in his crib. She was alarmed to see that each time he pulled himself to a standing position, he quickly fell down again, his left leg sticking strangely out from the hip. "I can't walk, Mommy, I can't walk!" he cried. In an instant, Edith knew: *polio.* Back home in Switzerland, the diagnosis was confirmed. Franky would need immediate attention and then months of therapy to stay the spread of paralysis.

Shortly before the end of the month, misfortune struck a second time. The Board informed the Schaeffers that their income would be cut by $100 per month, a substantial amount considering Franky's medical bills. Making matters worse, Susan began complaining of swollen, painful joints. The doctor diagnosed rheumatic fever and prescribed months of constant bed rest. *Constant bed rest?* Edith thought. *With Franky's therapy and continual houseguests? How will I manage it all?* To top things off, the resident permits they needed to stay in the country were by now long overdue.

Again Edith fell to her knees in prayer. In lengthy conversation with her heavenly Father, she poured out her questions and fears, always taking time to listen for God's response. Sometimes that response came in the form of guidance, other times comfort. Always it brought peace and a deep joy that sustained her for another day.

During this time one French word kept resurfacing in family conversation: *L'Abri*, or shelter. When everything around them seemed to be coming unglued, God's promise to be a shelter kept them going and gave them strength. Moreover, it seemed that Chalet *Bijou* had already become a shelter to the hundreds of people who had come seeking a safe place to ask questions and explore spiritual truths. One day Edith took a piece of art paper and sketched some pine trees and chalets on a hill dotted with skiing stick figures. "L'Abri . . . Come for morning coffee or afternoon tea, with your questions," the invitation read. Was it possible that God was opening the door to a different kind of work? Perhaps it was time to tell the Board about this outreach. Their reaction might well provide the direction they needed.

Amidst the avalanches and mudslides that wrecked havoc all around Champéry during the weeks leading up to the New Year 1955, a letter arrived from an unhappy Board asking, "What do you mean, you're inviting people in for *conversation?*" Meanwhile the government office responsible for processing their resident permits remained stone silent. More hardship, more discouragement, more prayer. Finally, in the middle of a Valentine's Day celebration, the postman arrived with two letters from the local authorities. One stated the family had until midnight of March 31 to leave the village of Champéry; the other stated that they had until the same date to leave Switzerland altogether. The reason given in both letters: "Having had a religious influence in the village of Champéry."

Leave? In six weeks?! Emotions ran high as the entire family discussed what to do. Was God telling them it was time to return to America? Or was he calling them to a new beginning in Switzerland, in which L'Abri was to play a role? Once again Edith spent hours in prayer. Sensing that God would not ask them to leave the work of sharing God's Messiah, Jesus, with the hundreds of visitors who were now coming from around the world, she began to search the surrounding villages for a suitable house to live in while Francis stayed home to pack. It seemed apparent, at least, that they could not stay where they were. God would have to take care of the resident permits if he wanted them to stay in the country; neither of them had the time or energy to worry about that.

With only a few precious days before the deadline, Edith's search was interrupted by a young Czechoslovakian couple. The woman had gone into premature labor, and they needed help getting to the hospital in Lausanne many miles away. The last thing Edith wanted was to take time away from her house hunting, yet how could she turn away from the couple's pleading eyes? At the hospital the woman gave birth to a tiny baby boy, but the doctors were doubtful he would survive.[2] Seeking to ease the couple's heartache, Edith remained with them, grateful that God had detoured her in their time of need. Still, after a sleepless night in the hospital, feelings of desperation began choking their way to the surface again. "Oh, Fran," she cried on the telephone. "What shall we do? I'm going to go out looking again; if I find something, will you come look at it tomorrow?"

"Yes, if you find something. But I doubt you will," Francis replied.

Her husband's gloomy response fueled Edith's determination. She *would* find something by the end of the day; *she had to*. But after tramping for miles through the snow in the village of Villars, she was in tears as the sun sank low on the horizon. Finding a bench, she sat down and began to pray. "Oh, heavenly Father, forgive me for insisting on my own will today. I really do want to want *your* will, not my own. Please help me to be sincere in this. Forgive me for closing the door on the possibility that you might have a totally different plan for the next step in our lives."[3]

Reaching the main street of Villars, Edith kept her head down, not wanting anyone to see her eyes red from weeping. She clung to a thought that had come to mind over and over again in recent months: "The way God turns things for our good and the good of His work, and His glory, does not mean He has sent disaster . . . but that the possibilities of what He can do in us and for us are breathtakingly endless."[4] But at the moment their possibilities seemed to be shrinking as fast as the setting sun.

Then she heard her name. Looking up, she saw a real estate broker whom she had visited days before. "Hop in," he said. "I think I have something that might interest you." The pair drove down the mountain to the village of Huémoz where a huge, vacant chalet sat behind a crossroads bus stop. Edith could see its tremendous possibilities, but it was not for rent; it was for sale.

"For sale!" Edith repeated to herself. "We have no money, and even if we were millionaires, who would buy a house in a country without a permit to live there?" Still, riding the train back to Champéry, she began reviewing the last few days. Had the markers of answered prayer been leading up to this moment? That night, fully aware that both she and Francis needed a miracle to convince them God wanted them to stay in Switzerland, she prayed in such specific terms that even she was startled at the words tumbling out of her mouth. "God, if you want us to buy this house, please give us $1,000 toward the deposit, and have it arrive by 10:00 o'clock tomorrow morning."

Just as Edith and Francis were leaving to catch the train to Huémoz the next day, the postman arrived on skis and handed them their mail. Aboard the train they opened a letter from a couple in Ohio who had been following their work in Switzerland and wanted to contribute something toward "a house that will always be open to young people." Inside the envelope was a check for $1,000. Arriving at the chalet they eventually named Chalet *Mélèzes*, Edith and Francis signed the sales agreement, confident that God would work out the details of the permit.[5]

On a clear weekend in May 1955, L'Abri was officially launched with a sudden influx of weekend guests. On June 5, Francis wrote to the Board with his resignation.

Over the years L'Abri grew to become a world famous sanctuary where people of all ages, locales, and walks of life could come for a day, a week, or a month, to explore, question, even debate biblical Christianity. From an European opera singer to a drunkard from Alabama, they came with valises full of anguish and anger. They came with a multitude of questions. For each and every one, Edith had a smile, a prayer, and a place at the table. "Life at L'Abri was never, ever easy, but it was always rewarding," recollects Edith.

Indeed, Edith's life in the Swiss Alps was a test of her skills and charity. She supervised the guests who poured through the chalet monthly as they helped with the daily baking, gardening, and surplus canning, as well as cleaning and laundry. Three of her four children suffered with long-term illnesses.[6] Eventually her mother-in-law, disabled by a stroke, moved into the chalet, along with another disabled woman with an ill temper and a penchant for hiding napkins under her mattress. Each guest and family member needed her attention, and her to-do list was endless.

No matter. Guests at L'Abri were warmed as much by Edith's gracious spirit as by the evening fire. Before long her hospitality became legendary. What enabled her to maintain her charity toward others in such a difficult environment? Edith's quick answer is prayer. "Nothing was too small for prayer. In those days I prayed about everything, giving everything over to God."

Following Francis's death in 1984, Edith was instrumental in L'Abri's expansion around the world.[7] While the environment of each location is unique, all have the same emphasis of communicating Christianity as objectively true and relevant to the human experience, as evidenced by Edith's life. Despite a number of strokes that have compromised her health, Edith is still an important part of everyday life at L'Abri in Switzerland. Although her participation now is limited, the generous hospitality she extended to all who cast a shadow on her doorstep in the early days of the Fellowship is still at the heart of the L'Abri experience.[8]

Questions/Thoughts for Reflection: The qualities that best describe Edith Schaeffer are *hope* in the possibilities of what God can do; *prayer,* believing that nothing is too small to bring before a caring heavenly Father; and an *openness* to share herself graciously with others through all of life's ups and downs. Write a short inventory of your own life, concentrating on these three areas. Are you hopeful that God can use your current circumstances? Are you prayerful as you face difficult situations? Do you freely share your thoughts and feelings with other people, allowing them to be an encouragement to you while letting God use your life to benefit others?

Prayer Focus: Gracious heavenly Father, help me trust you more and more each day so that I too can live a life full of hope, prayer, and generosity toward others.

Geeta Swamidass

(b. 1948 – d.—)

"As Christians, our lives should be characterized by obedience. There should be no conditions, just go. Rest assured, whatever God calls us to, he can also give us the joy that comes of our obedience."
—Geeta Swamidass, personal interview

Born in Bangalore, India, on November 23, 1948, Geeta Gnanaolivu grew up in a Christian home. Because of her mother's royal ancestry and her father's prestigious position as an army officer, her family lived a comfortable life unaffected by the Indian caste system or religious discrimination in the predominantly Hindu culture. Although her parents tried to instill in her a love for Jesus, Geeta's main concern growing up was her grades; her primary interest in God was his ability to help her achieve them. "If you will help me pass this exam," Geeta prayed on numerous occasions, "I'll trust in you." In high school, sensing that God had honored her prayers over the years, she felt she owed him her obedience and accepted Jesus as her Savior. Little did she know that this decision would lead to many challenging opportunities to express her faith and obedience to Christ.

Like many young adults, Geeta entered college wanting to make a difference in life. Along with three other students, she embarked on a study of the book of Daniel. What a man of God the prophet was. What an impact he had! If only she could have that same kind of influence on her world. Coming across Daniel 11:32, she read: "The people who know their God shall be strong, and carry out great exploits." This verse had a profound affect on Geeta. She realized she must first come to know God intimately, be obedient to him as an expression of her love and devotion, before he would lead her to do great things. No longer could she pursue her own plans first.

All her life Geeta loved animals. She was continually bringing home sick or injured creatures and treating them with homemade concoctions, rejoicing when they became well. She wanted to pursue veterinary medicine, but her father was not pleased with the choice. "You have long fingers and a healing touch, you would make a great surgeon," he said. He would financially support her only if she went to medical school. Disappointed but respectful of her father's wishes, Geeta decided to apply to the top medical school in the country, Christian Medical College in Vellore, India, praying that she would be accepted only if it was God's will for her. To ensure this, although the school was extremely competitive and sponsorship would have greatly enhanced her chances of admittance, Geeta refused all sponsorship opportunities. If God wanted her there, she would make it on her own.

Out of thousands of applicants who applied to the college each year, only 120 names were picked to proceed through the application process after a one-day exam. To keep anonymity and ensure fairness, each of these applicants was assigned a number. A three-day interview whittled the list down to sixty finalists, most of whom were sponsored students. Only two spaces were reserved for open applicants such as Geeta.

Repeatedly the principal of the school told Geeta he wanted her in but that her chances were slim without sponsorship. But Geeta remained adamant. "No, I need to know if this is God's will. If I accept a sponsorship, I'll never know for sure." After three days of waiting, Geeta's number was called. She entered Christian Medical College in 1966.

In 1973, following medical school and a one-year internship, Geeta accepted a position at a small facility called Christian Fellowship Hospital, where she worked primarily with female patients. One day a friend, another doctor in her early 40s, called asking if Geeta would accompany her while she underwent some surgery. Without inquiring what the surgery was, Geeta agreed and met her friend at the hospital. In the operating room, she learned that her friend was three months pregnant. With her family complete and her career in full swing, she had come for an abortion.

A hysterotomy was to be performed, a procedure Geeta had never seen before, in which the uterus is opened and the fetus removed. Several minutes into the operation, the surgeon gently withdrew the fully formed fetus. Although Geeta had seen many embryos and fetuses in various stages of development preserved in jars of formaldehyde, she was totally unprepared to see this little life now squirming in the palm of the surgeon's hand. The baby struggled to breathe, its tiny hands and feet flailing as its premature lungs gasped for air but could not. Within moments it died. Geeta was shaken. She had not given any thought to abortion before; now it was as if the issue were suspended, inescapable, in midair right before her eyes. She vowed never to participate in an abortion.

In 1974, Geeta moved on to another hospital in Kedagaon, India, called Pandita Ramabai Mukti Mission Hospital/Orphanage. While there an intern at another hospital called to tell her about a newborn baby girl named Lekha. Born without arms or legs, the doctors were practicing euthanasia by starving her, a common practice in a country whose population was exploding. Deep inside, Geeta knew Lekha's life had great value and that what was happening was wrong. But a baby with no limbs? Who would want such a child, and how would they care for her? Despite her own questions, she told the intern to bring the baby to the mission hospital. There the nurses loved and nurtured little Lekha, who smiled and laughed as she grew. After five years, Lekha was adopted by a Christian family in New Jersey, where she thrived and became accomplished in a variety of endeavors.

For years Geeta envisioned the kind of man she would marry. Foremost he would be a doctor. Like her father, who left the army in order to become a pastor, he would be obedient to God's call on his life. Her friends wanted her to meet Jaipaul Swamidass, a man of high character, but Geeta would not even consider him. He was an army engineer not a doctor.

That year Geeta was asked to participate in a conference called the Evangelical Union of India, the first major Christian evangelical meeting in the country. A few days before the conference, on Christmas Eve, Geeta felt unsettled over the issue of marriage and sought some solitary time away from the bustle of Christmas preparations. Her parents had tried to arrange several marriages for her over the years; they were all fine men, but they had not fit her concept of the perfect husband. She had said no to each, and her parents were exasperated. That afternoon she got down on her knees and prayed. "What's wrong with me?" she cried. "Lord, show me what *you* want me to do. I can't go on unless you give me an answer."

As she struggled with her feelings, trying to be sensitive to God's voice, Jaipaul's name came to mind. *Why not him?* Geeta immediately sat down and wrote a list of reasons why she did not want to marry Jaipaul, though she had never met him. Topping the list of objections was the fact that he was not a doctor. For the first time she asked herself why this detail was so important. Her conclusion, prestige and security, surprised her. Realizing this, she bowed her head in prayer. With Jaipaul's name foremost in her thoughts, she thanked God for his guidance. Instant peace came over her. She knew whom she was to marry.

On the train heading for the conference, Geeta's friends introduced her to Jaipaul. The two spoke for a short time, agreeing to get together for lunch the first day of the conference. After fulfilling her morning responsibilities at the medical registration booth, Geeta met Jaipaul in the cafeteria. Having chatted only briefly on the train, she expected to spend the hour getting to know him better. Instead, Jaipaul proposed marriage. "But you hardly know me," Geeta objected. "Why would you want to marry me?"

"Because God told me you are the one I am supposed to marry," Jaipaul said.

Geeta was stunned. "God also told me that I was suppose to marry you!" she replied. By the end of lunch, they were engaged.

Geeta's parents, rather than being pleased, were dismayed. Jaipaul was in the process of leaving the army to go back to school in search of God's calling for him. With no job or clearly defined career goals, he was not their idea of the ideal son-in-law. Trusting their faith, Geeta and Jaipaul agreed they would wait for her parents' blessing.

Two months later Geeta's father traveled to the United States on business. He wrote a letter describing America as "a prosperous country with lots of money, but they have no God." He noted that the divorce rate was high, a fact he attributed to Americans' godless living, and began thinking over his daughter's choice for a husband. He still did not like Jaipaul's lack of employment, but he admired the man's desire to be obedient to God. He approved the marriage, and in August 1975 Geeta and Jaipaul were married.

In the spring of 1976, still unsure what the future held, the couple felt called to come to the United States as missionaries. Jaipaul had heard about Biola University in California and decided this was where he was meant to go. But they had no means to pay for an exit visa, travel expenses, or college tuition. On top of all this, Geeta would not be allowed to practice medicine in the States until passing the required medical exams. Where would they come up with all the necessary money? As fall approached, the couple sold everything they had to fund the journey. Within days of their departure, a family friend gave the couple enough money to cover the first semester's tuition. They arrived in California one week before classes started.

As Jaipaul attended lectures, Geeta studied for the California medical exams and worked for an OB/GYN in the Orange County area. From 1978 to 1982, she gave birth to two sons and a daughter. Finally, in 1984, she passed her exams and was ready to do her internship. But God had other ideas for her life.

By this time Jaipaul was working in real estate, where he met many prominent people in the community. One man, the owner of a successful contracting business who had recently accepted Christ, felt inclined to give a significant financial gift to charity. Alarmed at the staggering rate of abortions being performed following the *Roe v. Wade* ruling in 1973, he, together with three other businessmen and Jaipaul, decided to start a crisis pregnancy center. Three more men, all local obstetricians wanting to help their patients find alternatives to abortion, joined them in the venture. A date was set for the first meeting of the newly formed board.

As the men brainstormed about the practicality of opening a clinic, one gaping hole emerged in their plan. They needed a woman doctor to direct the work. Immediately Jaipaul thought of Geeta. "With her background in missions and her work assisting unwed mothers, she would be perfect for the job," he said.

That night, listening to Jaipaul describe the group's vision, Geeta felt trapped. Although she had a heart for the unborn, being the director of a clinic was not her dream. For the next few days, a thought kept nagging at her mind: Might God be asking her to set aside her own desires for a medical practice to make a crisis pregnancy clinic a reality? She agreed to be on the steering committee to help get the project started. As the time approached for the clinic to open and no director had been found, she struggled again in prayer over the growing feeling that directing the clinic was her God-ordained destiny.

In January 1985, the board approached Geeta again. "We're calling it LivingWell.[1] It will be the first medical clinic in the country to specifically address crisis pregnancies, and we want you to run it," they urged.

"Do what you feel God wants you to do," Jaipaul said when the couple spoke that evening. Reminding Geeta of the abortion she had witnessed in India, he added: "If you really believe that was wrong, why don't you do something about it?"

Remembering that experience, Geeta committed herself to directing the clinic for one year. On April 15, 1985, LivingWell Medical Clinic opened in the city of Orange, where she performed free pregnancy testing, initial medical exams, and counseling to women in crisis. However, it did not take long for her to realize that for each pregnant woman who came through the doors, many more were hurting deeply from past abortions. Whether a medical necessity or a painful solution to a difficult predicament, abortion had left these women emotionally wounded. Now, months or even years later, they were paying the price. Geeta decided to add another facet to her growing ministry by extending the healing hand of forgiveness to these women who were unable to forgive themselves.

Throughout the year Jaipaul's income was unsteady, and Geeta was not on salary. But God provided for their needs in many ways. Occasionally the Christian preschool their children attended allowed the bill to go unpaid; they believed in what Geeta was doing and wanted to support the work.

The next year the board asked Geeta to stay on. She agreed. She had just begun to see the fruits of her labor—women accepting Christ, babies being born, healing taking place—and knew she wasn't ready to quit.

Geeta has been the director of LivingWell Medical Clinic ever since. Being the first crisis pregnancy medical clinic in the United States, LivingWell is the model after which all subsequent crisis pregnancy medical clinics have followed. At the time of writing, more than sixty-eight thousand women have been seen in half a dozen LivingWell clinics statewide. More than fifteen thousand babies have been born that might otherwise have been aborted, and over one thousand women have received postabortion counseling. A much sought-after speaker to Christian and secular groups, Geeta has addressed more than thirty thousand people on the subject of abstinence and the consequences of "safe sex."

Questions/Thoughts for Reflection: Obedience is difficult for most of us. We are rebellious by nature, tending toward a self-serving attitude. While some cultures provide a more rigid framework within which a young woman can mature, there are always choices to be made and opportunities to go one's own way, as evidenced by Geeta Swamidass's life. In today's society, where independence and a strong will are prized, what do you think of Geeta's willingness to defer to her father's wishes regarding her education and her husband's advice to pursue a different career choice? What part did these events play in her God-given destiny? What part did her own obedience play in following the path she felt God was calling her to pursue?

Prayer Focus: Dear Father, the psalmist says you knew the course of my life before I was even conceived, yet in birth you gave me the freedom to determine my own path. Please help me day by day to prayerfully consider what I will say and do and what I will become by my choices.

Joni Eareckson Tada and Renée Bondi

(b. 1949 – d.— and b. 1958 – d.—)

"Our sufferings matter to God because they bond us and bind us to the Man of Sorrows like nothing else. We have something eternally precious in common with Christ and that is our suffering—our own scars and our own anguish, all the times we've felt rejection and pain. . . . All these things have given us at least a tiny taste of what the Savior endured to purchase our redemption."
—Joni Eareckson Tada

Seventeen-year-old Joni Eareckson embraced life in 1967 as only a teenager fresh out of high school could. Named after her father, Johnny, she inherited his adventurous spirit and love for the outdoors. She cherished her accomplishments as a member of the National Honor Society at her high school in Baltimore, Maryland, and was looking forward to attending Western Maryland College, where she planned to study to become a physical therapist. And she was dating two nice boys, both of whom seemed like potential marriage material. Life was ideal until a swim in nearby Chesapeake Bay on a picture-perfect July day changed everything. Diving into what she thought was a deep recess, she hit bottom. Unable to move, she was rushed by ambulance to a hospital where tests confirmed the doctors' suspicions: Joni had broken her neck. She would be a quadriplegic—paralyzed from the neck down, needing help with every function of her existence—for the rest of her life.

Renée Lacouague went to sleep one balmy night in May 1988, twirling a new engagement ring around her finger. A twenty-nine-year-old professional singer and high school choral music teacher in San Juan Capistrano, California, she had just accepted a proposal of marriage the night before; she could now look forward to being a bride, and some-day, a mother. Like Joni, she, too, led an ideal life. But later that night she woke, her arms sweeping the air in a futile attempt to feel the mattress beneath her, the sheets surrounding her or the pillow that should have been under her head. She was suspended momentarily in midair, with her head aimed toward the floor. She hit with a thud.[1]

She tried to call out to her roommate, but all that issued from her mouth was a whisper. Within a few minutes her roommate came through the door, unaware of what had awakened her. While they waited for an ambulance, what Renée later described as a "wave of silence" crept over her body, beginning with her neck and then spreading to her chest, torso, and limbs. *Wait a minute,* she thought. *I can't be paralyzed; all I did was go to bed.* But a CAT scan confirmed that she was a quadriplegic.

For weeks both women lay in traction with nothing on their hands but time. Time to count the square tiles on the hospital floor and ceiling as the Stryker Frame that kept their bodies immobile was turned 180 degrees every few hours; time to sleep if only because there was nothing else to do; time to wonder, *Why.* Why would God allow such tragic, sense-less accidents? What purpose could their lives possibly serve now? Both women had been raised in Christian homes—Joni, Protestant, and Renée, Catholic. Yet neither had had to face such deep, probing questions before, questions that no Scripture verse could easily gloss over. Because Joni's accident occurred before medical advancements in the field of spinal cord injury promised much hope of recovery, she wondered if life would ever be worth the suffering she had experienced and hardship she would face. Renée at least still had the love of her fiancé, Mike Bondi, who promised that her new challenges would not deter him from marrying her.

Thus began both women's journey down a long road to discover what God had in store for their lives and whether they would be up to the challenge.

After spending nearly two years in and out of hospitals, rehabilitation, and occupational therapy, Joni went home to the Baltimore suburbs, then to the family horse ranch in the rolling hills of nearby Sykesville. Her boyfriends slowly fading from her life, she wondered if she would ever marry. Who would want a quadriplegic for a bride? She had learned how to write and draw holding implements in her mouth and found sketching nature to be a healing pastime. While answers to her many questions did not come easily, prayer, reading Scripture, and talking with friends about her doubts and fears were opening her mind to possibilities she had not previously considered. Being raised by parents whose lives were devoted to God, she had adopted their Christian heritage until adolescence, when more popular pursuits began to occupy her time. Even after accepting Jesus Christ as her Savior in her sophomore year, her faith lacked the depth and vibrancy she desired. Just weeks before her accident, she had prayed that God would do something in her life that would turn her around. Was her current situation God's response to that prayer, or was it a meaningless coincidence?

In 1972, a group of family and close friends gathered to lay hands on Joni and pray for healing, but nothing changed. Off and on she fought bouts of depression as she struggled to grasp God's purpose for her life. Slowly a thought crept into her consciousness. Is it possible that God wanted to use her disability for a greater purpose than a miraculous intervention might accomplish? While she had always understood that God would never leave or forsake her, she was beginning to realize that promise did not mean a life free from trouble. With each agonizing question and her painstaking search for answers, her faith grew.

"It took a long time," Joni has said recently, "but I now view my accident from the Ephesians 1:11 perspective. It's part of a grand plan that years ago I never would have foreseen. I am convinced God 'hated' the isolated incident of my suffering; but He 'delights' in how my spinal cord injury is fitting into his marvelous mosaic for my good and his glory."

Renée's hospital stay lasted five months. Although her injury was more severe than Joni's,[2] medical advancements had allowed her to regain more movement and coordination in her upper body. But her voice remained weak, and she spoke in a whisper. "I'm sorry Renée," her doctor informed her one day. "Because of the location of your injury, you will never sing again." Lying in her hospital bed, she wondered about her freak accident. Her whole life revolved around singing. Was that talent truly gone forever? And what about her dream to someday be a mother? Without answers all she could do was patiently surrender her daily circumstances to Jesus, something her contemplative upbringing had well prepared her to do.

One evening, four months into her hospital stay, Renée tried to pray as she often did. But she had trouble focusing; her thoughts scattered. She closed her eyes and put all her effort toward concentrating. To her surprise the words to a familiar refrain leapt to the forefront of her mind: *"Be not afraid. I go before you always. Come, follow me, and I will give you rest."*[3] "It was then I knew I was going to be OK," Renée remembers. "But I also knew the definition of *OK* had radically changed."[4]

One day a visiting friend who was a vocal coach noticed how Renée breathed as she whispered. The friend returned with a one-pound ankle weight and placed it across Renée's diaphragm, the muscle used to control voice volume and strength. By the end of her hospital stay, Renée could lift fifty-five pounds of weight using her diaphragm, and her normal speaking voice had returned. Still, the doctor warned, she would never be able to sing in the powerful voice she once had. Because she was now able to talk, she took a job at her church as the choir director, a task she performed from a wheelchair. The next year she and Mike married.

In late 1972 a business associate of Joni's father stopped by for a visit and noticed some of Joni's drawings. Amazed to hear that she was a quadriplegic who drew with pens, pencils, and paintbrushes between her teeth, he organized an art exhibit featuring her work at a Baltimore restaurant. Several branches of the local media attended the event, and Joni became an instant celebrity. Her face beamed as she interacted with the crowd. More exciting than the exposure her artwork received was a conversation she had with a young fireman in attendance who had lost his hands in a fire. Ashamed of his stumps and unable to go back to work, he had become bitter and full of rage. Joni powered her chair to a quiet corner of the restaurant and shared with him for half an hour what she had learned about tragedy and suffering and how God had sustained her over the years. As she spoke, the young man's face brightened. "You've helped me, thanks," he said, and left. Joni later learned that the man became a spokesman for the local fire department.

Over the next two years, Joni's artwork drew the attention of television and radio shows around the country, including an interview on the *Today Show* with Barbara Walters in 1974. Her phone rang with invitations to share her story with church groups and other organizations from coast to coast. At the encouragement of family, friends, and audiences who heard her speak, she wrote her first book (*Joni*[5]) about her experiences and all she had learned. Within weeks of its release, letters flooded her doorstep from people with and without disabilities who related to her story of suffering. Knowing she could not possibly respond personally to the thousands of touching letters she eventually received, Joni began taking mental notes of their contents. While each letter was unique, most fell within similar categories of questions. She knew she must write a sequel (*A Step Further*[6]) to address these questions and bring hope to the thousands of people who had turned to her for help. During this same time she was contacted by World Wide Pictures. They wanted to shoot a film about her life story, featuring Joni playing herself. No sooner had she finished *A Step Further* than she was off to California.[7]

In 1992 a friend came to Renée's home to visit. A professional Broadway musician, he had performed hundreds of songs in his career. He sat down at Renée's piano and began to play a medley of tunes. "Come on, Renée, get over here and sing with me," he said.

Renée began to cry. "I can't."

"Just try," he coaxed. He changed keys and played again. "Be not afraid," he sang. "I go before you always. Come, follow me, and I will give you rest."

Choked up over her friend's choice of songs—out of the hundreds in his repertoire, why would he pick this song, which had given her so much encouragement in the hospital years before?—Renée began singing softly. As they sang each verse and repeated the refrain, her voice grew stronger. She sang until the shock of hearing her own Broadway voice returning overwhelmed her. Jim stopped playing and together they wept. What had just happened was medically impossible. Weeks of practice proved the incident was not a fluke; Renée could sing again! In 1992, she recorded her first CD, *Inner Voice,* and began singing for audiences, sharing her story of faith and hope. Four more CDs followed. Soon she was in demand around the country.

In 1979, back home on the farm in Maryland, Joni had time to review the direction her life was heading. The books, the letters, the movie, the speaking engagements, everything pointed to filling a void in the lives of people who, like her, suffered with a severe disability but still had dreams of living a normal life. A thought began to fill her days, a ministry to help handicapped people's dreams become a reality. A ministry called Joni and Friends. Just a couple of years before, she would not have had a clue how to begin such an organization. Now, with friends in World Wide Pictures, Grace Community Church in Los Angeles where she attended services while filming *Joni,* the Center of Achievement for the Physically Disabled at California State University, Northridge, and others throughout the nation who could promote such a work, it felt within her grasp. But it wouldn't happen in the rural farmland of Maryland. She must go to Los Angeles. Now thirty years old, it was time to strike out on her own and test the faith that had thus far been cradled in the nurturing soil of family and close friends.

In Los Angeles, Joni learned to drive. Through the process she met a young woman, Vicki, who, as a newly divorced young mother, became paralyzed due to a gunshot wound to the neck. Cynical and bitter, she scoffed at Joni's first attempts to share God's love. Determined to stick with Vicki no matter what, offering friendship as her trust was earned, Joni's genuine love finally won Vicki's heart. One day a letter arrived, among the dozens that were being directed to the Joni and Friends office in Los Angeles, from a young mother who had become paralyzed after a drunk driver hit her car. Her husband could not handle the disability and left her. Like Vicki, she was a quadriplegic trying to raise a child on her own. Joni handed the letter to Vicki. "I'm having a tough time answering this letter, would you mind taking a look at it? Maybe even answering it?"

Disabled people helping disabled people. Joni and Friends was beginning to work.

"I have always believed that it is my responsibility to deepen my life and its message," Joni said recently in recollection of the early days of Joni and Friends. "It is God's responsibility to broaden the scope of influence of my life and the impact of my message. Years ago I wrote out my life's mission statement, to be God's best audiovisual aid of how his strength shows up best in my weakness. In the wake of doing that, I knew he may (or may not!) give me the stewardship of influence."

Influence is one thing Joni now has in abundance. Her ministry, Joni and Friends,[8] has grown to become an organization with worldwide impact. With the help of Ken Tada, whom Joni married on July 3, 1982, and a staff of several dozen others, Joni and Friends has distributed thousands of wheelchairs to disabled people in more than fifty countries. Annual family retreats, held at retreat centers across the country, draw hundreds of handicapped people and their families to the outdoors, where they can enjoy fun and fellowship. Numerous ministry offices across the country and in Europe, as well as partnerships with local disability organizations and government entities worldwide, work to raise awareness of the world's six hundred million disabled people.

Besides her work with Joni and Friends, Joni has served on the National Council on Disability and was a proponent of the Americans with Disabilities Act. Her nearly three dozen books are enjoyed the world over by adults and children alike. She continues to host a daily five-minute radio program that began in 1982, and she writes a monthly column for *Moody Monthly* magazine. Along with her personal assistant, she travels around the country advocating for the disabled, and more recently, warning against overstepping the ethical boundaries of biotechnology and stem cell research. "Life value must never be determined by 'quality of life' criteria, which is subjective and constantly shifting. I want to underscore that life value has its roots in the creative authority of God . . . that our lives have worth and meaning no matter what the disability."

Married to a wonderful man, singing again and sharing her story with audiences across the country, Renée felt fulfilled and happy. Yet strong maternal yearnings continued to nag at her like an unquenchable thirst. As far as her doctor knew, no c-4 quadriplegic had ever given birth to a baby; the odds of it happening to Renée were enormous. After many nights of soul-searching prayer, she and Mike decided to try. In 1994 she heard the news: she was expecting! With many possibilities for danger to both her and the baby, it was a high-risk pregnancy from the start. A team of doctors and nurses assigned to Renée and her child monitored her progress each month.

Nine days before the scheduled birth, Renée's family called. Her sister, Michelle, had been critically injured in a dirt bike accident. Besides both lungs being punctured, she was now a paraplegic. On March 20, 1995, while Michelle fought for her life,[9] Renée was induced. A few hours later, she felt goose bumps around her neck, telling her something was happening to her lower body.

"Am I having a contraction?" she asked her attending nurse. The nurse nodded. Five minutes later she felt the tingling again. The nurse checked her and saw the baby's head crowning. While she raced for the doctor, Renée sobbed as thoughts of her own disability and her sister's paralysis filled her mind. "Lord," she cried aloud, "my family can't take one more tragedy. This baby has to be perfect!"

In what seemed like a miracle, Renée's body responded perfectly to the Pitocin and baby Daniel traveled down the birth canal without a hitch. As medical teams attended to both Daniel and Renée, she looked anxiously at Mike and the obstetrician. The doctor leaned down and patted Renée's shoulder. "He's perfect, Renée."[10]

In 2002, Renée's life story appeared in print through her book, *The Last Dance but Not the Last Song*.[11] A year later she began Bondi Ministries[12] to help financially support her speaking and singing (Renée and Mike both donate their time to the ministry). Today she balances her days between being a wife and mother and the work to which she feels called so strongly. As a quadriplegic whose activities and schedule are totally dependent on others, she still struggles at times with a host of unanswered questions. But through faith she keeps going.

"I still can't comprehend how I got in this chair. It surpasses my understanding. But Philippians 4:7 (NIV) says, 'The peace of God, which transcends all understanding, will guard your hearts and your minds in Christ Jesus.' I've bowed my head, many times in tears, and prayed, 'Lord, I give this to you.' I've found that in doing this, God gives me the strength and clarity of mind to face the challenge of the next day."[13]

Questions/Thoughts for Reflection: The challenges of any physical or mental disability can be overwhelming. When the disability is severe, as with Joni Eareckson-Tada and Renée Bondi, the challenges can seem insurmountable, and life can appear hopeless and meaningless. If you are suffering from a disability or handicap, or if you have experienced some other form of mental or emotional anguish, remember that you are not alone. Seek help from your church or community. And remember God's promise to you in Deuteronomy 31:6: "Be strong and courageous. Do not be afraid . . . for the LORD your God goes with you; he will never leave you nor forsake you" (NIV).

Prayer Focus: "Be not afraid. I go before you always. Come, follow me, and I will give you rest."

Corrie ten Boom

(b. 1892 – d. 1983)

"Jesus will blot out your sins like a cloud. A cloud does not return.
He will put your sins away as far as the east is from the west. If you
repent, he casts them into the depths of the sea, forgiven and
forgotten. Then he puts out a sign, 'No Fishing Allowed.'"
—**Corrie ten Boom,** *Her Life and Faith*

Corrie ten Boom was born in Amsterdam, Holland on April 15, 1892. The youngest of four children, her earliest remembrances include stories told around the dinner table of her Grandfather Willem. Though not Jewish himself, Willem founded local weekly prayer meetings for the Jews, focusing on world peace and the regathering of a Jewish nation in Jerusalem. This love and respect for the Jews was passed down through Willem's son, Casper, to Corrie, who saw her devout Christian father form lifelong friendships with the Jews in the community.

Sensing that marriage was not in her future, Corrie went to school in Switzerland in 1920 to learn her father's craft of watchmaking, so that she could work beside him in the shop beneath their home. She became the first licensed female watchmaker in Holland. In 1939, with German troops looming on its doorstep, Holland issued a declaration of neutrality. But in May 1940, bombs began to fall all over Holland, including the airport near Haarlem. Hearing the nearby explosions, Corrie ran into her sister Betsie's room. As the women clung to each other, Corrie saw a vision in which she, Betsie, and their father, along with many others, were crammed into a wagon and pulled out of Haarlem by a team of massive black horses. Terrified, she told Betsie what she had seen. With bombs lighting the night sky, they treaded softly down to the kitchen for coffee. "If God has shown us bad times ahead," Betsie responded, "it's enough for me that He knows about them. That's why He sometimes shows us things you know—to tell us that this too is in His hands."[1]

Within five days German paratroopers and tanks had overwhelmed the ill-equipped Dutch army. For then forty-eight-year-old Corrie, who spent most of her nights with teenage girls as a Girls Guide leader[2] and thus hadn't lost her taste for adventure, the challenges of the occupation were exhilarating at first. By the fall, however, restrictions imposed by the new town administration tightened, and its anti-Semitic agenda became clear. The resistance, initially more symbolic than active, grew along with the repression of Dutch freedom and persecution of the Jews.

"We will continue to support the Jews," Casper insisted, noticing other Dutch businesses and families withdrawing from their Hebrew neighbors.

Corrie and Betsie readily agreed with their father. While he kept the watch shop open and Betsie cared for the growing number of Dutch Jews and other Hollanders who were taking refuge from the gestapo in their home, Corrie began to organize a systematic approach to helping these "underdivers," as they were called, escape. Deception now became a way of life for Corrie, whose prewar reputation for honesty had been uncompromising.

As the activities of "The Beje Gang"[3] became more and more obvious to the Haarlem community, the danger to the ten Booms increased. Casper prayed frequently with his family that God would post a watch of angels around them. One day, however, it seemed that the hedge of protection fell. On the morning of February 28, 1944, a man secretly working for the gestapo came to the door, claiming that his wife had been arrested in nearby Alkmaar, where she had purportedly been helping the

Jews. A policeman there said he would free her for six hundred guilders. Could Corrie help?

Corrie, who was sick with a high fever, promised that she would do what she could. Pulling together a team of people, she instructed them to come up with as much money as they could within an hour, four hundred guilders if possible. The man returned at the appointed time and collected the six hundred guilders Corrie had gathered, including two hundred of her own. Within five minutes, a squad of gestapo agents stormed the Beje. Thirty-five people were arrested, including Corrie, her father, all three siblings, and her nephew Kik.[4]

In the prison at Scheveningen, Corrie was separated from her family. Her heart broke as she watched her aged father shuffle down a long corridor out of sight. For the first ten days of her imprisonment, she shared a tiny cell with five other women. As she grew sicker, she was given a cell of her own. Someone else might have been delighted over the sudden space and privacy. Not Corrie, who had never been alone a day in her life. Soon the loneliness became intolerable. To keep from going crazy, she befriended the ants who came daily to her cell to collect bread crumbs from off the floor. Later, using a stay from her corset, she began digging a little hole between the bricks separating her cell from the one next door. Within weeks she was able to carry on whispered conversations with her neighbors, sharing with them passages of Scripture from the Bible she had smuggled out of the Beje.

Two months into her confinement, Corrie learned through a letter from her sister Nollie, who had been freed along with her brother Willem, that their father had died ten days after his arrest. But Corrie did not have long to grieve. Within a couple of weeks, she was ordered into a van to a train station, where she was reunited with her sister Betsie. Together they traveled to their new destination: Vught, a concentration camp in Noord-Brabant.

Once in the barracks of Vught, life was a study of contrasts. Some days were bearable, when a parcel was allowed to reach a prisoner, its contents shared by all. Other days a simple infraction of the camp rules would bring the guards flying into the bunker to indiscriminately pull prisoners from their cells to be shot. During these dark days Corrie prayed constantly. "Give me your Holy Spirit, Lord, that I may bring this great sorrow to you and leave it with you. Protect me from the hatred I feel stirring in my heart."

Late in the summer Vught was emptied as Allied troops drew closer to Holland. Corrie and Betsie were again driven like cattle into a boxcar, this time headed for the heart of Germany. After three days of travel, they arrived at their new home: Ravensbrück. Seeing rows and rows of emaciated women reaching through the bars of their cells with skeletal-like hands, Corrie thought, *It doesn't look like anyone could remain alive here.*

The sisters' induction into the camp included walking naked past hooting guards into the showers. Waiting for her number to be called, Corrie prayed, "Lord, save us. Betsie is so frail, I'm not sure she can do this." Turning to her sister, she asked, "Betsie, are you ready?"

"I don't think I can," Betsie whispered.

Not knowing how to avoid the inevitable, fearful that gas might issue from the shower spigot instead of water, Corrie closed her eyes in prayer once more. "O Lord, if you ask this sacrifice of us, give us the willingness to do it."

"Do you have any objections to surrendering your clothes?" a guard barked at the pair. "We'll teach you Hollanders what Ravensbrück is like!"

Ignoring the man, the sisters kept their heads bowed. Suddenly they heard their numbers called over the loudspeaker. Opening her eyes, Betsie's weak voice broke the silence. "Corrie, I'm ready now."

Thus began their stay in the infamous German concentration camp. While Corrie struggled through the passing weeks to keep the surrounding despair from swallowing her up, Betsie grew more serene and sickly. Once she was so weak that Corrie and another prisoner had to carry her outside for roll call, propping her up against their own bodies.[5] In her more lucid moments, Betsie talked about life after Ravensbrück. "When we return to Holland, we will open up a home for people who need healing after the war. It will be a big, beautiful house, with inlaid wood floors and bas-relief statues along the walls, with lovely grounds and a garden for growing flowers. We'll be released by the New Year, Corrie. Just you wait and see."

The sicker Betsie got, the clearer her vision of life after Ravensbrück became. "After the home is established, we'll return to Germany and turn one of these camps into a refugee center for the homeless. There will be millions of refugees in Germany, Corrie. They too will need a place to heal. Then we'll travel all around the world. People need to hear that no pit is so deep that Jesus' love is not deeper still. His light is stronger than the darkest of places. They will believe us because we were here. We'll go together, you and me."

But as the end of the year approached, Betsie's dreams seemed to fade with her health. Just days before Christmas, she died. Four days later Corrie's name was called. She had been Prisoner 66730 for so long, she almost didn't respond when the words, "ten Boom, Cornelia!" boomed over the loudspeaker. Would she be gassed or released? By this time it no longer mattered. She'd seen hell on earth; heaven would be a welcome sight. To her surprise she was given discharge papers, made to sign a statement testifying that she had not been mistreated, and handed a lovely new outfit to wear, complete with hat and shoes. Little did she know at the time that her release had been the result of a clerical error.[6]

After a few days in the camp hospital to bring down the grotesque swelling in her legs due to malnutrition, she dressed and approached the heavy iron gates. She limped slowly, weak and emaciated, into the surrounding forest, leaving behind memories of her father and sister while many questions filled her mind: What about her nephew Kik, and all the others who had been arrested in the Beje that day?[7] En route to the train station, Betsie's words rang more loudly than ever in Corrie's mind. She had been right: it was New Year's Day 1945, and they were both free. But what about the rest of the vision? Were her sister's ideas the delusions of a sick woman or divine inspiration?

The long train ride back to her homeland left Corrie in even worse condition; the boxcar was frigid and damp, and she had lost the food coupons she had been given. After three days she arrived in Groningen, in Holland's free south, where she made her way to a Christian hospital. Entering its doors, doctors and nurses alike stared at her. They had seen few return from the camps of Germany, and Corrie was a sight, with fine clothing hanging on her foul-smelling, wasted body like a child playing dress-up. Finally, a nurse with a warm friendly smile approached her and began tending to her needs. Hearing that Corrie was from the village of Haarlem, she asked, "Have you heard of Corrie ten Boom? I wonder what's become of her."

Corrie looked at the young nurse, her eyes widening in recognition. She was one of the hundreds of girls she had mentored as a Girls Guide leader not too many years before. "I *am* Corrie ten Boom," she replied. The nurse clung to her and wept.

Home at the Beje, Corrie never forgot Betsie's words. How could any of it come to pass? She had no money with which to purchase a house such as her sister had envisioned or to travel outside the country. But there was one thing she could do. She could share her story and Betsie's vision with fellow Hollanders. At one meeting set up for that purpose, she met Mrs. Bierens de Hann, a widow with five sons in the resistance. One had been captured and sent to Germany; she had not heard from him since. "If my son Jan returns home safely, I will dedicate my estate, Schapenduinen in Bloemendaal, to your cause."

Two weeks later a scented letter arrived from Mrs. de Haan, with a single line written in purple ink, "Jan is home," and an invitation to visit Schapenduinen. Meeting Mrs. de Haan at the front door of the huge estate, Corrie's imagination was reeling. Could this mansion be the house Betsie had dreamed of? Unable to move her feet, she stammered, "Are there—does this house have inlaid floors, and bas-relief statues lining the walls?"

"Why, yes, how did you know?" Mrs. de Haan replied. The estate, with its fifty-six rooms and vast lawns and gardens, was the perfect place for Dutch refugees needing clean air to breath and a garden to tend as they recuperated from the war.

Months passed; the war ended. As Corrie continued to speak, God provided funds not only to maintain Schapenduinen but also to meet the expenses of an expanding speaking schedule that took her to other parts of Europe and the United States. With each address she told about the constant presence of Jesus in the German concentration camp, along with Betsie's vision. In 1946 she felt the tug of God to return to Germany, this time to encourage the nine million refugees there. Her feelings were mixed as she obediently followed the Lord's command. More often than not she pitied the German people, most of whom were ashamed of the atrocities that had occurred in their country. Visiting a factory overflowing with German refugees, the director of a relief organization approached her. He had heard about her rehabilitation work in Holland and wondered if she would take on a similar project in Germany.

"I don't think I am the one you want," Corrie began. "I have no formal training."

"We have located the perfect place," the man continued. "A former concentration camp that has just been released from the government, at Darmstadt."

Hearing the location, Corrie knew this was the next fulfillment of Betsie's vision. With so many refugees living in inhumane conditions throughout Germany, the camp would make a perfect sanctuary for about one hundred and sixty people. A few days later she walked up a cinder path between two barracks where prisoners had once been held. The scene looked surreal, as thought she were walking in a dream. But was it a bad dream or a good one? How she responded would make the difference.

"Window boxes," she declared. "We'll add them to every window. And bright green and yellow paint . . . the color of things washed anew in a spring rain."

Soon after the renovations were completed, families began pouring into the camp.[8] In the midst of the work, Corrie continued to speak in cities large and small throughout the country. During one meeting she saw a man standing on the outskirts of the audience who caused her to feel uneasy, though she didn't know why. At the end of the meeting, he approached her.

"Can I help you?" Corrie asked. But the man remained silent and would not look up.

"I can't help you if you don't talk to me," she coaxed.

Finally he began to speak. Immediately Corrie recognized him and bristled. He was the guard in the shower room at Ravensbrück who had jeered at her and Betsie for not wanting to remove their clothes.

"I was one of the guards at Ravensbrück during the time you were there. I accepted Jesus Christ as my Savior this past Christmas and asked him to forgive my sins. I also asked him to give me the opportunity to ask one of my victims for forgiveness. When I heard you were coming to town, I knew I must speak to you. Will you forgive me?"

The man stretched out his hand. Corrie looked at it, a lump of hatred filling her chest until she felt she might suffocate. Just as her mind told her that she could not possibly forgive him for the part he played in her own suffering and the deaths of her family members, a quiet voice filled her heart, saying, "I forgive you everything." Knowing the depths of God's forgiveness for her own sins, including the hatred she felt at that moment, she knew she could not withhold forgiveness from this man standing before her. Still, every inch her hand moved to meet his was excruciatingly difficult. Finally, she grasped the hand of the ex-guard. At that moment God's love surged through her arm like a bolt of electricity. Looking the man in the eyes with genuine love, she stated, "Yes, I forgive you."

The man covered his face with his hands and began sobbing. "But I can't forget—"

"Jesus will blot out your sins like a cloud," Corrie said, her voice soft and soothing. "A cloud does not return. He will put your sins away as far as the east is from the west. If you repent, he casts them into the depths of the sea, forgiven and forgotten. Then he puts out a sign, 'No Fishing Allowed.'"[9]

Corrie traveled to more than sixty countries during the next three decades. In that time she encountered several people who shared some responsibility in her family's hardship and suffering during the war years in Haarlem or in the prison camps. With each she shared the same love and forgiveness God had given her for the ex-guard from Ravensbrück. Forgiveness is also the theme of several of the more than two dozen books she wrote prior to 1978, when a stroke left her paralyzed. She died on her ninety-first birthday, April 15, 1983, in Anaheim, California.

Questions/Thoughts for Reflection: Stories such as Corrie ten Boom's leave us marveling at the amount of fortitude required to relinquish hatred for wrongs committed and truly forgive the wrongdoer. Who has such strength? No one does. Whether the injustice is a mere slanderous remark or a brutal murder, forgiveness does not come naturally to anyone; it comes from God alone. As he forgives us, so we are to forgive others.

It does not take much effort before the insults of our lives come flooding anew to the forefront of our minds. Take a few minutes now to pray about your own memories of injustice, asking God to help you release them and truly forgive.

Prayer Focus: Dear God, like an open wound that never heals, the pain of these memories has festered from unforgiveness. But I do not know how to forgive. Please show me the way.

Phillis Wheatley

(b. Cira 1753 – d. 1784)

> *"'Twas mercy brought me from my pagan land,*
> *Taught my benighted soul to understand*
> *That there's a God, that there's a Savior too:*
> *Once I redemption neither sought nor knew.*
> *Some view our sable race with scornful eye*
> *'Their colour is a diabolic die.'*
> *Remember, Christians, Negros, black as Cain,*
> *May be refin'd, and join th' angelic train."*
> —Phillis Wheatley, *On Being Brought from Africa to America*

Susanna Wheatley's eyes burned as she tried to hold back hot tears. She could hardly watch the auctioneer as he yanked the filth-encrusted little girl into position along with the other slaves, still blinking from the light after being shackled in the bowels of the ship. It was a foggy June morning in Boston, 1761. Covered only with a raveling piece of carpet, the child shivered relentlessly.

"Step right up, make your purchase! Ev'ry one a' them, healthy and strong, fresh off the boat from Africa!" the auctioneer called to passersby.

"Buy her, John," Susanna said in a voice just loud enough to be heard in her husband's ear.

"Be reasonable, dear," John Wheatley said, glancing at the slave. A successful businessman, he looked at the little waif with a more practical eye. "We're looking for a girl who will be of some use to you. This pitiful thing looks like she would blow over in the next breeze."

But Susanna's heart had completely taken over her senses. "Please John!" she cried. "I cannot bear to think what will become of her otherwise."

"How old is this one?" John asked the auctioneer.

"I dunno, seven, eight maybe. Good stock, she is."

John looked once more into his wife's pleading eyes. Against his better judgment, he bid for the child. She now belonged to them; he hoped she would turn out to be a worthwhile purchase.

The rest of the day was spent in bathing the new slave, finding clothes for her to wear and trying to acquaint her with the household. They intended to house her in outdoor quarters along with the other help. But the girl, whom they decided to name Phillis,[1] seemed too sickly and frail for the time being. When the Wheatley's daughter, Mary, just a couple of years older than Phillis, offered the second bed in her bedroom, they agreed.

As the days passed, Mary was happy for Phillis's presence. It was like having a little sister to keep her company around the big house. Like a mother hen, she took the child under her wing and began showing her not only the household chores, but the library as well, with its cherished copies of the Bible and the Latin classics, along with books on astronomy and the English poets. When Phillis began to show signs of an insatiable curiosity and a quick mind, housework quickly gave way to Mary's efforts to provide Phillis with an honest education. Although the other servants warned that most slaves were not capable of higher learning, Phillis proved to the contrary; every day she was learning to read and draw her letters at an astonishing rate, as well as exhibiting a keen aptitude for art and science. She was assigned a few light chores around the house but nothing like the Wheatleys had originally envisioned for their new help. As the months passed, John complained that thus far Phillis was more trouble than she was help. But Susanna was happy; he would have to be satisfied with that.

By the fall of 1762, Phillis was accomplished in both English and Latin, reading the Holy Scriptures and the classics with great proficiency. She found the poets Milton, Pope, and Gray especially meaningful. Even after her health improved, Susanna refused to turn Phillis out to the drafty servants' quarters, choosing instead to refurbish a small room inside the house, a room belonging to Phillis alone. When Susanna insisted that Phillis sit with the family during services at King's Chapel rather than up in the gallery with the other slaves, both became the center of gossip.

On October 19, 1765, the British Parliament passed the Stamp Act, levying heavy duties on the American colonies. Boston was in an uproar of protest. As the city's agitation rose, so did Phillis's desire to do what she could to help. She had already begun to write poetry, but John thought it an outlandish pastime for a slave and had forbidden her to pursue it. But was not time spent in her bedroom her own? She pulled out a quill and began writing, using what she'd read in the newspaper as resource material for her poetic voice. Concluding the poem, an idea sprang to mind. What would his Majesty the King think of her poem? She copied it to a fresh sheet of paper, folded and sealed it. On the outside she wrote: "To the King's Most Excellent Majesty, George III, London, England." The following morning, the letter was posted.

In 1767, the Stamp Act was repealed, but that was not the end of Phillis's involvement in the matter. A short time later a local city official came to the Wheatley home to inquire if Phillis had written a letter to the king. The problem was the king did not believe that a slave could have written the letter; and if Phillis had, how could she be so educated? A commission of seventeen men—including the esteemed attorney John Hancock and Governor Thomas Hutchinson—plus John Wheatley, was assigned to look into the matter. Establishing to the commission that Phillis had written the poem was simple, as the writing matched that of her own hand in several other poems she kept in her room. For the next hour the commission questioned her on the English and Latin poets and classics, proving that her knowledge was not superficially learned for their benefit but was the result of true intellectual prowess. When a declaration was signed and sealed for delivery back to the king, even John Wheatley was proud of Phillis.

Phillis's letter to King George, published in the local paper, was just the beginning of a prolific writing career. Soon numerous small publishing successes around Boston brought her minor acclaim. In 1770, a broadside of her poems was circulated throughout the colonies, including a poem that was later reprinted in major newspapers, called, "On the Death of the Rev. Mr. George Whitefield." With rumors of revolution and acts of rebellion becoming more commonplace with each passing day, Phillis's inspiring poem about the beloved circuit preacher lifted the hearts and spirits of New Englanders, if only for a brief moment.

Although Phillis enjoyed seeing her poems in print, she never gave a thought to publishing a book of her work. However, a fan in England, the Countess of Huntingdon, having become familiar with Phillis's poetry through mutual friend Rev. Samson Occum, decided to gather several of her poems into a bound collection. Susanna Wheatley was aware of the effort but did not say a word to the poet. In 1773, she sent Phillis to England under the guise that the climate would improve her perpetual poor health. In London Phillis was met by the Countess, who explained the real reason for her visit. The collection of thirty-nine poems, called *Poems on Various Subjects, Religious and Moral,* was published the same year.

Phillis remained in England until just months before Susanna's death in March 1774, when she returned to Boston to be near the woman who had been unfailingly kind to her. She stayed with the family until after John's death three years later. Meanwhile, her poems circulated around New England, inspiring everyone with their melodic prose—some exhibiting her deep Christian faith, many being elegies and honorific verses celebrating the lives of friends and famous contemporaries, while others commemorated important events. Having written a poem about General George Washington, she was invited to visit him personally in 1776.

In 1778, Phillis married a free man, John Peters, who was educated as a lawyer. But with the tough post-Revolutionary economic times, work was scarce. He found employment at a grocery with the intention of buying the store, even gambling in hopes of collecting the necessary money. Following the birth of the Peters' three children, two daughters and one son, John was imprisoned for his gambling debts. Compensation for Phillis's published poems long since gone, what little money she had soon disappeared. She and her children were subjected to severe poverty. In 1783, the two eldest children died of dysentery. Phillis tried to work as a scullery maid at a Boston boarding house, but being sickly herself and unused to physical labor, she eventually lost her job. She and her youngest daughter passed away on the same day in December 1784. However, her legacy of writing lived on, experiencing a resurgence of popularity during the Civil War. She is still honored today for her remarkable literary achievements in the face of overwhelming odds.

Questions/Thoughts for Reflection: Phillis Wheatley's poems are a celebration of life. They expressed her deep faith, shared in the grief of some, and delighted in the joys and accomplishments of her friends, acquaintances, even celebrities she never met. She wrote about historical events with a unique perspective. While a few references to slavery are scattered throughout her work, she was never bitter, always looking for God's hand in the twists and turns of life. What a beautiful attitude! As you face your own difficulties, remember Phillis's courage and ability to savor life in all its complexities.

Prayer Focus: God, today, help me to make the best of what I am given. Help me to look for your hand in the ordinary and extraordinary events of my day.

The Woman at the Well

(b. "unavailable" – d. "unavailable")

"Come see a man who knew all about the things I did, who knows me inside and out. Do you think this could be the Messiah?"
—The woman at the well (John 4:1–30)

Jesus' public ministry had barely begun when the Pharisees first took notice of him. Who was this man who had allegedly turned water into wine at a wedding feast and brazenly disrupted the recent Passover celebration in Jerusalem by pitching the money changers' tables upside down? Now here he was, making his way around the waters of the Jordan River in the Judean countryside, drawing a bigger crowd than the menace, John the Baptist. What were this man's intentions?

But Jesus wanted to avoid questions for now. Time to move on to Galilee, where he would spend much of the next couple years. He decided to take the most direct route, through Samaria, rather than crossing over to the eastern side of the Jordan and traveling north along the King's Highway. His disciples balked. Jews had no dealings with the Samaritan "half-breeds,"[1] they argued. But Jesus was insistent; he had to go through Samaria. As usual, the disciples gave in to their teacher's wishes. Who knows? Maybe he had arranged to meet someone in that detestable land.

Approaching the city of Sychar, the disciples went into the city to buy food while Jesus rested against the ancient brick surface of Jacob's well. Parched from his journey, he stayed near the well instead of seeking shelter from the noonday heat. Shortly, a woman approached, her worn expression and tired posture suggesting the kind of woman who had come to apologize simply for living. Her head was shielded from the scorching sun by the hood of her *kesut*. In her hand she carried a water pot attached to a long rope.

"Qedemtaakh brikhtaa"

"Blessed be your morning as well," the woman responded. "But as you can see, the sun is high overhead. It is noon."

"You are right, and it is hot. May I ask you to fetch me a drink?"

The woman dropped her hood and scrutinized Jesus. "How is it that you, a Jew, ask a Samaritan for a drink, and a woman no less? Don't you know that Jews have nothing to do with Samaritans?"

"If you knew who it is speaking to you, and the gift of God that I offer, you would be asking me for a drink, and I would give you living water."

The woman laughed. "What is this water you speak of? There is no water around here except in this well, which is deep." Her eyes narrowed as she looked Jesus over. "And you have nothing to draw with. Are you greater than our father Jacob, who dug this well for his family and livestock?"

Jesus smiled at her defiance. *This is how she has survived; she knows nothing else.* He grew serious. "Whoever draws water from this well will thirst again. But whoever drinks the water I offer will never thirst again, for it shall become a fountain springing up to everlasting life."

"Give me this water, so that I will never have to come again in the heat to draw!"

"Go, call your husband and return."

The woman scowled. "What is this, a trick? I have no husband."

Jesus nodded. "You are an honest woman. In fact, you have had five husbands, and the man you are living with now is not your husband." Jesus went on to tell her the story of her life. As he related each detail, the water pot slid from her fingers and landed with a thud on the ground.

"Sir, you—you must be a prophet. How else could you know these things about me?"

Jesus smiled again but said nothing, allowing the truth of the woman's own words to sink into her soul. He could see she was beginning to feel uncomfortable with the direction the conversation was taking.

"You know, *our* fathers worshipped on this mountain, while you Jews say that Jerusalem is the correct place to worship."[2]

"Woman," Jesus replied softly, "there will come a day when you will worship neither on this mountain nor in Jerusalem. You see, you Samaritans do not understand who you worship, but the Jews know, for salvation comes through them. From now on, true worshippers will worship God the Father in spirit and truth. God is spirit, and those who wish to worship him must do so in spirit and truth. If you are worshipping with truth of mind and heart and sincerity of spirit, this is what the heavenly Father is seeking."

The woman shrugged. "Think what you want. When the Messiah comes, he will teach us all things."

Jesus lifted his arms to the woman, his palms up and open in a gesture of invitation. "I am the Messiah."

For an instant the woman looked stunned. Her arms and legs felt like clay, and she could barely move. At that moment the disciples appeared, their faces revealing what was on their minds: why was Jesus talking with this Samaritan woman? But they held their tongues. All at once the woman took flight into the town without even looking back to see whether Jesus was still there. *He has to stay there. . . . They must meet him!*

Entering the gates of Sychar, she began calling out to the men and women milling around in the square and the surrounding shops, to anyone who would listen: "Come see a man who knew all about the things I did, who knows me inside and out. Do you think this could be the Messiah?"

Immediately, a throng of people stopped what they were doing and followed the woman outside the city to meet Jesus.

Questions/Thoughts for Reflection: The woman at the well is an unlikely hero. She was a woman with a seedy reputation, disdained by the other villagers. So great was their scorn that she could not even draw water in the cool morning air with the rest of the women but was forced instead to go to the well in the sweltering noonday heat. After years of experiencing such contempt, she was hardened and bitter.

But think for a moment. Who among us, if we had to endure the same ridicule at the hands of our friends and neighbors as the woman at the well did, would be willing to go to those same people with the message of living water and eternal life? How tempting it would be to keep such knowledge to ourselves! After all, they hardly deserve to meet Jesus. Then again, neither did she; nor do we. Are you willing to share what little you know about Jesus with others, even those whom you deem undeserving?

Prayer Focus: Jesus, how little I deserved to hear the message of salvation, yet you chose to bring me that message so that I might be called your intimate friend, even the bride of Christ. Help me to share what I know about you with others, even to my enemies.

Sabina Wurmbrand

(b. 1913 – d. 2000)

"People were so frightened, yet they were 'free.' In prison, even at the worst times, we'd seen God's hand at work. We came to know that although we suffered, he would not leave us. We could trust him. So a vital part of work in our Underground Church was to teach people this. And, with a prison background, it was easier to win their trust."

—Sabina Wurmbrand, *The Pastor's Wife*

They're coming, the Russians are coming!" a boy announced as he ran ahead of gray tanks flying red flags into the main square of Bucharest. Few people were out that day, August 23, 1944, which marked the end to Nazi terror in Romania. Among the scattered crowd were thirty-one-year-old Sabina Wurmbrand, her pastor-husband Richard, and their five-year-old son, Mihai. As the tanks screeched by, Sabina passed Bibles into the hands of the young men sprouting from the turrets.

As Jewish converts to Christianity, the Wurmbrands had lived in constant fear under the Nazis. Both of Sabina's parents and three siblings had died in their hometown, of starvation or in concentration camps.

She and Richard had narrowly escaped the fate of millions of Jews on several occasions. Now, watching the heavy tanks rumble through the square, they felt cautiously optimistic. Surely these liberators would be more tolerant of ethnic and religious diversity than their Nazi predecessors.

Within a year the troops they had welcomed into the country took power. While Romanians continued to hold important government posts, they were handpicked by the Communists. Stalin was named honorary head of Congress. In the fall the new government called for a "Congress of Cults," a gathering of delegates from every religion and confession in the country. The Wurmbrands knew that in Russia the official church was controlled by the state. Was this the beginning of state-run religion in Romania?

The convention opened with a speech by the new premier, Petru Groza, who avowed in his most convincing manner that the new Romanian government was in favor of faith. Sabina knew immediately that the event was a farce. Communism was dedicated to the destruction of faith, its speeches only a show to lull the Western world into a state of blindness and apathy. Still, the hall exploded with thunderous applause from men representing dozens of faiths and denominations in a mock show of support. One by one they stood up to microphones posted around the room and gave the government authorities what they wanted to hear.

Sabina turned to her husband. "Will you not wash this shame from the face of Christ?"

"If I speak, you will lose a husband."

"I don't need a coward for a husband," Sabina replied.[1]

Richard stood up to the microphone, saying it was the duty of everyone present not to praise earthly powers that come and go but to glorify God the Creator and Christ the Savior, who died on the cross for all. The sound was cut off before he could finish; the session ended abruptly. Over the next four years, the Wurmbrands distributed Bibles camouflaged as Communist propaganda to the occupying Russian troops. As official church gatherings became more dangerous, congregations began to meet in houses under the guise of birthday and anniversary parties. Richard led worship in many homes but kept his own parish church open on Sundays as well. He knew secret informers filled his pews, and he was taken in for questioning more than once. But he was released each time. Then, one icy Sunday morning in February 1948, he walked out the door of his home in the direction of the church and vanished.

In those days pastors disappeared by the hundreds. With no formal training their wives continued the work of the church. Few of these women were as well versed in Scripture as Sabina, so they looked to her for leadership. Juggling pastoral work in an increasingly underground church and visits with officials to locate her husband, Sabina had to find creative ways to support herself and her son.[2] Friends generously gave of their resources. A woman living in the countryside took Mihai for extended periods so that Sabina could keep up her schedule. During one such visit, in August 1950, she came home late after an exhausting day working as a charwoman. She fell into bed and slept soundly until loud blows on the door in the early morning awakened her.

"Sabina Wurmbrand? We know you're hiding arms here.[3] Show us where they are!"

Sabina climbed out of bed and stood before her accusers. "The only weapon we have in this house is here." She picked up a Bible from the floor, where it had been thrown by one of the officers. As two policemen dragged her to the door, she managed to grab a robe and wool socks.

For weeks, Sabina was interrogated in Ghencea, a transit prison camp, about her background, acquaintances and activities. She and Richard had discussed on several occasions how to handle such cross-examinations. Communism is unreasonable madness and subject to God's higher laws, they concluded. They had a spiritual and moral responsibility to protect the innocent and mislead those whose sole aim is to destroy. However, nothing could have prepared her for the verbal harassment and physical abuse she experienced. Only one comforting result came of her "interviews": she learned that her husband was still alive, sentenced to twenty years in prison as a counterrevolutionary.

Although she was never formally charged with a crime and had not been given a trial, Sabina was moved through the prison system, finally landing in a work project the Communist government considered their crown jewel, the Danube River Canal. For hours on end every day of the week, she gathered rocks from a quarry. At night, packed with eighty other women into a hut intended to house twenty, she passed the evening hours with her neighbors by telling stories, talking politics, and sharing their different faith traditions. After months of work, subsisting only on watery soup and small portions of black bread, Sabina looked like a waif, her hands and feet crushed from the rocks, and her skin covered with abrasions and ulcers.

Months later the women were moved from the quarry to nearby fields where they dug up dirt and transported it in wheelbarrows to waiting trucks. Working under the hot sun, they took every opportunity to graze on the surrounding grass, collecting frogs and snakes in their pockets to be eaten at night. One morning, they were awakened to the shouts of guards. The entire camp was being evacuated and the prisoners moved. Sabina was reassigned to a sewing shop at one camp, then to a pig farm at another facility, where she succumbed to exhaustion. She was moved to a prison hospital where, for the first time, she was spoken to kindly and given nourishing food to eat. *Why the good treatment after two years of hard labor?* she wondered. The answer came in the form of rumors. Changes were afoot; the Canal project was being scrapped due to a serious design flaw, its engineers and overseers arrested.

In the spring of 1953, Sabina was moved back to Ghencea where she had initially been interrogated. This time, when her name was called, the prison officials and guards smiled and addressed her politely. What did she think of her reeducation in prison? Had she discovered that socialism was a productive way of life? That nothing could turn back the tide of Communism? That God was dead? Sabina knew she should simply agree with the line of questioning, but she could not. "I see that you are powerful. Probably you have papers and documents there about me that I've never seen, which can decide my fate. But God keeps records, too, and neither you nor I would have life without him. So whether he keeps me here or sets me free, I'll accept that as best for me."[4]

The major conducting the interview pounded his fists on the desk in front of him, shaking the gold braids on his epaulettes. "Ungrateful, Mrs. Wurmbrand! I see you have not learned your lesson. I shall make a report to that effect!"[5]

Three days later Sabina's name was called again. Rather than going to her death as she expected, she was handed a Certificate of Liberation. Someone more powerful than the major had determined her fate. She made her way home to Mihai on the kindness of strangers. A week later loudspeakers throughout the city announced the death of Stalin. In the weeks to come, rumors of a general amnesty flew throughout Romania, with more prisoners than usual being released. But the tide turned as Nikita Khrushchev began working his way into the Kremlin, and more arrests were made. Sabina returned to her work in the underground church, where she and a handful of trusted workers decided on a pro-active approach to the problem of informers and arrests. To catch a thief, one must be a thief and a half, they decided. If they sent their own informers into the Communists' midst, they might learn who the enemy informers were, as well as plans for arrests, which could then be averted. Workers were planted in strategic places; soon the plan began to work.

The year 1956 began with the release of thousands of political prisoners. One evening in June, Richard came home, his frame looking like a skeleton and his body bearing the scars of unthinkable torture. Notwithstanding, he immediately began making plans to share his story of how God had met him in the mass cells and solitary confinement of prison. Sabina wanted him to relax, take time to recuperate. Why must he immediately raise the sword against the dragon of Communism? But repose was not Richard's way. Within weeks he was preaching in the official churches as well as the underground gatherings and teaching against Communism at the universities. Sabina knew it would not be long before he was rearrested. In January 1959 the secret police burst into the Wurmbrands' tiny attic apartment and whisked Richard away for the second time.

The ensuing years were especially difficult for Sabina. Richard's new sentence of twenty-five years carried with it a heavy fine. Every few weeks collectors came to her door demanding cash or property. Other officials came too. If she divorced Richard, they said, she could legally return to work and collect food rations. Sabina refused, choosing instead to sell thread spun from silk worms molting in her kitchen and hand-knitted jerseys for food money.

At long last a June 1964 paper displayed a bold headline: AMNESTY. Days later a neighbor's phone rang. After nearly six more years of imprisonment, Richard was in Cluj; he would be home the next day! By this time rumors of the pastor who had survived a total of fourteen years in prison had made Richard a celebrity. Daily dozens of people came to hear him teach and receive a prayer or blessing. News of the couple's courage had even reached other parts of Europe. With so many people coming and going, there could be no pretense of hiding from the secret police. A cloistered gathering of church leaders decided that the Wurmbrand family must be removed from the country. It was Richard's only hope for survival, plus with him on the outside, he could tell the world what was really happening in the People's Republic of Romania. A ransom of ten thousand dollars, collected from friends and family around the globe, was paid to the Communist government in exchange for exit visas.

On December 6, 1965, Richard, Sabina, and Mihai boarded a DC7 for Norway, then England, where Richard wrote his first declaration of Christian persecution. Audiences in England and the United States invited the couple to come and share their story, including a United States Senate International Security Subcommittee, before which Richard stripped to the waist and revealed eighteen deep scars on his neck and torso, evidence of his testimony. After a move to the United States, the Wurmbrands began The Voice of the Martyrs,[6] a ministry committed to serving the worldwide persecuted church. Since its inception in 1967, the organization has given millions of dollars in relief, medical aid and teaching materials to persecuted Christians and their families in over forty countries. Both Sabina and her husband remained actively involved in The Voice of the Martyrs until their deaths.[7]

Questions/Thoughts for Reflection: Most of us live lives of relative comfort and ease; it is hard to imagine an existence as difficult as Sabina Wurmbrand's. If we suddenly began to experience life as she lived it, we might wonder if God had abandoned us. But Sabina's story demonstrates the opposite. In times of hardship God holds us the closest, albeit in unexpected ways. In both good times and bad, we can trust him to guide us and help us not to succumb to evil, thereby preserving us for eternal life.

Prayer Focus: Heavenly Father, help me to trust you though I cannot see you. Help me remain faithful to you even when the path is difficult to follow.

Notes

Introduction

1. Rolland Hein, *Christian Mythmakers* (Chicago: Cornerstone Press, 1998), 3.

2. Robert Coles, *The Call of Service: A Witness to Idealism* (Boston: Mariner Books, 1994), xxiii.

3. Max Lucado, *When God Whispers Your Name* (Nashville: W. Publishing Group, 1994, 1999), 27.

Kay Arthur

1. Kay Arthur, *Lord, I Want to Know You* (Sisters, Oreg.: Multnomah, 1992), 43.

2. Ibid., 85.

3. Ibid.

4. Ibid., 86.

5. The inductive Bible study method is described fully in Kay's book, *How to Study Your Bible* (Eugene, Oreg.: Harvest House, 1994).

6. Kay Arthur, *How to Study Your Bible* , 5.

7. Precept Ministries can be reached through its Web site: www.precept.org, or by contacting Precept Ministries, P.O. Box 182218, Chattanooga, TN 37422, (800) 763-8280.

Mary Kay Ash

1. Quote taken from www.marykay.com.

2. *Mary Kay* (New York: Harper and Row, 1981), rereleased as *Miracles Happen* (New York: Quill, 2003); *Mary Kay on People Management* (New York: Warner Books, 1984); *You Can Have It All* (New York: Prima Lifestyles, 1995).

Jill Briscoe

1. Torchbearers began as a ministry to disillusioned German youth after WWII. By this time its work had spread to England as well.

2. Taken from an interview with *Leadership Journal* on www.ChristianityToday.com, Spring 2001.

3. Jill wrote three of these books with her daughter, Dr. Judy Briscoe Golz.

Amy Carmichael

1. Sam Wellman, *Amy Carmichael—A Life Abandoned to God* (Uhrichsville, Ohio: Barbour Publishing, 1998), 32.

Edith Cavell

1. Taken from Brand Whitlock, *Belgium Under the German Occupation, A Personal Narrative* (1919), as posted on www.phobos.spaceports.com.

2. There may be some truth to this story, as a young German soldier's body was found buried beside Edith's grave.

Jerrie Cobb

1. Within one year, Jerrie earned her Multi-Engine, Instrument, Flight Instructor, and Ground Instructor ratings, as well as her Airline Transport license.

2. Latifa Lyles, "Now Launches Campaign to Send Pilot Jerrie Cobb Into Space," www.now.org, Winter 1999.

3. Amazonia, as the Amazon Basin is called, covers over two million square miles, an area larger than the United States, and encompasses parts of Brazil, Colombia, Bolivia, Peru, Venezuela, and Ecuador.

4. The Jerrie Cobb Foundation can be reached by contacting the Director, Jerrie Cobb Foundation, Inc. 1008 Beach Blvd., Sun City, FL 33573, www.jerrie-cobb-foundation.org.

5. Revolutionary Armed Forces of Colombia.

6. This brief note was typed on a postcard and mailed to the crisis committee, along with the handwritten postscript, John 5:13, under Jerrie's signature.

Deborah, Judge of Israel

1. After the death of Joshua, who led the Hebrew people across the Jordan River into the promised land, God called a series of individuals known as "judges" over a period of about 325 years to lead the children of Israel in their new homeland. These judges were well-known for their relationship with God, practical wisdom, leadership skills, and occasional military brilliance. Deborah was the fourth of twelve judges and the only woman. Her term as judge began in 1209 BC and lasted forty years. Her story is told in Judges 4–5.

2. When the Israelites entered the promised land in 1406 BC, the Canaanites were one of the first people Joshua and his army conquered. Now Jabin was bent on taking back the land the Israelites had taken from his ancestors two hundred years earlier.

3. A prophet or prophetess was a person whose main role was to encourage the people of Israel to obey God.

4. History has not revealed why Jael, whose husband was a friend of Jabin king of Canaan and thus was most likely known as an ally to Sisera, would betray the commander and commit murder.

Shirley Dobson

1. Helen Kooiman Hosier, *100 Christian Women Who Changed the 20th Century* (Grand Rapids: Revell, 2000), 307.

2. Taken from an interview with Elisabeth Elliott, "Gateway to Joy" radio broadcast as published on www.backtothebible.org, Friday, April 27, 2001.

3. Ibid.

Elizabeth Hanford Dole

1. Helen Kooiman Hosier, *100 Christian Women Who Changed the 20th Century*, 219.

Elisabeth Elliott

1. The stretch of beach along the Curaray River where the missionaries landed is known as Palm Beach.

2. Interview with Mission Frontiers, The Bulletin of the U.S. Center for World Mission, www.missionfrontier.org, August 1999.

3. *The Elisabeth Elliot Newsletter* was published from 1982 to 2003 to give encouragement and hope to those struggling from a variety of "sicknesses of the heart," including suffering. Many of the devotionals found in the newsletter have since been revamped and are now being used as part of a daily devotional series sponsored by Back to the Bible's Internet ministry on the World Wide Web.

4. "Gateway to Joy" was broadcast daily for thirteen years on approximately 250 English-speaking stations and another 250 non-English stations. The last broadcast was on Friday, August 31, 2001.

5. Of Elisabeth's books, perhaps the most beloved is her husband Jim Elliot's biography, called *In the Shadow of the Almighty*, published by Harper and Row in 1958.

6. Ibid., 50.

Esther, Queen of Persia

1. Esther's story is told in the Old Testament Book of Esther.

Gloria Gaither

1. Now Anderson University.

2. Helen Kooiman Hosier, *100 Christian Women Who Changed the 20th Century*, 123.

3. For the past thirty years, the Praise Gathering has remained a yearly highlight for thousands of people, uniting believers through music and meaningful worship, life-changing testimonies, and genuine fellowship.

4. Gloria received her master's degree from Ball State University in Muncie, Indiana in 1986.

5. Helen Kooiman Hosier, *100 Christian Women Who Changed the 20th Century*, 123.

6. Taken from the Gaither Family Resources, www.gaitherfamily resources.com.

7. To learn more about Gloria and Bill Gaither's many ventures and ministries, go to their Web site at www.gaithernet.com.

8. Gloria is currently working on a stage musical adaptation of John Steinbeck's novel, *To a God Unknown*.

9. Awarded by the Association of Songwriters, Composers, and Performers (ASCAP) to Gloria and Bill in 2000.

10. From Gloria Gaither's official biography.

Lakita Garth

1. Vanessa Bush, "Not Until My Wedding Night," *Essence*, December 2003.

2. Speech given by Lakita Garth before the U.S. Congressional Subcommittee, July 16, 1998.

3. As reported in Meg Meeker, M.D., *Epidemic: How Teen Sex Is Killing Our Kids* (Washington, D.C.: Lifeline Press, California, 2002), 32.

4. "Not Until My Wedding Night," *Essence*, December 2003, 45.

5. Ibid., 65.

6. Ibid.

7. Ibid.

Helena, Mother of Constantine the Great

1. Helena's son, Emperor Constantine I, later rebuilt this city and renamed it Helenopolis, causing most historians to think this was the likely place of her birth.

2. France.

3. At this time the Roman Empire was ruled by two emperors: Diocletian, who ruled over the east (Asia Minor), and Constantius Chlorus, who ruled over the west (most of Europe). When Constantius died in 306, Constantine's troops named him emperor in his father's stead. However, it would take nearly two decades of battles for Constantine to secure his rule, establishing himself as sole emperor of the entire Roman Empire in 324.

4. These original basilicas were later destroyed. Construction of the current-day Church of the Nativity and underground Grotto was completed in AD 565 on the same site as the church built by Helena.

5. Some historians believe the crosses were found by construction workers at the church site on Golgotha long after Helena had died and that only later was the discovery attributed to her.

6. Current-day Istanbul.

7. Historians presume Helena died in AD 330 because this was the last year a coin was cast bearing her image. Helena was eventually named a saint in the Catholic church. Her feast day is August 18.

Roberta Hestenes

1. Roberta earned her master of divinity in 1979 and her doctor of ministry in 1984.

2. Now Eastern University.

3. A coalition of over three hundred colleges.

Hildegard of Bingen

1. Hildegard from *Scivias*, as quoted in Barbara Newman's *Voice of the Living Light: Hildegard of Bingen and Her World* (Berkeley, Calif.: University of California Press, 1998), 17.

2. Latin for "know the ways of the Lord."

3. Many of Hildegard's illustrations used the mandala form, with round central patterns bringing order to multiple random elements. In recent migraine studies this pattern is often seen in study participants' drawings.

4. Rupertsberg flourished with fifty residents, running water, and a sewage system. In 1165, Hildegard founded a daughter house across the Rhine River in Eibingen, but she spent the rest of her life at the convent at Bingen.

5. Liturgical psalms to be sung during worship.

6. *Physica*, a scientific and medical encyclopedia, and *Causae and Curae,* a book of causes and cures for two hundred physical and mental ailments. These books reflect Hildegard's view that the body and soul are interconnected, a radical idea for her day.

7. The Rituals of the Virtues.

8. Fiona Bowie and Oliver Davies, eds., *Hildegard of Birgen: Mystical Writings* (New York: Crossroad Publishing Co., 1992), 39. It has not been determined which pope this was.

9. Regine Pernoud, *Hildegard of Bingen: Inspired Conscience of the Twentieth Century*, translated by Paul Duggan (New York: Marlowe and Company, 1998), 74.

Kay Coles James

1. Susan Graham Mathis, "One Amazing Lady: Kay Coles James," *Focus on the Family*, October/November 2003.

2. Interview in *The Reformed Quarterly*, vol. 19, no. 1, 2000; an online publication of Reformed Theological Seminary, www.rts.edu.

3. Susan Graham Mathis, "One Amazing Lady: Kay Coles James," *Focus on the Family*, October/November 2003.

4. Interview in *The Reformed Quarterly*, vol. 19, no. 1, 2000.

Madeleine L'Engle

1. Madeleine L'Engle, *Two-Part Invention* (New York: Farrar, Straus & Giroux, 1988), 39. Not every opinion expressed in Madeleine L'Engle's works represents the views of the author or the publisher.

2. Madeleine L'Engle, *The Small Rain* (New York: Vanguard Press, 1945, reprinted by Farrar Straus & Giroux, 1985).

3. Hugh Franklin is best known for his role as Dr. Charles Tyler in *All My Children*.

4. Madeleine L'Engle, *A Wrinkle in Time* (New York: Farrar, Straus & Giroux, 1962).

5. Madeleine L'Engle, *Two-Part Invention*, 145.

6. Maria Ruiz Scaperlanda, "Madeleine L'Engles: An Epic in Time," *St. Anthony Messenger*, www.AmericanCatholic.org, June 2000.

7. Ibid.

8. Ibid.

9. Ibid.

Mary of Magdala

1. *Rabboni* means "Master" or "Teacher" in Aramaic.

Mary, Mother of Jesus

1. *Nunc Dimittis,* the Latin translation of the first few words of the passage of Scripture found in Luke 2:29–32, is also the name given to this canticle.

Dayna Curry Masterson and Heather Mercer

1. Camerin Courtney, "A Higher Calling," *Today's Christian Woman,* November/December 2002.

2. Ibid.

3. Ibid.

4. According to Taliban law, Afghan women were forbidden to be seen in public unless covered from head to toe with a costume called a *burqa,* which afforded complete body coverage except for a mesh screen around the eyes for visibility.

5. Under the Taliban's strict interpretation of fundamentalist Islamic law, it was forbidden for a native or foreigner to talk to a Muslim about Christianity. Many SNI aid workers believed the Taliban interpreted proselytizing as offering humanitarian aid in exchange for conversations about Jesus, a crime usually punishable by imprisonment or death.

6. Taliban representatives.

7. The prisoners were allowed to write some correspondence. They were also allowed a few visitors, including their parents and the pastor of Antioch Church, Jimmy Seibert. Staying in Islamabad and Kabul, Dayna's and Heather's parents wrote letters to Taliban supreme leader Mullah Mohammed Omar asking for "Islamic compassion."

8. Jeff M. Sellers, "Dayna Curry Will Celebrate Her 30th Birthday in a Taliban Prison," *Christianity Today,* www.ChristianityToday.com, 29 October 2001.

9. Meg Culler, "Strength in Prayer," *The Baylor Line,* Winter 2002.

10. Excerpts from *Prisoners of Hope,* in "From Afghanistan Aid Workers to Hostages of the Taliban," *Christianity Today,* www.ChristianityToday.com, 8 July 2002.

11. Sheryl Henderson Blunt, "Caught in the Crossfire," *Christianity Today,* www.ChristianityToday.com, 12 November 2001.

12. Dayna Curry and Heather Mercer, *Prisoners of Hope* (New York: Doubleday and Colorado Springs: Waterbrook Press, 2002).

13. The Hope Afghanistan Foundation can be reached through its Web site: www.hopeafghanistan.net.

14. Taken from the Edward Mote hymn, "My Hope Is Built on Nothing Less (The Solid Rock)," Circa 1834.

Fern Nichols

1. Moms In Touch International can be reached by writing to P.O. Box 1120, Poway, CA 92074–1120, via e-mail at info@momsintouch.org, or through their Web site at www.momsintouch.org.

2. Interview with Laura Leathers for *Just Between Us*, Spring 2003.

3. Per Focus on the Family Correspondence Department, this broadcast remains one of Focus on the Family's most popular and is re-aired on a regular basis.

4. Currently, 105 countries around the world have MITI prayer groups.

5. Ibid.

6. Fern Nichols, *Prayers from a Mom's Heart* (Grand Rapids: Inspirio, 2003); and *Every Child Needs a Praying Mom* (Grand Rapids: Zondervan, 2003).

7. From the prayer of Lancelot Andrewes, Bishop of Winchester, who died in 1626.

Anna Nitschman

1. Circa 1715.

2. Moravia was part of the present-day Czech Republic, near the eastern border of Germany.

3. Unity of Brethren. The Moravian church has always accepted the Apostles' and Nicene creeds and the sacraments common to the Christian church. Later it adopted the Augsburg Confession and took as its motto: "In essentials, unity; in nonessentials, liberty; and in all things, love."

4. Since ancient times the casting of lots has been a common form of discerning God's will.

5. In a painting by Johann Valentin Haidt of the synod held at Herrnhut in 1750, Anna can be seen two seats away from Count Zinzendorf.

Kathleeen Norris

1. Kathleen Norris, *Amazing Grace: A Vocabulary of Faith* (New York: Riverhead Books, 1998), 2.

2. Kathleen Norris, *Dakota: A Spiritual Geography* (New York: Houghton Mifflin Company, 1993), 96.

3. Kathleen Norris, *Falling Off* (Chicago: Big Table Publishing Co., 1971).

4. Kathleen Norris, *Dakota: A Spiritual Geography*, 94.

5. In *Dakota: A Spiritual Geography*, Kathleen describes her spiritual geography as "the place where I've wrestled my story out of the circumstances of landscape and inheritance."

6. Interview with Dick Staub for *Christianity Today*, www.Christianity Today.com, 15 July 2002.

7. The Liturgy of the Hour is a compilation of the daily prayers of the Catholic Church, to be prayed at designated hours. Examples include Lauds (morning), Vespers (evening), Compline (nighttime), and others.

8. *Lectio divina* is Latin for "holy reading," in which one reads more for the heart, to enhance the life of faith, than for the intellect to gain knowledge.

9. *Ora et labora,* or "pray and work."

10. St. Benedict's Rule is actually a set of guidelines to govern monastic life. The Rule includes such instructions as "remain open to change," "receive all guests as Christ," "look for God at work in the world," etc.

11. The term *Desert Fathers* refers to fourth-century monks who chose to live outside the confines of (mostly) Egyptian society in order to follow God more closely.

12. Lay associate.

13. Kathleen Norris, *The Cloister Walk* (New York: Riverhead Books, 1996), xviii.

14. Kathleen Norris, *Dakota: A Spiritual Geography; The Cloister Walk;* and *Amazing Grace: A Vocabulary of Faith* . Not every opinion expressed in these works represents the views of the author or the publisher.

Janette Oke

1. Helen Kooiman Hosier, *100 Christian Women Who Changed the 20th Century,* 60.

2. See www.janetteoke.com.

3. Janette Oke, *Love Comes Softly* (Minneapolis: Bethany House Publishers, 1979).

4. Ibid., 59.

5. See www.janetteoke.com.

6. Helen Kooiman Hosier, *100 Christian Women Who Changed the 20th Century,* 60.

7. Ibid., 61.

Janet Parshall

1. Jane Johnson Struck, "Facing the Future," *Today's Christian Woman,* September/October 2003.

2. Interview with Janet Chismar, *Religion Today,* www.crosswalk.com, 5 June 2002.

3. Interview with Darla J. Knoth, "Advancing—Not Retreating!," Profiles, Inspirational Portraits of Woman of Faith series, *Woman's Touch.*

4. Helen Kooiman Hosier, *100 Christian Women Who Changed the 20th Century,* 140.

5. *Janet Parshall's America* can be reached through its Web site: www.jpamerica.com, or by contacting Janet Parshall at 1901 N. Moore Street, Suite 201A, Arlington, VA 22209, (703) 276-8594.

6. Janet's popularity crosses both Christian and secular boundaries, as does the respect she draws from her contemporaries.

7. Jane Johnson Struck, "Facing the Future," *Today's Christian Woman*, September/October 2003.

8. Ibid.

9. Ibid.

Perpetua and Felicitias

1. Perpetua's journal published as *The Passion of Saints Perpetua and Felicity*, is the first known Christian document in history written by a woman. Over two hundred years later, this journal had become such a beloved text in North Africa that Augustine of Hippo felt compelled to warn people not to give it the same weight and reverence as Scripture. The narrative set forth in this chapter is paraphrased from Perpetua's journal as it is presented in the *Medieval Source Book* Web site at www.ford ham.edu/ha/sall/sbook.html.

2. By *passion* and *deliverance*, Perpetua's brother referred to whether her imprisonment would lead to suffering and death or freedom.

3. By this time their jailer had become a Christian and had lightened their suffering.

4. "Agape feast" is the name given to a communal meal the early Christians traditionally shared together before taking Communion.

5. Geta was Septimius Severus's child by his wife, Julia Domna.

6. The following account was written by a member of the church at Carthage and added posthumously to Perpetua's journal.

7. Saturn was premier among the mythical Roman gods and was worshipped in a temple in Rome.

8. Ceres was the daughter of the Roman gods Saturn and Rhea.

9. Tradition has it that many of the spectators, inspired by the martyrs' courage, converted to Christianity on the spot. As copies of Perpetua's journal, with its subsequent epilogue, were spread throughout North Africa over the next two centuries, the witness of Perpetua, Felicitas, and that of their friends, stirred many to consider Jesus Christ as Lord, while encouraging thousands more to hold fast to their faith in the face of persecution. In the Catholic Church, the Feast of Saints Perpetua and Felicita is celebrated on March 7.

Patti Pierce

1. This group of women later became the board of Women at the Well.

2. Women at the Well can be contacted at 993 Santa Cruz Ave., Menlo Park, CA 94025, (650) 328-8966, or on the Internet at www.womenatthewell.org.

3. *Spiritual formation* is a term given to the process by which the Holy Spirit molds our lives into the likeness of Jesus Christ. We cooperate with this process

through certain practices, called spiritual disciplines, which make us more open and receptive to the Spirit's touch.

4. C. S. Lewis, *The Problem of Pain* (New York: Macmillan, 1944), 91.

Condoleezza Rice

1. This anecdote paraphrased from B. Denise Hawkins's article, "Condoleezza Rice's Secret Weapon," *Today's Christian Woman*, www.ChristianityToday.com, September/October 2002.

2. Jim Crow laws, enacted throughout much of the U.S. during the 1880s, imposed the segregation of blacks from their white counterparts. The laws were enforced through the 1960s. The term *Jim Crow*, referring to blacks, has been around since the 1830s, but it was popularized by a little ditty sung by a traveling minstrel who performed in the South during the 1930s.

3. In fact, Condoleezza is a brilliant pianist. She plays as time allows, her most celebrated performance being with the cellist Yo Yo Ma in 2002.

4. Ibid.

5. Taken from the media announcement of her nomination, November 16, 2004.

6. "Therefore, having been justified by faith, we have peace with God through our Lord Jesus Christ, through whom also we have access by faith into this grace in which we stand, and rejoice in hope of the glory of God. And not only that, but we also glory in tribulations, knowing that tribulation produces perseverance; and perseverance, character; and character, hope" (Rom. 5:1–4).

Rikka

1. Rikka's story is made available courtesy of The Voice of the Martyrs, P.O. Box 443, Bartlesville, OK 74005. Contact The Voice of the Martyrs at (800) 747-0085, www.thevoice@vom-usa.org, or visit their Web site at www.persecution.org.

Edith Schaeffer

1. Edith Schaeffer, *The Tapestry: The Life and Times of Francis and Edith Schaeffer* (Waco: Word Books, 1981), 398.

2. In fact, the child lived only two weeks.

3. Edith Schaeffer, *The Tapestry: The Life and Times of Francis and Edith Schaeffer*, 416.

4. Edith Schaeffer, *The Tapestry: The Life and Times of Francis and Edith Schaeffer*, 643.

5. Within hours of signing the sales agreement, Francis and Edith met two men of influence in the county, who, upon hearing their story, had the eviction papers reversed and permits granted.

6. Not long after Susan came down with rheumatic fever, Debbie also contracted the disease. Both girls remained bedridden intermittently over a period of three years.

7. Currently there are ten L'Abri locations in nine countries. For more information about L'Abri Fellowship, visit their Web site at www.labri.org.

8. Of the many books Edith wrote in her lifetime, the one that expresses her belief in gracious hospitality in all areas of life, *Hidden Art,* is perhaps most beloved (London: The Norfolk Press, 1971).

Geeta Swamidass

1. LivingWell Medical Clinic can be contacted at 2010 N. Tustin St., Suite D, Orange, CA 92865, (714) 633-HOPE, or at www.living-well.org.

Joni Eareckson Tada and Reneé Bondi

1. Not prone to sleepwalking or seizures, Reneé cannot explain her accident. In anticipation of receiving her engagement ring, she had had acrylic nails applied for the first time just days before. Because methyl methacrylate (MMA), a chemical substance commonly used in manicure shops to adhere acrylic nails, has been known to cause hallucinations, it is possible the substance entered her bloodstream, causing her to hallucinate.

2. Joni broke her neck at cervical vertebrae 5, Reneé at cervical vertebrae 4.

3. "Be Not Afraid" by Bob Dufford, S.J.

4. Jane Johnson Struck, "Spirited Surrender," *Today's Christian Woman,* May/June 2001.

5. Joni Eareckson with Joe Musser, *Joni* (Grand Rapids: Zondervan, 1976; rereleased in 1996).

6. Joni Eareckson with Steve Estes, *A Step Further* (Grand Rapids: Zondervan, 1978).

7. *Joni,* released by World Wide Pictures, 1979.

8. Joni and Friends can be contacted at: P.O. Box 3333, Agoura Hills, CA 91376, (818) 707-5664, or at www.joniandfriends.org.

9. A paraplegic wife and mother, Michelle eventually returned to work as a dental hygienist.

10. As far as Reneé's medical team is aware, to date Daniel is the only baby ever born to a c-4 quadriplegic.

11. Reneé Bondi with Nancy Curtis, *The Last Dance but Not the Last Song* (Grand Rapids: Baker Book House, 2002).

12. Bondi Ministries can be reached through Reneé's Web site at www.bondiministries.org, or by calling (800) 795-5757. As of 2004, Bondi Ministries is an affiliate of Joni and Friends.

13. Reneé Bondi with Nancy Curtis, *The Last Dance but Not the Last Song* (Grand Rapids: Baker Book House, 2002).

Corrie ten Boom

1. Corrie ten Boom, *The Hiding Place* (New York: Bantam Books (by arrangement with Fleming H. Revell Company), 1974), 62–63.

2. Corrie founded the first organized girls club in the country, which later became part of the Girls Guide movement, similar to the Girl Scouts.

3. The Beje Gang consisted of thirty boys and twenty girls along with twenty men and ten women, entirely organized and directed by Corrie. It's main purpose was to hide underdivers and dispatch them safely out of the country.

4. At the time six underdivers were hiding in a secret compartment behind a wall in an upper bedroom, called the Angelscrib. Two days later, under the very noses of the police who had taken over the Beje, these men and women were rescued by another police officer who had secretly remained loyal to the Dutch crown.

5. Roll call convened daily at 3:30 a.m. Regardless of the weather, the prisoners were forced to stand in place outside their barracks, sometimes for hours at a time. Anyone who fell out of line was beaten on the spot. Corrie would frequently take her Bible with her to roll call and, shielded from the guards' view by the back of the person in front of her, read to whomever was standing nearby.

6. In 1959, Corrie returned to Ravensbrück to honor the ninety-six thousand women who died there due to malnutrition, disease, or being shot or gassed, including her sister Betsie. There she learned that the week following her liberation, every female prisoner her age was gassed to death.

7. In 1953, the ten Boom family finally learned that Kik had died at the concentration camp in Bergen-Belsen. He was twenty years old.

8. The former concentration camp in Darmstadt, Germany remained open for fourteen years as a place of renewal amid the chaos of rebuilding after the war. Schapenduinen in Bloemendaal, Holland served Dutch war victims exclusively until 1950, when it opened its doors to anyone in the general population needing rest and care.

9. Carole C. Carlson, *Corrie ten Boom—Her Life, Her Faith* (New Jersey: Fleming H. Revell, 1983), 159–60.

Phillis Wheatley

1 The Wheatleys presumably named Phillis after the ship, called *The Phillis,* which had carried her from the Senegal-Gambia region of Africa to America.

The Women at the Well

1. The city of Samaria was the capital of the Northern Kingdom of Israel before it fell to the Assyrians in 721 BC. While many Jews were taken captive to Assyria, thousands of foreigners, also under Assyrian rule, were moved into Israel where they intermarried with the remaining Jews there. Since that time until Jesus' day, the pure-bred Jews felt animosity toward their mixed-blood Samaritan neighbors.

2. After the split between the Northern Kingdom of Israel and the Southern Kingdom of Judea, Israel set up an alternate center of worship on Mt. Gerizim, not far from Jacob's well, so that the people would not have to travel to Jerusalem. The

worship center was destroyed approximately 150 years before this conversation took place.

Sabine Wurmbrand

1. From The Voice of the Martyrs Web site at www.persecution.com.

2. Being the wife of a political prisoner meant no work permit and no food rations card.

3. A common tactic of the police when they wanted to arrest someone was to plant firearms in the house, then "find" them during an arrest. This situation may have been a ruse, as no weapon was found in Sabina's home.

4. Sabina Wurmbrand, *The Pastor's Wife* (Bartlesville, Okla.: Living Sacrifice Book Company, 1970), 151.

6. The Voice of the Martyrs was originally named Jesus to the Communist World. The name was changed to encompass persecuted Christians living outside of Communist countries. You can reach The Voice of the Martyrs at (800) 747-0085, thevoice@vom-usa.org, or by visiting www.persecution.org.

7. Sabina died on August 11, 2000. Richard died on February 17, 2001.

Your Story

You have just read about a variety of women from different times and places, who have lived remarkable, God-directed lives that reaped great rewards for his kingdom. They made choices of obedience—sometimes in opposition to their personal preferences or at great personal cost . . . even potential life-threatening risk—for the benefit of others. Their stories are rich, full of personal fulfillment and without regrets.

Do you crave such an existence? The first step is to acknowledge the lordship of Jesus Christ over every aspect of your being: heart, mind, body, and soul. If you have not already done this, now is the time . . . don't wait to make this vital decision! If you have done this, you are ready for the next important step—write out a short testimony of faith, along with a personal mission statement of your life.

TESTIMONY OF FAITH

Writing your testimony of faith fulfills two purposes. Recollecting all that God has done helps you to recognize the many concrete ways in which he has moved in your life, deepening your awareness of your own salvation and redemption. Writing your testimony also implants it firmly in your mind, so that when the opportunity arises to share what God has done in your life, you can do so boldly and confidently. Jesus said, "Whoever therefore shall confess me before men, him will I confess also before my Father which is in heaven. But whosoever shall deny me before men, him will I also deny before my Father which is in heaven" (Matt. 10:32–33). As these words suggest, your ability (or inability) to share your story with others can serve as a strong indicator of where your own heart is before God.

Take some time to write out your testimony. Once you have it neatly written, keep a copy of it here so you can always refer back to it or add to it as time goes on.

PERSONAL MISSION STATEMENT

Writing a personal mission statement is a new concept to many, but it can help you clarify major life goals and make day-to-day decisions. Remember, to be faithful in the big things, you must start by being faithful in the little things, in the daily decisions to chose God's way over your own. Your personal mission statement should be a single concise phrase or sentence. It should encapsulate your deepest desire for how you want to live your life before God, in fairly broad sweeping terms. And it should be something that, hopefully, will remain with you and guide you throughout your life. While "to play in a worship band" is a terrific goal to shoot for, it is too narrow and short-sighted for a personal mission statement. More appropriate might be, "to glorify God through music." For example, my personal mission statement is: *To live in such a was as to make Jesus famous.*

Write out your personal mission statement below: